**British Library Cataloguing in Publication
Data**

A catalogue record for this book is available
from the British Library.

*A nation is a society united by delusions
about its ancestry and by common hatred of
its neighbours.*

William Ralph Inge

An Irish Soldier Foresees His Spiritual Death

David Stokes

October 7th. 2023. London.

What's going on? Where is Shin Bet? Mossad? Surely somebody would have known. Aren't there agents among Israel's enemies? Informants? Nobody knew? Nobody could help. Tech operators at listening posts didn't hear anything? No messages sent. No electronic codes cracked. How odd. Young people at a rave in the desert are attacked and hunted down by purposeful men carrying Russian-designed assault rifles. A number of them have green headbands inscribed with Arabic text. Muhammed al-Qussam. Martyr. Some wear keffiyehs or hattah, the traditional headdress from the Middle East that originates with the Bedouins.

As the day goes on it gets much worse. Hours pass. The scale of the atrocity against Israeli civilians, their friends and defenders are now more apparent on this October day. Images of terror and cruelty are filtered through to the world's media. It's grim. Much worse than anyone looking on from the security of a European state can imagine. For some moments in the day, I can picture in my mind the image of a terrified woman running from Stepan Bandera's militia in Lviv in 1941. Where have I seen that image? She's in her underwear, running for her life, her nose and mouth a blob of blood.

There's a loop of outrage and agony linking the Lviv of 1941 with the Israel of 2023. The Israeli flag is hoisted in sympathy on public buildings, at Westminster too. I'm relieved our city is outraged by this, reaching out to those so far away with their lives devastated by this vicious hate crime. On the main evening television news they mention the Supernova music festival in the desert, the death by encirclement of the young who had everything to live for. Instinctively my heart is with those young souls taken way before their time and in such a pitiless way, conscious too of a rage at the men who took it upon themselves to commit such crimes. Don't they have a God? Do they not believe in a judgement day? What could they possibly say to their creator to lessen their crimes? Unless that is they are tuning into a God of a different sun.

The bodies are not yet counted, the first day of this eruption of hate and terror is not even over when discordant voices are heard. What about? What about the? The staccato pops of automatic weapons are still heard in the villages and settlements attacked by terrorists from Gaza as argumentative, self-righteous voices are raised. What about the Palestinians? What about the people of Gaza? The battles are still happening between Israeli defenders and the terror-raiders of Hamas and Palestinian jihad. Nobody can tell where it will end or what's really happening but already the voices are raised. What about? What about the people of Gaza? What about the Palestinians?

We haven't yet got to the point where the dead can be identified much less buried and the voices calling for yet more violence against Israel are raised. Higher and yet higher. From the river to the sea. Death to Israel. It didn't start on October 7th. Palestinian flags and keffiyehs. Fists raised in anger. Soon the marches will begin in earnest. It's only the first day of this nightmare for millions of people in that region. As a Londoner I've been friendly with both Muslims and Jews, once had a Jewish landlord when I lived in the borough of Hackney, not far from the Orthodox community at Stamford Hill. I've worked with Ahmadis, Indian devotees of Jamme Masjid, Pashtuns, Iranians, British converts to Islam and Eastend Bengalis, always found Jews and Muslims interesting. I've always been more than happy to share with them whatever moments of solidarity and friendship somewhere like London allows over the course of its work-weary days. Why wouldn't I?

The old slurs about money-lending Jews I dislike, Orwell's ginger-headed Jew guiltily wolfing down bacon. Jewface in Tin Pan Alley. The same with the hatred slung at Muslims in modern Britain. It's wrong on every level. The true Londoner doesn't drag racial bigotry into conversations with fellow Londoners for most of us have roots and family elsewhere. I wouldn't say I'd any particularly informed view on the politics of the Middle East, except like many other Londoners there's a longing for peace in my heart.

There's a certain admiration of Israel's David against the Goliath of so many hostile states in that part of the world, often left unsaid because of the appalling hardship Arab populations have endured over decades of war and the consequences of war. The bravery of their soldiers and fliers, the sacrifice in every generation of young blood in defence of the motherland can't be overlooked. From the insignificant working-class suburbs of London it all seems abstract, a construct of media. Yeats' heavily built Falstaffian lieutenant comes to mind, cracking jokes about war. Off now to the Golan Heights.

There's something else too. Something that niggles on a deeply personal level. You see I wasn't always a Londoner. I was born and brought up in Ireland. I once viewed the world not as a Londoner with friends from Sri Lanka, Indian and the heartlands of Surrey and a wife from the Igbo people of Southern Nigeria, but rather from the insular view of a monoculture formed by old British colonial ways, Irish ultranationalism, the Irish hierarchy's interpretation of Roman Catholicism and the calloused-handed Irish working classes who were always one bad week or two away from disaster.

And now at this wounded moment in time it brings up something unexpected. Voices from Ireland are adding an unnecessarily bitter tone to an international criticism of Israel. And it's not just the radical left, the voices of anger from a fading world of hammers and sickles struggling to find new ways of saying the same old things. The president, leaders of the main parties, reputable journalists (as much as journalists can ever be reputable) and even the prime minister are not in synch with the sympathetic view from Western nations. Their dissent is languishing like something dead and rotten by the side of a road that populations of the modern world are hoping will lead to somewhere brighter.

Soon Ireland will find itself described as the most antisemitic country in Europe. For a country that's never had more than a miniscule number of Jewish citizens and has no significant relationship with Israel or the Middle East it seems odd. Where's all that coming from? On a level of national psychology, if there is such a thing, it may all stem from a sense of inferiority at having only one neighbour, and that neighbour being a far more significant force in the world. Big country, small country. And Ireland's the small country.

There's a perception too that Israel is the large and powerful country set against smaller Arab enclaves, just like Britain and Ireland. Big country, small country with Israel as the big country. Although the opposite is true. Israel is the small country, with its land mass less than the size of Wales or thereabouts, surrounded by large and formidable enemies. History too. History surely has a lot to do with it. When it comes to Irish affairs history tends to mean a lot. Of the few connections Ireland has with Israel one in particular comes to mind.

In the hills of Southern Lebanon overlooking the Northern border of Israel a not so important Irish institution has made a name for itself in a handful of villages and crossroads. The Irish army has sent a contingent of U.N blue berets to the area since the late nineteen seventies. It's a source of pride for many. For others the Irish army shouldn't even exist. Anti-militarism and a fear that an Irish army might threaten the body politic as it did once in the early days of the state were recurring factors over decades that undermined military funding, morale and effectiveness. Only very recently as new and unexpected threats raise their ugly heads from a more volatile Europe are the old attitudes slowly changing.

And yet there they are, in the hills of South Lebanon, decked out in the sky-blue trimmings of the United Nations. They are criticised out there too, told they are not doing the job they're meant to do, stopping the rockets of Hezbollah hitting the towns and villages of Northern Israel. They are there now on this day, this terrible day in October when purposeful men with Russian-designed assault rifles have broken into Israel and are killing civilians.

Back home in Ireland the capital city is one of the few capitals in Europe not to fly the Israeli flag in solidarity with a nation so cruelly wounded by terror. That doesn't go unnoticed. After all it's the nuances that matter. It's hard at such times to accept the view of Ireland as a nation siding with the Iranian-sponsored terror that kills Israeli civilians rather than with a Western worldview that sees Israel as part of the Western family of nations and stands with it in cooperation and friendship. DeValera is again mentioned as the only leader to send a letter of condolence to his German ambassador on the death of Hitler. That follows us through history. The stubbornness of the man.

It's late on the night of October 7th. The radio is bringing more news from Israel, all of it bad. They murdered and murdered. Took hostages too. And the voices that support such a thing or qualify it as something that didn't just begin on October 7th are already heard. From the perspective of a Londoner my heart is comforted by our government's sensitive response to the deaths of those young people. The part of me that's Irish is wounded.

April 1981. Ireland.

RTE radio has just announced two soldiers are missing, presumed dead in Lebanon. They're not the first to die in the few years the Irish government have sent a battalion-sized contingent to UNIFIL (United Nations Interim Force In Lebanon). It's a grey morning on the Curragh Camp in County Kildare. The presumed deaths of the two soldiers are close to home as I am a serving Irish soldier, on my way as it happens to Lebanon. I don't know how much of it is my own weakness for melancholic thoughts or how much of it is the miserable weather, but the news of the soldiers' fate is overly depressing. Death and its nuances are so much closer this morning.

The tricolour flies at half-mast on the Fire station Tower on the Curragh, the highest point hereabouts. The flag stirs in the lightest breeze in deference to the two missing men. They must be dead if the flag is at half-mast. Plato's argument from incompatibility is a simple trick of logic, based on the observation that opposite forms can't exist in the one object. So, the concept of huge does not belong in the same descriptive sentence as tiny. The house cannot be both huge and tiny. The dog cannot be both skinny and fat. Plato brings this logic to the human soul, concluding that the human soul cannot imply the opposites of death and life. Hence death cannot be assigned to the human soul. The human soul survives death.

But even by this reasoning death is the end of the organism we know through our senses and personalities. The ancient Greeks believed the soul ready to be reincarnated drinks from the River Lethe, the river of forgetfulness. This is why it has no knowledge of its previous life. So, if our souls survive but have no knowledge of us or of the lives we led then any kind of survival after death is rather abstract. For the ordinary person it all just sounds like death.

An idea of absolute death with no redemption or no hope for the soul to drink from the river of forgetfulness is easier to swallow around here. Maybe it has to do with how Irish skies press down with such force on the horizons, the alarming absence of sunlight. Death feels like death, total and everlasting. Surely Plato couldn't have worked out his more hopeful spiritual theories if he'd lived here under these skies.

The mood in the camp is sombre. Have the spirits of so many fallen soldiers from centuries of militarism on the Curragh come together to mourn the latest death? The shell-shocked trooper wounded at the Somme who hung himself in the week before he had to re-join his unit in France. The young Irish Army officer who killed himself for no obvious reason while on duty in the post-war torpor of a newly named republic. They are never fully absent here. The Curragh absorbs the spirit of the men who march on its squares and eat in its canteens and sleep in its billets.

At eighteen I'm in the middle of an important transformation, hoping to somehow get past a not unexpected teenage angst and then take up the usual roles of adulthood, or whatever roles are left to take. Inside is nearly always dark. Either it's some kind of depression or I've somehow internalised the sadness left behind by a legion of unhappy souls once part of this old military camp in the middle of Kildare. Or is this just life? Is this just how we're meant to feel quite a lot of the time?

I'm in the green uniform of the Irish Defence Forces and wear the standard black felt beret with a red patch as background for the cap-badge. The shiny and cheap metal cap-badge issued to the enlisted ranks is a sunburst with the words Oglaigh na hEireann on it, which translates as Irish volunteer. An old '48 era British steel helmet painted in the sky-blue of the U.N dangles from my British army surplus web-belt. I'm waiting outside the orderly office of my home unit in Ceannt Barracks. The morning sinks into a greyer, more death-disorientated mood.

The Curragh's military past stretches back centuries. There were military settlements and tented camps here before the first permanent structures were built by the British Army in 1879. The first of the seven barracks was Beresford Barracks, which after 1922 became Ceannt Barracks. The other barracks were named Ponsonby, Stewart, A.S.C, Gough, Engineer and Keane. In the optimistic days after the birth of a free state the barracks were renamed in honour of the signatories of the 1916 Proclamation, Pearse, Plunkett, Ceannt, McDermott, Clarke, McDonagh and Connolly.

The signatories of the proclamation were executed by firing squad in Kilmainham Jail in the febrile days after the 1916 Easter Rising. It's another link between a soldier's death and the Curragh Camp. In the annals of the Four Masters an ancient king of Ireland was killed on the Curragh. Elizabethan commanders galloped their horses here and deployed columns of men in preparation for the Williamite Wars of the 1690s.

The royalist Richard Talbot mustered his Irish Army on the Curragh before marching on Derry. Another hundred years on the Croppies sang these lines from the Shan Van Vocht-

On the Curragh of Kildare

the boys will be there,

with their pikes in good repair.

Gibbet Rath on the edge of the Curragh plains was the site of the massacre of hundreds of Irish rebels against the Crown as they surrounded after the 1798 Rising. One of the Yeomanry officers who helped in the killing of the surrendering men left these words as a requiem of sorts.

... avenged - 500 rebels bleaching on the Curragh of Kildare - that Curragh over which my sweet innocent girls walked with me last summer, that Curragh was strewed

*with the vile carcasses of popish rebels and
the accursed town of Kildare has been
reduced to a heap of ashes by our hands.*

Queen Vic herself visited the humble
Curragh in 1861 to review the troops
stationed there, which included her son
Prince Edward. In Victorian times many a
soldier left these barracks to fight in faraway
wars and many never returned. Many a song
was composed in their honour. The Curragh
Mutiny of 1914 proved yet again that British
army officers in Ireland would turn against
the interests of the native Irish at critical
moments in history, even if it meant defying
their own government in London.

Waiting outside the orderly room in Ceannt
Barracks I'm not really worried about going
to Lebanon. Overall, it's interesting by the
standards of working-class Ireland in the
early nineteen eighties, to have a chance to
go anywhere outside our province of
Leinster. The darkness of my soul is more
connected to the actual mood in this part of
the world. There's something about the Irish
countryside, something a little troubling and
tricky to work out and to put down in words.
Maybe too many people suffered bad deaths
here or left too much bitterness behind in
the wake of the lives they lived here. At night

it's more apparent but it's apparent in the daylight too.

George Sayer's conversation with J.R.R Tolkien comes to mind. Sayer wrote that Tolkien had this to say about Ireland.

He described Ireland as a country naturally evil. He said he could feel evil coming from the earth, from the peat bogs, from the clumps of trees, even from the cliffs, and this evil was only held in check by the great devotion of the southern Irish to their religion.

A land-rover pulls up outside the orderly room with two NCOs sitting up front alongside the driver. I jump in the back and the vehicle pulls off. The two NCOs are career men, determined to make something out of this army business. They are not in a talking mood. Reports of two missing-presumed-dead soldiers in Lebanon have soured the morning. I know both NCOs a little and travelling to the Middle East to run any kind of risk of getting killed out there is not why they swore on the bible and the tricolour. Like so many others they're in the green uniform from financial necessity. The dread of unemployment takes on pathological symptoms after all. They've both had a taste of the dole, swallowed the shame of standing in a workless queue in their hometown to palm the state's pittance.

Not that a regular wage is the only instinct rallying men to the recruitment office in the Curragh. In swearing on the flag and the bible there's a sense of offering oneself as a human sacrifice for the sanctity of the state. In those moments at least it's obvious we're swearing an oath not so much to kill but to die for Ireland. Although in a world of such beastly necessity such high-mindedness is often short-lived.

One of the NCOs is pensive, smoking a cigarette he's taken slyly from its red and white box. Offering a ciggie to other soldiers is common but he's not in a sharing mood. The NCOs in the front of the land-rover are quiet as we begin the sixty miles or so journey from the Curragh to Dublin. The guy who's smoking looks worried and sucks more vigorously on his fag. He didn't sign up for any of this, flying to a faraway warzone on the same morning two Irish soldiers are announced as missing, presumed dead. He has young children, a wife and a small colony of relatives to think about.

In the deeper reaches of mind I know I shouldn't be here either. Brute reality and the dull and often miserable causality down at this level of life are the big factors at play. This is the mental servitude the great thinkers have written about. It's Sartrean Bad Faith and the bum-end of Nietzsche's master and slave theorem. It's a Vodou Wanga curse and a hex from a thousand forefathers. Deep in my soul I know it's not where I want to be. Billet-room conversations hereabouts are enough in themselves to drop a few brain-cells. A man of ordinary intelligence could lower his I.Q by several points just by hanging around the barrack-squares, canteens and billets of this army.

The Irish military had long since settled into a torpor created by political interference and mistrust, social inferiority, a dislike by many citizens and no significant role worthy of an armed body of men. Our battles were fought a long time ago at Kilmichael and Pettigo. We take very much a secondary role to the national police force (An Garda Siochana) against terrorists, Republicans idealists and others animated by a political impasse in the North of the country. It's very much a macho thing in a macho country. The police are personified by the canny, Gaelic football-loving, two-fisted, whisky-drinking police sergeant pulling on his cap and raincoat and jumping into an old Renault patrol car for to sort out the latest trouble outside a pub or involving locals gathering at a halting-site.

He wouldn't have needed a bunch of townies in army uniforms to help him sort it all out. We're his social inferiors after all, the boot-boys and Saturday night booze-fighters he had to deal with as a younger man out on the beat. If he needs support he has plenty of colleagues from nearby towns. He has detectives too he can call on, armed with Smith and Wesson thirty eights and Israeli-made Uzi submachine guns. Only reluctantly do such men accept orders from on-high to work alongside the enlisted soldiers of the Defence Forces.

It can seem as if we're a kind of national embarrassment, an anomaly from an often-overlooked war of independence that nobody's quite sure of what to do with. Yet for all that we carry out what roles they give us to the letter, guarding arms and munitions in the old barracks handed over to us by the British army when they left in 1922. Soldiers sit in the back of land-rovers on long journeys escorting cash and prisoners, choking on diesel fumes and rattled to the bone by the roads. We stand on the walls of Portlaoise Prison, guarding convicted gunmen and bombers who slag us off as British lackies, insulting us by yelling out that we're a form of pond-life Irishness known as Free Staters.

Our colonels and brigadiers are not actually in command of us. All orders must be cleared by civilians from the Ministry of Defence. These civilians are briefed by whatever politicians are in office at the time. They are wary of us always, miserly with everything issued to us. On duty we never have anything more than forty rounds for our standard Belgium-made assault rifle, the FN 7.62mm. That means if we ever did get into trouble we're very limited in a situation that calls for sustained fire. Forty rounds is the exact reckoning with every round jealously counted before and after. Maybe they're worried we'd steal ten or twenty rounds and sell them to a shifty character with a Belfast accent in one of those pubs where everyone stands at the end of the night for the national anthem.

Very shortly after passing out from basic training the Irish soldier will get the message, keep your head down and shut up. Don't expect much from your betters or from anyone else. Take what's going and be grateful for it. U.N service saved the enlisted Irish soldier from a barracks-confined existence with crushing psychological outcomes. Many went into the nearest beer or whisky bottle and didn't come back out again. U.N adventures in the Congo, Cyprus and now Lebanon saved an entire caste of Irishmen from the indignity of a soldier's life with only an historic or imaginary enemy and without much to do.

The armies and militias we'd encounter in Lebanon were lethal in thought and action and consumed with purpose, often willing to fight to the death for their cause. In reality we had no cause. In Lebanon we'd find a cause in kind as defenders of the Shiite Arabs in the villages where we were stationed. It was better than nothing. The Israelis and their allies in the Christian militias were often viewed with mistrust and hostility for in the absence of a political education or a proper briefing we didn't really know why they were fighting so zealously to defend their borders. Nobody had bothered to tell us.

A number of Irish soldiers in Lebanon hated everyone, particularly the Arabs. They made fun of them and used all the gross stereotypes that are interchangeable throughout the ages and known to the family of nations. Without any cause to win in Ireland we hoped to find a cause in Lebanon. Wasn't it a little noble to be going to such a place? Didn't all the idealistic words and solemn motions passed in the U.N General Assembly mean something? Weren't we of some use, to somebody?

It's not the actual circumstances in themselves that are a problem, the reality of heading to the Lebanon as an eighteen-year-old Irish soldier. As far as it goes there are many worse things in Ireland and elsewhere. It's more about the knowledge that there might be something different to this. If there were no options or no other way of going about things, then there'd be no anxiety. But I know I shouldn't be here. I should be studying for an academic course or getting a portfolio together for to submit to an art-college or at least sending in applications to train as a nurse in a psychiatric hospital. Or anything really. Anything other than this. But none of this is possible. There is nothing other than this. Survive, move on. Find a way out. It's just a bump on the road, nothing personal.

In the longer historical timeframe, we're lucky. We're not heading to the Somme or to Sion Kop like so many Irish soldier laddies before us. They're not asking us to run a bayonet through another economically oppressed sap wearing a different coloured uniform to ours. It's just the United Nations. The guys who've already been to Lebanon are looking forward to more sun-bathing and off-duty boozing, more visits to the brothels and bars of Northern Israel.

Post October 7ᵗʰ attack. Germany.

I'm in Spottinger Cemetery in Landsberg. I came out on the train from Munich. There's about three hundred of the condemned buried here. Snowdrops are in flower. It's a little jarring to see snowdrops on such hated ground. I spoke with a few people in Munich and it's amazing after all this time how people skirt around certain facts. Not that they say it outright. War is war. Stuff happens. From history as it's written in English in the Western lands it's cut and dried. They were tried and convicted. Then executed by hanging.

The nameless crosses at Landsberg are linked to the most dismal time. The bishops in Munich back then were not unsympathetic. They made statements in support of the men when they were on trial. Snowdrops are now growing on such graves. Apparently two Conservative party members of parliament back in England also spoke up on behalf of the men, the same kind of characters who had a record of speaking up for Nazi Germany.

The night before I opened the pages of a book and read several pages stretched out on a comfortable bed in a Munich hotel room. It was from Primo Levi's The Truce.

As I wandered around the streets of Munich, full of ruins, near the station where our train lay stranded once more, I felt I was moving among throngs of insolvent debtors, as if everyone owed me something, and refused to pay. I was among them, in the enemy camp, among the Herrenvolk; but the men were few, many were mutilated, many dressed in rags like us. I felt that everyone should interrogate us, read in our faces who we were, and listen to our tale in humility. But no one looked us in the eyes, no one accepted the challenge; they were deaf, blind and dumb, imprisoned in their ruins, as in a fortress of wilful ignorance, still strong, still capable of hatred and contempt, still prisoners of their old tangle of pride and guilt.

I found myself searching for them, among that anonymous crowd of sealed faces, for other faces clearly stamped in my memory, many bearing a name: the name of someone who could not but know, remember, reply; who had commanded and obeyed, killed, humiliated, corrupted. A vain and foolish

search; because not they, but others, the few
just ones, would reply for them.

There's not much to see on the streets where Primo Levi walked. Nothing sinister. It's the beginning of Spargelzeit. It's like a season for asparagus. It's a kind of asparagus that grows under the earth. The Germans call it white gold and they eat tons of it. That's what people are talking about on the streets near the Hauptbannhof. I hear the word mentioned too in a busy Turkish café near Munich central rail station. The horrors of what Levi went through at Dachau can't be sensed around here. Not even a bit. There are connections, I guess. But a person would have to have a lot of time for to dig about for them.

On an online site dedicated to German history I find the following.

Diary entry on 2ⁿᵈ July 1941 of Felix Landau, a member of Einsatzgruppe C in Ukraine.

Shortly after our arrival we shot our first Jews. As usual a few of the new officers became megalomaniacs and really go for it wholeheartedly.

The following day after returning from a mass execution Landau wrote home to his sweetheart in Germany.

We have just come back. Five hundred Jews were lined up ready to be shot ... One of them simply would not die. The first layer of sand had already been thrown on the first group when a hand emerged out of the sand ... A couple more shots rang out ... Strange, I am unmoved, no pity, nothing.

Speaking about the men who carried out such killings a German Red Cross nurse, Annette Schuckling, wrote home to her mother.

What Papa says is true; people with no moral inhibitions exude a strange odour. I can now pick out these people, and many of them really do smell like blood. Oh Mama, what an enormous slaughterhouse the world is.

They covered the protests on the main evening news. I watched it on TV in the hotel room. They were chanting from *the river to the sea*. Sometimes I think our memory-banks have been erased. People chant such things and others might not get their meaning. We might not even think it's such a bad thing. It might just be a problem with how we think.

April 1981. Ireland

The land-rover takes us along the camp's middle road and onto the main road cutting through the belly of our little world. We pass the crossroads so long the centre of all which happens on the Curragh, past Farrell's shop and the post-office and on up the hill past the main garrison church and the fire station with the flag of our nation flapping gloomily at half-mast. The Marion Shrine at the entrance to the camp reminds us of the foremost tradition around here. There's a Wesleyan Hall at the crossroads too, a link to a principally working-class spiritual movement brought from England and inaugurated in Dublin in 1745.

Further on there's the Curragh Military Cemetery with its stone outer walls and sparse trees so other-worldly in certain conditions of light. The Commonwealth War Graves Commission cares for the graves of the one hundred and four British servicemen who died during WW1 and are buried there. The bones in the earth hereabouts are mute corroborations of an empire's history. In John Huston's touching tribute to James Joyce's Dublin 'The Dead' the final scene when Gabriel Conroy is reflecting on his love for his wife in his hotel room includes a beautifully lit still of the Curragh Military Cemetery.

Huston was dealing with his final illness at the time and didn't live to see the film's release. The leading female role was played by his daughter Angelica. In the final scene Angelica's character is lying in the hotel bed of a snow-covered Dublin, describing to her husband Gabriel Conroy how her first sweetheart in effect sacrificed his life for her. Gabriel Conroy is played with remarkable sensitivity by Donal McCann.

The closing scene where McCann's lines are taken from Joyce's text with the snow falling on an already snow-covered Dublin belongs to the higher achievements of Irish artistic expression. And with a parting touch of poetic cinematography Huston uses an image of the Curragh Military Cemetery with its trees inanimate spectres from a lost world. The Commonwealth Graves Commission would have approved.

The old British army cavalry barracks at Newbridge was on a scale to match any barracks in the empire. Now there's not much remaining to remind us of the dimensions of the barracks. The garrison's Methodist church was in use after the closure of the barracks in the nineteen twenties. Later it was de-consecrated and used as Newbridge's Town Hall. The barracks was designed by the Leeds-born architect and freemason Abraham Hargrave in 1813.

We pass Newbridge Town Hall on our way to Lebanon as it's on the main street, a link with an empire on which the sun never set. How many cavalrymen found spiritual succour here in this very Methodist chapel before the Crimea, Sion Kop and Mesopotamia called? Are the spirits of John Wesley's preachers and the faithfully departed somewhere on the other side of this stone portal? Spiritual links between the present and the British army in Kildare come to life at unexpected moments.

In 1922 the empire's soldiers marched away and the tricolours of a new nation were set at full mast over the old forts and barracks. It was better for the sake of expediency for local people to forget their emotional connections and blood links with the empire's garrisons. But moods and nuances not easily decoded into words can yet be found here. There's a physical vibe at times to remind us of our imperial dragoons and hussars in the old buildings and walls yet standing. There's a palpable mood too, reminding us of the void we are all moving towards. There are words of life and words of death and there are the old towns of Leinster on a grey, dreary morning.

The driver of the land-rover and one of the corporals in the front seats live around here. Their eyes are skinned for familiar faces as we drive through the near-deserted morning streets. The town has a natural relationship with the rituals of life on the Curragh and is only a couple of miles away from the Curragh Camp. Many of the older families around here have a subliminal bond to the military history of the area. At one point sixty nine of the British army's one hundred and seven line regiments were stationed in Ireland. Thousands of British soldiers populated the seven barracks on the Curragh, the cavalry barracks in Newbridge and the barracks in the neighbouring towns of Naas and Kildare Town. Many stayed and married local women. There's no shortage of English and Scottish surnames around here.

The military population of the Curragh became a part of life in these Kildare parishes. In a pub a couple of miles away an old farmer from a neighbouring townland reminisces about walking miles on damp, cold nights to the Curragh Camp for to bum cigarettes from soldiers. That was back in the nineteen thirties when poverty and hunger were as real as rain and frost. The poor man of the land said he usually managed to scrounge a smoke from the national soldiers.

Such characters were linked by class and geography to the tenants of the O'Kelly estate on the other side of Newbridge at Clongorey. Those small holders were so poor they lived on the most modest crops of potatoes and whatever they could make from selling turf cut from humble plots of bog. Their only pay-days were when they dried and then sold their turf to the local military. They lived on credit from shops in Newbridge, paying off their debts when they got paid for their turf. They were poor but proud people with religion, folklore, strong stone houses and kinship ties to support them through the trials of life.

Clongorey and its equivalents throughout Ireland are the key to understanding our sympathy with underdogs. It's part of a national psyche that resonates with the oppressed and can translate as a sense of rage at injustice or perceived injustice. The world's media stand on Israel's soil and file negative report after negative report about the country hosting them. Such blanket negativity over time seeps into the psyche of populations at a distance from it all and dependent on media for insight and analysis. How could it not? Never once is it mentioned what might happen if a country in Israel's situation stepped back from its retaliatory strikes, hyper-vigilance and often fanatical defence of its population and borders.

For the BBC, RTE and most other Western media outlets Israel is not on solid ground. The argument for its very existence is questioned. Anything it does in its defence is diligently reported and added to a list of grievances that formidable tribes and regimes from the Muslim world and powers in an ideological war with the Western democracies confabulate into a great beast of apocalyptic horror. The demonization reactivates the injustices of Clongorey in the Irish psyche and prompts the invective and poorly worded comment on a conflict a very long way from Paddy's green shamrock shore. So often it can come across as grossly insensitive to Jews and an insult to the state of Israel and its standing in the world.

In the 1880s the weather turned bad and the Liffey burst its banks and flooded the small potato plots and boglands of Clongorey. The hardship was such that the people could barely eat enough for to stand upright for a full day. They could not pay the rent on their small holdings. In the centuries before the establishment of a national Irish state a little over six hundred English landlords owned eighty percent of the land in Ireland. So many people were little more than serfs.

Their land was owned by strangers from England to whom they were obliged to pay heavy rents. English armies empowered by the Pope had forced the old Celtic Church, which had flourished in the first eight hundred years of Christianity in Ireland, to bow to the Latinate and Catholic dictates of London and Rome. So much Pagan wisdom and reverence for nature was subsumed under a vociferous Popery enforced by England. Then when Henry broke with Rome the native Irish were again obliged to adopt another spiritual creed, the Protestantism of the English king. Quite a number of them did.

Most clung to the old faith with its traces of the Pagan-Celtic church and the Polytheism of Iron Age Celts. Not that many ordinary people sat around turf fires in the evening discussing the Tuatha De Danann or the

Tain Bo Cuailnge but the old gods of the land and the sea god Manannan mac Lir were ghosts never fully exorcised from the Irish psyche. Yet today a simple triskelion can transfix the Irish mind.

How much were the devotions to a Hebrew healer-God a reawakening of the Tuaths' and Druids' devotions to an ancient serpent-god and to the spirits of the forest? Not every murmur around a turf fire in a time of oppression is necessarily written down in annals. The people of Clongorey like people throughout Ireland were dispossessed not just of land and livelihoods but of the fuller implications of their human existence. Take away a people's spiritual and mystical past and it is then much easier for them to lose their confidence and succumb to subjugation.

The evictions at Clongorey were as heartless and absolute as the evictions from the Famine era. Hundreds of Royal Irish Constabulary officers and specially appointed emergency men marched to Clongorey to smash the walls of stone cottages and set thatch-roofs alight. The elderly, the sick, young children and anyone else in the houses were thrown out on the side of the road like dogs. Little wonder there's a harshness of tone around here, a bitterness people hardly bother trying to hide.

The emergency men who so energetically tore down the walls of the houses of the people of Clongorey were the hated gombeen men of Irish history, the lackeys of absentee landlordism that live on in the Irish psyche as demonic parasites. During the eviction of the Fullam family in 1889 at Clongorey the police and gombeen-men were joined by a detachment of the Black Watch regiment stationed at the time on the Curragh.

The home of the Fullam family was smashed and burnt almost to the ground and then neighbouring cottages were smashed and burnt almost to the ground. Not long before the small holders were more than happy to drive their donkeys and carts filled with turf to the Curragh for to heat the billets of the soldiers. Now the soldiers were driving the smallholders out, burning out the poorest people in the county. The evictions were as spiteful as they were merciless for what fiscal gain or any kind of gain could be had by burning paupers out of their homes. The natural disaster caused by the Liffey bursting its banks ruined the small holdings so as they were incapable of generating any incomes or rents.

There's a photograph in the archives of a Mrs Kelly sitting by the ruins of cottages at Clongorey just after her eviction. She's dressed in head to toe in widow's black, her posture stiff-backed and dignified in the circumstances. Is there a messiah in the history of humanity who could morally command Mrs Kelly to forgive the absentee landlord and the wider society's crimes against her? There probably isn't but she more than likely forgave them anyhow.

Is it a co-incidence how the most exploitative types of capitalism and colonialism have promoted the Christian messiah above all other deities? Certain impositions need to be forgiven more than others. The machismo of the messiah taking on the sins of the world is just about gracious enough to allow the absentee landlord and the colonial whip-master off the hook. In moral terms nothing else could.

The names of the families from the Clongorey evictions are common hereabouts, much like the surnames of English soldiers from the old British garrison are common. The evicted families' rights and dignity were later restored by the Land Commission in the first decade of the twentieth century. Most of the families returned to re-build their lives at Clongorey.

That's what's awakened in the Irish psyche when negative reports are filed by Western journalists on a sojourn to Israel. As it's the only country in that region to allow negative reports on what's happening out there it's by far the most popular destination for Western journalists always keen to appear edgy and at the cusp of world events. They'll don a flak-jacket and maybe a helmet and stand with their backs to a bunch of bored kids on the West Bank chucking stones at military vehicles. They'll make it all sound apocalyptic as that's their stock-in-trade.

Then they'll be driven back to Jerusalem or Tel Aviv to a four or five star hotel. After a hot bath, a good dinner and a gin and tonic they'll enjoy the privilege of reporting as negatively as possible on the actions of their host nation. It's good work if you can get it. The negative reports are then played on a loop on television screens throughout what we know as the democratic nations. Not much is ruled out in pursuit of the sought-after narrative that shows Israel as a pariah state in breach of every convention ever signed into law.

This misreporting on events involving Israel is confirmed by Andrew Fox's December 2024 report entitled 'Questionable Counting: Analysing the death toll from the Hamas-run Ministry of Health in Gaza.' Western news' agencies repeat Hamas lies about casualties and fail to mention that Israeli forces killed 17'000 Hamas fighters in Gaza after October 7th and this figure should not be included in a casualty list of civilians. In 2022, the year before the conflict in Gaza, 5000 people died of natural causes in Gaza but this figure, much like the number of Hamas fighters killed, is not deducted from the overall casualty figures.

From 1,378 articles published in English-language media outlets Andrew Fox's researchers found that 84% made no distinction between civilian deaths and combatant deaths. On it goes. Two plus two is five. Eurasia are our enemies. They've always been our enemies. The biased media reports mount up and ordinary people who rely on such reports for their main source of information about world events are incensed. They've been played of course as all of us are played. What bumps up television news' ratings and does something good for the media professionals involved is more important than the actual truth.

This endless barrage of misinformation, incomplete information and criticism of Israel brings to life the ghosts of Clongorey in the Irish psyche. Rage fostered in the Irish nationalist consciousness is awoken and the evicted, the exiled, the unjustly imprisoned, the Famine dead and the martyred of Irish nationalist history are joined with the televised images of Arab civilians caught up in a brutal war. The Irish psyche faced with all this is horrified by a sense of communal suffering linked to a national struggle for survival and self-determination. Hence a country regurgitating its historical suffering and transferring it onto a media-honed narrative from a distant war is now rated as the most antisemitic country in Europe.

Such are the ways of the world. We drag our personal suffering and our national suffering with us through the years so it's hardly surprising when it's fanned into grotesque imaginings by media professionals that care little if anything about the consequence of what they send forth into the living-rooms of millions of unsuspecting viewers.

Post October 7th attack on Israel. Germany

It's dark by the time I get to Landsberg Prison. There's something weird about being near such a place at night. I definitely sense something odd. I read somewhere that medieval Parisians needed permission from the king or the bishops or the masters of the guild to work at night. They'd work by the burning wicks of goats' tallow. Something is happening at night outside that prison. If I could I'd have gone up close to it and ran my fingers along the exterior. But it's still an actual prison so I couldn't do that. I think there's something in the air that's too subtle to catch with a non-German mind, especially at certain hours of night.

Once, for almost a year, I read the psalms every evening. In the hotel room that night after I'd returned from Landsberg to Munich I found a line in a psalm and it made sense of what I felt at Landsberg Prison. I held the page of scripture open against my chest as a token of protection.

At midnight I rise to praise you.

Ireland. April. 1981.

We drive through the town of Newbridge on our way to Lebanon, passing a small road which would take us to Clongorey if we had any interest in going there, or if we had the time to go anywhere except towards the next stage in the journey to Lebanon. History is a living force here, as real as the ravens swooping by an old stone bridge on the edge of town.

The soldiers who were announced as missing presumed dead on the day before we set out for Lebanon were young men. Private Hugh Doherty came from Donegal and Private Kevin Joyce from the Aran Islands. They found the body of young Doherty near the outpost where he died. The body of Private Joyce was never found. There were stories in the billets about how Joyce was taken and held in Beirut and killed during an Israeli air attack. But it is now by and large accepted that he was killed by the PLO at Deir Ntar not long after he went missing.

Much later the Minister of Defence received a report commissioned into the deaths of Joyce and Doherty. Friends and family of the soldiers killed in a lonely part of South Lebanon in 1981 believe there was a cover-up. Was there a cover-up? Or do we really believe people in authority speak the truth when things go wrong?

Nothing happens in a vacuum. The deaths of Joyce and Doherty were foreshadowed by complex causal factors. What two young peacekeepers were doing at such an isolated post where PLO guerrillas moved about at will is a question which must have crossed the minds of those who looked into the young soldiers' deaths. Why were they allowed to remain at such an isolated post after a fatal conflict between the PLO and Fijian soldiers at nearby Deir Amis? Everyone in South Lebanon would have known the PLO fighters were out for U.N blood.

The PLO knew the tough and militarily adept Fijians were ready for any reprisal attacks so it wouldn't have taken very much lateral thinking to have figured out how easier it'd be to attack the two-man U.N outpost at Deir Ntar instead. Why Irish battalion operations at Camp Shamrock didn't withdraw all personnel from isolated outposts when everyone knew the PLO were out for blood is another question left unanswered. Were the Irish battalion staff officers reassured by

Dublin that the PLO would not attack an Irish post?

Both Private Joyce and Private Doherty would have carried forty rounds apiece for their rifles. In the simplest terms they shouldn't have been anywhere near an isolated outpost in an area where the PLO and other militias came and went at will. The authors of the report into what happened at Deir Ntar must have reflected on the apathetic or ill-informed or confused thinking behind the decision to send two men to an isolated outpost so soon after the conflict between the PLO and U.N soldiers in the nearby Fijian area of operation.

Like everything else in the world, the causality involved is the key to anything that might be learned. Whether we were very much aware of it or not Irish soldiers serving with the U.N on the Lebanon-Israeli border were vulnerable to any change of nuance in Dublin's foreign policy. The Bahrain Declaration of 1980 was a call for the establishment of a Palestinian state and was strongly backed by Brian Lenihan, our foreign minister at the time. Lenihan said the PLO was no longer a terrorist organisation and that Yasser Arafat was a moderate. It must have caused embarrassment in governmental circles in Dublin when shortly after Lenihan's statement the PLO killed two Irish soldiers in South Lebanon.

When Yasser Arafat visited Ireland in 1993 Foreign Minister Lenihan assured the PLO chairman of the *genuine warmth in Ireland for you and your cause.* The words were not good news for Irish U.N soldiers in Lebanon as the Irish area of operations was flanked on its southern side by an Israeli-backed militia highly sensitive to political or cultural bias. Ireland's foreign policy was read as pro-PLO and anti-Israeli. This perception, confirmed by Brian Lenihan's official statements, was a causal factor in the harassment of Irish U.N positions by the Israeli-backed South Lebanese Army. When the harassment came in the form of mortar rounds or machine-gun fire there was every chance of more Irish blood staining the soil of Lebanon.

At the time of Foreign Minister Lenihan's pro-PLO statements Ireland was the only EEC/EU country not to have an Israeli embassy. Our Chief Rabbi at the time was Dr. David Rosen who thought it was a bad idea for the Irish government to make partisan statements about the Middle East. Dr. Rosen understood the importance of words when they are echoed on the world stage. The Chief Rabbi said he was concerned about the safety of Irish soldiers on the Lebanon-Israeli border when the Irish government was seen to take one side against the other in a volatile, complex conflict where every syllable was weighed for any possible hint of bias or insensitivity. It was nice to hear someone in Dublin was worried about us.

Foreign Minister Lenihan's wisdom was linked to the school of provincial wisdom known as cute hoorism. But there wasn't anything cute about jeopardising the safety of Irish soldiers with poorly judged governmental statements, especially when such statements did not advance the cause of Ireland or its people in any tangible way. And anyhow the *genuine warmth* of the Irish people as proclaimed by the Irish government didn't reduce the killing penchant of PLO guerrillas at Deir Ntar.

Around the same time as the Bahrain Declaration Brian Lenihan said that the PLO had no contact with the IRA. Irish U.N soldiers who'd passed through the town of Tyre or its environs on their way from the Irish area of operations to U.N headquarters at Naquoura could only smile at Lenihan's words, as others had smiled. The bearded IRA volunteers manning the checkpoints with their PLO comrades at Tyre were from the IRA's Dublin Brigade. They laughed, joked and shook hands with the Irish U.N soldiers, chuffed at the curious sequence of events which situated Irishmen on either side of a PLO checkpoint in Lebanon.

So much for politicians and the exalted circles they move in. The Irish government's slanted criticism of Israel and support for the PLO was heard clearly by the South Lebanese Army, the Israeli-backed militia with machine-guns and mortars zeroed in on Irish U.N positions. With the vulnerability of Irish soldiers on the Lebanon-Israel border in mind a little more sensitivity might have been used when the Irish government felt in the mood for issuing statements to the world. There was no Israeli diplomat in Dublin at the time for to get in touch with for to try and find a more neutral tone. But we had a gifted Chief Rabbi in Dr. David Rosen who'd have been more than happy to advise Leinster House on the situation in and around the Lebanon-Israel border. With a less partisan and more diplomatically-informed line in foreign affairs the life of an Irish soldier or two might have been saved.

Post October 9th attack on Israel. Germany.

I catch a train from Munich to Berlin. When I get there, I hang around the Reichstag building, wondering if I'm standing above Hitler's bunker. They haven't marked it of course as the Neo-Nazis would show up in record time. They'd hold a commemoration or whatever they do. Give the Nazi salute. Chant the old slogans yet again. I don't think we really get it here in the English-speaking world, how the modern Germans see themselves as victims of the Nazis as much as anyone else. As I am wandering about near the Reichstag I meet two Federal police officers.

We get talking and one of them says his grandfather was held in Dachau as a political prisoner. His pronunciation of the word is chilling. Konzentrationslager. Standing close to the bunker where Hitler spent his last hours a German policeman with a gun is pronouncing a dreaded word just as those who were about to die would have heard it. Both officers are very diplomatic for street cops. There's a sense when walking around Berlin of walking on liberated streets where political power is not unfairly used. There's nothing sinister here, except for the history of the place. And the protestors chanting, calling again for the mass killing of Jews.

Yet the shocking crimes and fraud that Hitler and his crew visited on so many is alive here in Germany. People are still enchanted by the simplicity of that message. It's like as if the sufferings and complexities of the world are too much to take. There's a sense too that a messiah with a jackboot ready to smash into the faces of all enemies is just too tempting to fully rule out as an option. There's a building on Kurfurstendamm that was once the famous Cafe Wien. Now it's an Apple store and there's a bunch of people queuing up to buy phones or gadgets or whatever they're now selling in such places. That's Europe today, the hill of bones we walk on. I hung around there for a little while to try to imagine Berlin in the nineteen thirties. There are streets where houses survived all the bombs and mayhem. I stood outside one noble old house for nearly an hour. Maybe it was more than an hour or maybe less. I didn't time it. I just found it strangely comforting. Somebody had lived there who is now reaching out to the world of the living.

There was a sense of comfort and love from the old building. Someone or other, maybe someone who once lived there, was calling out in some strange way nonverbal way from that house. Is it plausible to believe that old buildings can hold onto something from the past that's loving? After a while I rang the bell, but nobody answered. For several more minutes I waited outside that old house, not knowing why I was waiting. I could sense it. It was like waiting in a corridor for someone you love that you know is going to appear in a minute or two. Then I suddenly felt very tired. The house was just the house of a stranger in a strange city. I took one last look at it and went on about my business. It was near the U-station at Charlottenberg. If I ever return to Berlin I'm sure I'd be able to find it. In fact, I could probably find it blindfolded.

The politics out here are going bad again. There's a party called Alternative fur Deutschland. They've been marching through the streets. They say Germany is broken and it's mostly because of immigration. After all these years, after everything that's happened, Jews in Berlin are being told to stay out of certain neighbourhoods. I come across a post online from the Israeli embassy.

'In Berlin houses where Jews live will be marked again. This brings back the worse memories, especially in Germany. They want to destroy us all, without exception.'

April 1981. Ireland.

On the day before Lebanon the dark green army land-rover taking us from the Curragh to Dublin picks up speed on the road between Newbridge and Naas. The corporal in the front with the Fu Manchu moustache is smoking another cigarette as he gazes mournfully out the window at a monotonously grey morning. Enlisted soldiers are often from the roughest or poorest families in the land, many from the garrison towns once very familiar to the old empire's recruiting sergeants. Conversations in land-rovers or in billet-rooms or canteens are not known for erudition, academic reference or wit. If politicians are ever mentioned it's in very vulgar terms. Mostly conversations down at the lower rung of army life revolve around bodily functions, anything to do with sex, football, booze and boozing culture, duty rosters and what NCO or officer is a total prick.

Foreign Minister Lenihan's remarks on the politics of the Middle East are not discussed or referenced. Down here in the mire of beastly soldering a carefully pieced together fortress of ignorance can never be breached. Lies, rumours, obscenity, violence or the threat of violence and endless talk of porn, booze and sex are the norm. To talk about anything to do with politics or foreign affairs would be like asking someone out for a fight. How dare a private soldier with an interest in reading newspapers mention politics when ordinary, decent soldiers are talking about porno-films, venereal disease, getting drunk and worse than that.

It's an act, like so much of our lives are an act. Behave like a squaddie in an art college or a university humanities' site and it's not appreciated. Behave like someone interested in the arts in the dining-rooms and canteens of the Irish Army in the eighties and it's absolutely not appreciated. I'm not the only one to have wandered as a lost soul in the Defence Forces as an insecure teenager trying to find a role in life or struggling to get from one psychic stage of development to the next. One guy from our battalion in Lebanon loved Elvis Presley so much he joined the most convenient army he could find to mimic Elvis in GI Blues. He wore his blue U.N forage cap with the peak tipped so far forward it shadowed his eyes and the top part of his face. The guy's cap was tilted so far forward that he had to hold his head up high and peer down his nose for to see where he was going.

He was enjoying himself, listening to Elvis track after Elvis track on his cassette-player when he wasn't on duty. He was a good-natured guy, popular with the locals, enjoying his army fantasy. When he looked in the mirror did he see a young Irish soldier serving with the U.N in Lebanon? Or did he see the great Elvis cavorting with the girls in GI Blues? In time the good-natured Elvis fan shook off his army fantasies and did something else in life, just as I eventually shook off the demons rooting me to probably the last place in the world I wanted to be. Sense comes gradually to human beings, although this is not a general rule in all cases.

When we reach the town of Naas one of the corporals in the front of the land-rover wants to stop to buy fags. It's not the corporal with the Fu Manchu moustache who's been slyly smoking without offering anyone a ciggie. It's the other corporal in the middle who is sitting next to the driver. Fu Manchu is grouchy. He's not happy about having to shift from his seat to allow the second corporal to jump from the land-rover to the pavement.

The driver and the two corporals are married with young children. They don't seem convinced about this Lebanon business, especially when the national flag on top of the Curragh Fire Station is flying in honour of two dead soldiers. The corporal hurrying to the shop to buy fags is a dab hand at snooker and practises for hours each day on a snooker table in the NCO's mess. He's not looking forward to losing six months' practise by living in a Nissan hut in the hills of South Lebanon. He's insecure too, worried about leaving a precocious young wife alone for possibly one too many lonely Saturday nights. It's the eighties after all. There are no mobile phones or anything much by way of electronic communication. Soldiers stay in touch with loved ones and friends by writing letters and making the occasional phone-call from a telephone at battalion headquarters. Postal deliveries are a godsend. A number of soldiers in the battalion are semi-literate and at least one is illiterate.

At one point during our Lebanon sojourn I ghost-write love letters for an armoured car driver. When his sweetheart wrote back he'd ask me to read her letters to him. He was an easy-going guy and good behind the wheel of an armoured car. But he couldn't read or write a word. The letters we wrote together must have been okay as shortly after the armoured car guy got back to Ireland he married his sweetheart.

In Naas the corporal returns to the land-rover with a fag from a newly bought pack dangling from his lips. As he jumps into the front seats he's joking about Fu Manchu not sharing any of his fags. There's no malice in his words. In the long stagnant hours in the life of our odd and sometimes even lovable military outfit jokes and jibing are as important as Mars bars and cigarettes.

When we get to the Irish area of operations in South Lebanon I'll be assigned as a radio operator to Recce Company. Later, as soon as it's possible I'll transfer to A Coy. I'll have enough practical work to keep my mind busy for most of the time. There'll be aerials and radio-sets to play about with, generators and checkpoint spotlights to maintain and operate. There'll be old Vietnam-era American 77 sets to operate and lug about. I'll get to walk into the wadis of South Lebanon laying field-telephone wire or tracing old lines for faults. The wadis in their barren quietude are transcendent.

The officers and men of A Coy are Eastern Command men from the old British Army-built barracks of Dublin. Sergeant-major

Bennett the bruiser of Portobello set out to fight Dublin's pet lamb from what was to become Cathal Brugha Barracks. The armoured car drivers from A Coy are Cathal Brugha Barracks' men. They are generally okay, brutal-tongued most of the time. Many of the A Coy enlisted men come from families from the old tenement slums of Behan, James Plunkett and O'Casey. When they speak about home, they mention streets and housing estates where much of the drug-wars and crime of the nineteen eighties are generated from.

One of the young A Coy soldiers was an Artane Boy, an orphan from the North Dublin Industrial School run by the Christian Brothers. This made more sense. There was a raging energy in the guy's eyes, something broken that couldn't ever really be fixed. The military had its fair share of the nation's orphans and alumni from the state's correction schools and detention centres. Now and then we'd hear the ugly names of Daingean and Letterfrack spat out in the billets like something vile that can never be swallowed.

Later in London I'd meet the walking wounded from such places. One guy was a gentle soul who'd been schooled by the religious at Dominic Street and who'd smoked and over-ate himself to death in his late forties. He didn't care about Jews or Arabs and cared little about his jaunt with UNIFIL. His anxiety was a living force haunting every facet of his existence. Whatever he'd gone through with the religious order who'd schooled him at Dominic Street it eventually broke something very important inside him. He'd been told his grandfather was his father too. He said he'd been punished from day one, slapped about as if his sole reason to be in the world was to be slapped about by unkind men who were strangers to him. The Dominican priests had taken the old line of scripture literally and acted accordingly.

Behold, I was brought forth in inequity, and in sin did my mother conceive me.

Another guy who washed up in London was sent as a thirteen-year-old runaway to a Christian Brothers' house in County Wicklow. On the first night there he was woken in the early hours by two ghouls with torchlights, wearing the black robes of Ignatius Rice's teaching order. They violated his anus with some implement or other, loosening him up for the nights to come. He ran away the next day with his childhood confidence and so many hopes for the future crushed by the state's hired pederasts.

The young A Coy soldier from Artane was going through his own agonies of betrayal and hurt. What did the torments of the Jewish-Arab conflict mean to him? Parents had let kids down or had died and then the state stepped in and handed them over to an unregulated brotherhood with more than one strap-happy pederast or sadist among them. It's harder now to interpret it in a more humane light. Religious solutions to complex human problems are rarely if ever successful. The cities of England took in their fair share of the Irish state's religious institutional outrages, a state's walking wounded, a kind of revenge on the old enemy.

Who knows what roads the young A Coy soldier from Artane eventually took? There was remarkable hurt in his eyes. Something had happened to him to ruin his self-belief. At least in the billets of our humble army he found a comradeship of flawed souls and fellow travellers in the avenues of cynicism and pain, an acceptance of the darker shadows in the human psyche.

On the day before Lebanon the land-rover taking us from the Curragh to Dublin speeds up as we get past the town of Naas and onto the Naas dual carriageway. Naas, for the student of military history, is interesting insofar as it was the headquarters of the Royal Dublin Fusiliers. The barracks of the famous Dublins passed into the hands of the newly created Free State army in 1922. Many of the soldiers in the fledgling Free State army of the nineteen twenties were former Royal Dublin Fusiliers, redoubtable infantrymen who'd crawled through the mud and slime of the Somme with hell bursting over their heads. And they were joined too by quick killers from the IRA campaigns of 1918 to 1921, men who'd killed other men close up. How different we are from them. None of us has killed anyone, except for one of the cooks who killed a civilian in a pub fight a few years back.

The first and only battle in Ireland between the newly formed national army and the forces of the Crown took place in Pettigo-Belleek in 1922. The one hundred and fifty volunteers who took part were a combination of Anti-Treaty and Pro-Treaty forces under the faraway command of Collins. They faced nearly two thousand British soldiers, armed police and Orange militiamen over two weeks of fighting. They were serious men, a proper crew with a knack for putting holes in the vital parts of others. After two weeks they withdrew from the Pettigo-Belleek area just as Collins ordered. The student of Irish Republican history might conclude that they'd have returned with more men and better arms and equipment if their leader Collins had lived.

In keeping with the common and expected propaganda of national governments the London newspapers at the time described Pettigo-Belleek as a salient, as if using war coverage terms from the Western Front to talk about the northern slopes of Lough Erne could be in any way helpful. The Pettigo-Belleek area in 1922 was damp farmland, bogs and boreens on the northern shore of Lower Lough Erne, a forty-two-kilometre lake dotted with tiny islands.

The townlands of Pettigo extended to the northeast of the lake with Belleek to the southeast. A branch-line of the Great Northern Railway defied the sullen wetlands by coursing through the villages of Irvinestown, Kesh, Pettigo, Castle Caldwell, Belleek and then to the seaside town of Bundoran. To try and capture something of the mood of the time in the area we could picture in our minds the Protestant militia gathered at Pettigo under the command of Sir Basil Brooke. These men were later discredited by their actions against civilians. Brooke gave an infamous and inflammatory speech at an Orange rally when he urged his fellow Orangemen not to have a Catholic about the place. It was yet another backward step for the island of Ireland when decades later Brooke became prime minister of the Northern Ireland statelet.

The trouble at Pettigo-Belleek began when Brooke and his Orange militia crossed Lough Erne on a flotilla of small boats towed by a steamer. Once safely on the other side of the lake they kicked the Sinn Fein priest Lorcan O'Ciarain from his parish house at Magheramenagh Castle. The Pettigo-Belleek battles of May and June of 1922 set another unholy precedent whereby any military action from the South or even a misinterpreted false move brought a quick pogrom against nationalist ghettoes or an outrage against individual Catholics in the Northern enclaves. If a nationalist rifle cracked off a shot on the border, then a petrol-bomb or brick went through the window of a Catholic home in Belfast or Lurgan. The lessons of Pettigo-Belleek were absorbed into the collective unconsciousness of nationalists throughout the country as thousands of Northern Ireland Catholics fled murderous assaults by their Protestant neighbours.

Years later the first murders of the more recent troubles were justified by Gusty Spence by pointing to the 1966 bi-centennial celebrations in Dublin of the 1916 Rising. Spence was so worried about what he saw as nationalist sabre-rattling in Dublin that he went out and murdered three young innocent Catholics having a drink in a Belfast pub. A more pragmatic interpretation of the battles at Pettigo-Belleek is to see them as the predictable re-runs of working-class, property-less men doing their best to protect the privileges and proprietary rights of the ruling classes. If every individual from both sides totted up their overall wealth and assets in the world after the final shots echoed across Lough Erne would they have made very much improvement from what they had before the battle? Except for Sir Basil Brooke and the Catholic Church which owned the castle and grounds of Magheramenagh there would have been little real gain for the ordinary men on either side.

Nationalist consciousness can never be underestimated. It's a consciousness perfected from the womb. Peasants and the children of peasants and the property-less are so easily shepherded into a national consciousness that the centralised powers don't have to try very hard to perfect it. The cups and saucers are already spinning on the ends of the juggler's sticks with only an occasional deft touch of hand needed to keep them spinning. A shared consciousness of past hurts and nationalist boundaries is the arms' manufacturer's best friend.

Pettigo-Belleek scarred the heart of nationalist Ireland with a stalemate whereby nationalist militarism or threat of militarism on the border must always add up to threats or actual violence against Catholics in the North. With such a stalemate in mind the restrained subservience of the Irish army to An Gardai Siochana when security duties are mentioned is more understandable. It's a dead-end, a checkmate played out before any of us bound for the Lebanon on this coming flight were born.

We carry the incomplete moves of old battles in our unconscious minds as much as Protestants north of the border carry in their unconscious minds the fear that late one night they'll be murdered in their beds by their Catholic neighbours. The soldiering experience after all is so often an exercise in protracted frustration. Pettigo-Belleek confined us in a giant rattrap where any false move threatens the lives and wellbeing of our compatriots in Northern Ireland. Hiroshima and Nagasaki confined millions of soldiers globally in a more complex rattrap where nuclear annihilation of entire populations and ecological apocalypse were the jaws of the trap ready to snap shut at the first grave error of judgement.

In the Free State army of 1922/23 were thousands of men who'd fired thousands of rounds in action. Men who'd killed and maimed other men in combat and who'd fought as frontline British infantry in the infamous battles of WW1. Men who'd split the skulls of German storm-troopers in hand-to-hand fighting and who'd been choked almost to death by gas attacks, taken wounds to both body and psyche. There were men too who fought in the 1916 Easter Rising with Pearse, Connolly and De Valera and who'd killed with the coldness of heart needed to kill. Men who'd fought and killed and maimed in skirmishes and ambushes all over Ireland.

These veterans of death and mayhem were joined by thousands of young recruits keen to serve and kill under the leadership of Collins and his IRB and Irish Volunteer comrades. If anything can be judged by Collins' life and character he'd have not squandered such an army. He'd have strengthened and reinforced them, toughened them and honed their killing instincts. Within a few years they'd have been back at Pettigo-Belleek where the question of Irish national independence would be played out in further battles.

But Collins was killed while Irish national army rifle-barrels were yet piping hot from the exchanges at Pettigo-Belleek. Conservatives from the Catholic-educated middle-classes formed the first government of a modern Irish state with the revolutionary zeal of a bishop's tea-party. After several years of violence and disorder the population demanded peace and an unarmed police force. The heady days of 1921 and 1922 when Michael Collins was alive and at the head of a proud army with its fair share of seasoned cut-throats were soon forgotten. In a peaceful, neutral land there'd be no real need for an army.

We are linked to the fledgling National Army at Pettigo-Belleek, although it takes a fair leap of imagination to link us in a tangible way with any serious army unfettered from the neurotic civil servants who hate us. The only possible field of conflict on this island of Ireland is in the six counties of Ulster, partitioned and dominated by the descendants of Scottish Lowland Protestants, agents of the British state, and the remnants of Anglo-Irish landed gentry. Such a conflict is now more remote because so many of the Catholics of Northern Ireland are fairly content for the most part living in a United Kingdom of diversity. It's not the Northern Ireland of 1969 or even 1998. Discrimination is analysed and addressed, looked at through the lens of human rights legislation. The economic future of Catholics in the North is better served as part of the UK and in more candid moments this is admitted in private conversations at least. The Sinn Fein voter may be happy to be represented by an energised party, but this doesn't necessarily mean they would vote for a united Ireland if given the chance in a border poll.

After Pettigo-Belleek the powers behind the Dublin government accepted they could not march on the North in the spirit of Richard

Talbot and Sarsfield marching on Derry. London's heavy-handed reinforcing of Pettigo-Belleek set the ground-rules for any likely action on the border. It would not be a conflict between the national forces of the South against Northern Orangeism. It would be a contest between the South and the North with the full might of the British Empire supporting the North's Orange brigades in the field and everywhere else they were needed. With Collins dead there was nobody crazy enough or capable enough to even contemplate such a mad thing.

Much like so many conflicts around the globe the conflict in Ireland between North and South defaulted to a tense border, to mind-games and diplomatic exchanges of words and gestures. Actual violence when it happened was contained by British or Irish authorities, depending on whose jurisdiction it occurred in. From 1923 onwards Irish soldiery were on a peacetime footing. There was no enemy as such to fight. The bravery and sacrifice of Irishmen from Ireland and of Irish descent fighting in the British military and with the other allied forces in WWII redeemed the soul of neutral Ireland in the eyes of Churchill and Roosevelt. Hitler's ambitions in these wet islands were limited and after the Battle of Britain in 1940 there was no active German threat of invasion.

Psychologically Irish soldiers found themselves in a not dissimilar situation to the ground-crews of minuteman nuclear missiles or the flying crews of nuclear-armed USAF B52s in later decades. They could not actually fulfil the potential of their arms. The minuteman crew could not fire a nuclear missile at Russia, much like the Irish army could not band together its most resilient cut-throats and have another go at Pettigo-Belleek.

Serving the limited ambitions of the Irish government stunted the growth, professionalism and spirit de corps of Ireland's military. Several National Army senior officers simply resigned and immigrated to the USA. Others were transferred to the newly created police force, An Garda Siochana. Two former National Army generals, McEoin and Murphy, were later Garda commissioners. Murphy fought as a British army officer at Loos and the Somme, rising to the rank of Lieutenant Colonel before returning to Ireland to serve under Collins.

After the heady days of the formation of the state the army regressed to a torpor it has never really shook off. Many Irish citizens were annoyed or perplexed at the very idea of the new Irish state having an army at all. On closer analysis this is interesting as it concentrates the power of the state on the police, confident that any security duties could be handled by the police once they were given the arms and resources they needed.

In the rationale of the thoughtful citizen concerned with peace and stability the existence of an Irish army serves only one purpose, to present an actual or symbolic threat to the North. In the Irish national consciousness there's only one fight requiring a sacrifice of blood, suffering and death. And it's a very old fight, now only relevant in the context of what is seen by many as an armed and hostile legacy of settlers in the Northeast. If there's no effective Irish army then this spectre of war or conflict of some kind with the Orange North does not exist. Citizens can sleep easy at night.

In the Civil War of 1922-23 the National Army hunted down and killed De Valera's rebels with a ruthlessness to match the dreaded Black and Tans. Little wonder the Irish rational mind recoils at the very mention of an Irish National Army. These anxieties were addressed through the decades by shepherding the Irish military into the shadows, pretending they didn't really exist beyond occasional ceremonial jaunts, solemn flag-lowering occasions at the Garden of Remembrance and propaganda newsreels from Movietone and British Pathe News. Even when Ireland faced a real threat of invasion in 1939/40 the nation's most lucid minds pointed to our neutrality and to friends and kin in Britain and in the USA as a deterrent to invasion rather than relying on the National Army in the field.

U.N overseas service saved the spirit and morale of the Irish army. We can but try to imagine the weight of the torpor on the ordinary soldier in the army of the '40/50s. Hob-nailed boots and bulls-wool uniforms, quarter of a loaf ration per day per man and all the strong sweetened tea you could drink. Players or Woodbines, cold billet-rooms and morning Mass parades. British surplus .303 Lee Enfield rifles and Bren guns. Long marches in the rain from the Curragh Camp to the Glen of Imaal, a night or two under canvas and then back again.

Cathal Goulding and Sean Garland's IRA were active on the border in the late fifties and early sixties, attacking RUC stations and British army barracks where and when possible. The deaths of South and O'Hanlon added yet more mystique to the cause of blood and sacrifice to the nation, another stirring song added to the songbook of revolution. The National Army looked away as if it was of no concern to them. They were not led by ex-Flying Column men with short tempers or by former lieutenant colonels in the British Army who'd fought against the Kaiser's front-line at Loos and the Somme. It was not 1922 or 1923 when the IRA were hunted down and arrested by National soldiers and then knocked about a bit before getting thrown in a cell. It was not 1922 or 1923 when National Army soldiers jumped in a Crossley Tender or a commandeered civilian truck and raced to wherever they were needed to sort out matters through the barrel of a Mauser or the butt-end of a Lee Enfield.

The population and the institutions of the state insisted on peace and stability, so it made sense to ignore or play down the presence of IRA men on the border. There was no stomach for a role for the army in any way reminiscent of its vital role in the formation of the state. Besides, it was time for more rations of bread, cheese and bacon, for another load of damp turf to be wheel-barrowed to married quarters and another forced march to the Glen of Imaal.

Post October 7th attack on Israel. London.

A Jewish-owned business in London's Stamford Hill was vandalised by Palestine Action. Furniture, windows and computers were smashed, red paint sprayed from a cannister. Palestine Action said the attack was because the business had links to an arms industry company providing weapon components to Israel. The owners of the business said they have no such links.

It reminds me of when the British National Party marched on Hammersmith's Irish Centre. The staff working there on that day were scared. One of them rang her husband for to come and pick her up and she went home early. It must have been intimidating for those coming and going to and from the Irish Centre on that` day. Irish dancing classes for children were disrupted. There had never been any political events organised there before, or at least not events linked to the kind of causes the British National Party like to protest. Tony Benn gave a talk there after he'd retired from the active British Left. It was a cultural centre where Irish music and dancing were practised, and literary events were staged.

The Longford artist Bernard Canavan gave a series of talks on Irish history there once. In keeping with Bernard's erudite take on life the talks focused on romantic figures such as the brothers Yeats and Oscar Wilde. Perhaps the activists from the British National Party were protesting about culture. Maybe deep in their distrustful minds the very thought of people tuning into culture was a worrying and unhealthy thing to do. Maybe the thought of reading a book or listening to someone giving an informed talk on some aspect or other of history was the problem. Who can really say? After all, in fascist circles the art of following is more favoured than the process whereby an individual does their own thinking and comes up with their own conclusions.

The activists from the British National Party could have attacked the Hammersmith Irish Centre at night, just as Palestine Action attacked a Jewish business in Stamford Hill. They could have broken every window in the place, smashed the furniture and computers to pieces. But they chose a daytime protest instead, intimidating the few people who were working there at the time and causing a ripple of anxiety in the lives of locals with roots in Ireland.

Those who practised the tin whistle or the bodhran at the Hammersmith Irish Centre or who brought their children there for to learn Irish dancing had as much connection with those acting against the authorities in Northern Ireland on political grounds as the owners of a small business in Stamford Hill have with the operational decisions of the Israeli government. Yet they were targeted for intimidation and vandalism by the British National Party and by Palestine Action.

For the Irish who are quick to support direct action in support of the Palestinian cause it's worth remembering that we too were targeted by people with an abiding hatred for all we are and all we ever might be. The evicted at Clongorey and so many other sites of outrage from Irish history are activated in the national collective unconscious when conflicts in the world are presented to us in such a way that reenacts the tyranny of absent English landlords against oppressed Irish peasants. But impressions from deeper mind are not necessarily facts in the world.

If the principles of Palestine Action and the British National Party were normalised what would be the implications for society? Would it be okay to attack the house of someone who was born in a land where a tyrant seized power and is persecuting its people? What exact connection would warrant a protest, an act of criminal damage or a physical assault? Maybe in the future such a dystopia will exist, where conformity and homogeneity are so enforced that nothing outside the strictest criteria of sameness is accepted. It can seem at times that this is what many people want, or even crave, an existence of perfected conformity where even the most insignificant detail of difference or otherness is outlawed.

Meanwhile vandals have spray-painted the Israeli-owned Chez Marianne restaurant in Paris, along with the Belleville synagogue and two other synagogues. The Holocaust Memorial in the Marais district of the city was paint-bombed too. The European Union Agency for Fundamental Rights reported that seventy six percent of European Jews do not wear anything outside their homes and temples that might identify them as Jewish. If after such a relatively short time in history we begin to forget how Hitler's Holocaust began then what else can we forget? What use was our education in history if harassment and hatred is breaking out all over again?

From an Irish perspective will the evictions at Clongorey and elsewhere be forgotten too? Will we forget the nineteen seventies when every second joke on British television was an Irish joke? Will we forget the Irish children who listened to Irish joke after Irish joke on television shows to the point where they were led to belief that to be Irish was to be thick, backward and not quite human? That's what we do when we forget. We give the judicial crimes of the past a pardon. Within this civilisation we are part of and this epoch of time in which we are here on this planet there are certain happenings from the fairly recent past that we really shouldn't forget.

April 1981. Dublin.

In the land-rover enroute to Dublin's Collins' Barracks the conversation is livening up. The two corporals seem to have gotten over the worse of their earlier misery and are smoking and talking with the driver. At one point on the Naas Dual Carriageway, they remember they have somebody in the back and one of them turns around to ask if I am all right. Sure, I say. I'm all right. Then I'm forgotten about and the three guys in the front of the land-rover go on talking about the bread-and-butter details of army life conjoining all our destinies.

One of the corporals is hoping to pay for double-glazed windows for his house from the money he earns in Lebanon. The driver is not actually going to Lebanon this time around. His job is to drive us to Collins Barracks and then drive back to the Curragh. He's been to Lebanon a year ago and bought a decent second-hand car off his brother-in-law and paid off several small debts from his U.N pay. Money from Lebanon has paid for many a wedding and bought many a family car here in the county of Kildare and elsewhere too.

The conversation of the three guys sitting in the front of the land-rover is as banal as any conversation likely to be heard in any public house or workplace canteen. It echoes the concerns of three ordinary working men with family duties. It's not the talk of warriors or pillagers or men ready to stick bayonets into the guts or throats of other men. There's restraint in their words. Their anxieties are centred on money, the fidelity of women and the comforts of working-class Ireland. The conversation in the land-rover is not the conversation we'd have overheard at Pettigo-Belleek in 1922. It's not the talk of men psyched up to kill or of nationalist zealots who've sensed their moment in history has finally arrived.

In border-towns like Monaghan and Cavan in the eighties an occasional insult was heard from republican sympathisers. Usually, it was predicated by Free State. The term Free State was said with such venom it sounded like an insult in itself. In a re-interpretation of the mysticism and high-minded political ambitions of 1916 the republican purist was horrified by Free Statism as much as they were horrified by the demonic spectre of the Brits. When off-duty in the border towns we hung around in groups of six or seven, safety in numbers.

Further south we had a reputation almost as unlovely as the reputation of national traitors. We were damned as drunkards and wife-beaters, idle men with too much time to think about our inadequacies and failings in life.

The driver of the land-rover has cheered up and is talking about a recent Joe Dolan concert he went to with his wife and some friends. He's a big Joe Dolan fan and has all the LPs. He talks about the love and veneration of the fans, the swooning mothers circling the great Joe. The two corporals grin in approval. This is the kind of conversation they enjoy. This is where they are satisfied, talking about the moods and fancies of popular Ireland.

In reality we're part of a civilian militia rather than army men. The driver and the corporals in the front of the land-rover would swop their green uniforms tomorrow if they could for the overalls of a civilian job with the same pay, conditions and pension. It's just a job after all, a weekly paycheque. Men must live. There are only so many consistently gifted men in the land who can do skilled work from sun-up to sun-down, year-in, year-out. Somebody must drive a land-rover for the Irish army.

They haven't bothered giving us a psychological assessment before deploying to Lebanon. This is probably not such a bad thing. The psyche of the average enlisted man is best left unexplored. Probing the deeper mind of any of us will not advance the discipline of psychology or the evolution of the human species in any way. Watching another re-run of Debbie Goes To Dallas in the guardroom of Portlaoise Prison while swallowing garrison-strength tea and smoking the strongest fags to be had is not interesting in itself.

The experience of spending time in the Irish army is as much an individualised experience as it is defined by the roles we are meant to fill. There are dreamers in our ranks and others with ambitions beyond the barrack square. When I finally overcome the worse of my psychological problems and break free from Irish army barrack-rooms I'll drift to London like so many misfits before me. Where best to hide a tree but in the forest?

After about a year or so in London I bumped into a guy from my old unit. He was busy, rushing from a dump-truck to a pile of rubble in front of a house he was working on. He was friendly but very brief, clearly not wanting any jaunts down memory lane in the middle of his working day. I was surprised as I thought he'd like to chat for a few minutes at least about the old days. He didn't. Inside a minute he was gone, rushing back to the controls of his truck. As he went, he said one thing which stayed with me.

The four years in the Curragh was a waste 'a time boy. I could 'a been over here makin' money!

I began realising then what a waste of time it'd been. So much time is wasted anyhow but wasting time on the Curragh was an art-form. We wasted time sinfully and indulgently. We wasted time collectively and individually. We wasted time spitefully and guiltily. There was no situation we could not exploit fully by skilfully transforming it into a situation where we could waste time.

In fairness it wasn't only the humble enlisted soldier of the Irish army who skived and wasted time in the eighties. In London I worked with a Ukrainian who'd served with the Red Army around the time I was wasting time in the Irish army. One role he had was guarding MIG jets in a remote part of the old Soviet empire. The time-wasting, drunken shenanigans, skiving and general madness he described outshone anything I'd seen or heard of happening on the Curragh.

He and his comrades were at least involved in the Cold War, watching their radar-screens for signs of an impending Armageddon. In neutral Ireland it was hard to pretend anyone was interested in invading us. The RAF and Royal Navy were watching out for the wider air and sea defence of all the British Isles, including our ostensibly neutral country. Our defence budget was modest and influential voices questioned why we needed an army at all. Couldn't the police force, the Civil Defence and a small naval service for fishery protection do just as well?

Did we really need battalions of men with tanks and artillery? There were real concerns at times about Loyalist incursions from the North but the security threat as far as most people were concerned came from the Provisional IRA and a few splinter groups and oddballs on the far left. Irish soldiers guarded the walls of Portlaoise prison where the most dedicated IRA prisoners were held. During one attempted break-out at Portlaoise in the nineteen seventies an Irish soldier opened fire from his concrete sentry box. One of the rounds he fired ricocheted and killed an IRA prisoner.

A decade or so later Ireland's most dangerous rebel at the time tried to drive through an Irish army checkpoint. Irish soldiers opened fire on him and the man was badly injured. A fellow adventurer travelling in the car with him was shot dead. Internal security was more important than casual memory recalls. Movements of explosives, cash and high-risk prisoners were escorted by Irish army land-rovers. Soldiers with FN 7.62mm rifles and Carl Gustav 9mm machine-pistols travelled in the back of the land-rovers, watching and waiting.

In this regard we'd inherited the role of the National Army in the first few years after the founding of the Irish Free State. In support of the police, we were ready to kill if necessary or otherwise take on a modern-day version of the anti-Treaty IRA. Republican purists and bar-counter rebels enjoyed this curious historical loop and loved nothing better on beery Saturday nights than shouting out the insult 'Free State Bastards' to all connected to the Irish Defence Forces. However much we were lampooned we'd swore our lives to Ireland, offered ourselves as human sacrifices to the nation if such sacrifices were needed. That fact didn't seem appreciated very much in the day to day life of the country.

For the small number of citizens who took an interest in such things we were the devil incarnate, the enforcers of a parliament set up by the British in Dublin in 1922. They were incensed when we claimed our origins in the Easter Rising of 1916, damning us as the legacy of a counter-revolution in 1922/23 which abandoned the struggle for a thirty-two-county independent nation and settling instead for a partitioned twenty-six county capitalist pseudo-theocracy almost entirely dependent on Britain and with money posted home by immigrants.

I guess they were correct to a point but forgot how many of the volunteers of 1916 and 1919-1922 authenticated the twenty-six-county state by fully taking part in it. And of course, De Valera blessed the twenty-six-county parliament when he parted ways with Sinn Fein and went onto personify the modern Irish state. Our origins were in 1916 and in the revolutionary war in 1919-21 but also in the Free State army's campaigns against the irregulars in 1922-23. These fine points of history were often wholly academic as citizens could dislike us or hate us on sight simply because we were common soldiers. For the collective memory of the Irish Catholic people the very sight of a common soldier can have a repugnant connation.

In the front of the land-rover the driver and the two corporals are laughing at a crude, unfunny joke. It's a play on fanny-farts. The driver really enjoys the joke, laughing loudly and banging the heel of one hand on the steering-wheel. The moment captures the spirit of life in the army at that time. Fag smoke dense in the air, the baseness of sex-jokes and men laughing. Anything outside the empty vulgarity of barrack-room jokes and the necessity of everyday tasks doesn't exist. Or if it does exist it's better for ordinary soldiers not to mention it.

The more energetic Irish soldiers sometimes try to interpret the U.N experience in Lebanon as a jaunt on a par with the universal soldier going overseas. Photographs of Irish soldiers in Lebanon wearing flak-jackets and carrying general purpose machine guns with belts of 7.62mm ammo dangling from their mechanisms are common. Everyone poses for such photographs. We pose proudly from the turrets of armoured cars or from the roofs of sandbag positions. We pose in small groups with our FN rifles and Carl Gustav machine-pistols pointed jubilantly at the skies. The photographs are precious evidence to disclose to children and grandchildren in years to come, proof of manliness and a coming-of-age. We are not lazy semi-drunkards and wife-beaters the photographs declare. We went to a warzone and played a role in great events of global importance. Look, see how young we were. See the weapons we carried.

Posing and fantasy aside the presence of UNIFIL in South Lebanon really helped many of the simple people from those hilly towns and villages. The U.N brought field hospitals with brilliant medical professionals and x-ray units to scan the dislocated or fractured bones of locals. It brought dentists and female doctors to speak with subjugated women about age-old maladies. UNICEF opened schools and orphanages. Army engineers built roads and re-opened dormant water-supplies.

UNIFIL soldiers combed the dirt-roads and wadis of South Lebanon with mine-detectors, deactivating thousands of mines and lethal devices. The tiny bouncing betty mines dropped by the Israeli air force in the canisters of one-thousand-pound bombs littered South Lebanon. Routinely, a sheepherder or goat-herder from one of the villages stepped on a bouncing betty. The devices are spring-loaded, so they bounce a foot or so in the air. The idea is to put the victim out of action but often the unfortunate victim not only has a leg blown off but dies from shock and blood-loss.

One of the real heroes of Ireland's mission to Lebanon deactivated many of these devices as well as mines set by local militias. Lt. Aengus Murphy from Tuam in County Galway was a brave, fearless Irish army officer who defused Amal and Hezbollah mines and roadside booby-traps. Murphy was so good in his role that he was personally warned by Amal/Hezbollah to stop neutralising their explosive devices. This courageous lieutenant ignored their threat and went on about his work. He was killed in 1986 by an Amal/Hezbollah device intentionally set to kill him.

In the nineteen eighties the economy of South Lebanon was revitalised by the presence in medieval towns and villages of thousands of U.N soldiers with pocketfuls of U.S dollars to spend. Poor families opened their doors to fry egg and chips for soldiers and to sell Snickers bars and cans of Sprite and Pepsi. Arab merchants made money selling all kinds of junk to the soldiers. Watches, lighters, cartons of cigarettes, chintz, dubious gold chains for wives and fiancés back home, brass ornaments, fake brands, perfumes. All this and more were sold and bought at a fevered pitch. As practised consumers from the relative paucity of Irish working-class homes we filled bags and bags with all this junk and it was faithfully shipped home for us. We bought baubles for peace in Lebanon and ate egg and chips for the advancement of the South Lebanese people.

Our intended military role was subservient not so much to the U.N Secretary General but to the moods of the major players on the ground. When the PLO fancied firing a few rockets at Israel from their bases at Beaufort Castle or Tyre they just went ahead and did so. When Israel decided to invade Lebanon in 1982 it simply did so, ignoring the many UNIFIL posts and checkpoints it passed on the way. As idealistic, well-trained and well-motivated as many UNIFIL soldiers were we were subject to an often baffling and sometimes sinister remit from U.N headquarters in New York.

From the front of the land-rover Fu Manchu has snapped out of his introspection and is offering cigarettes to others. There's now a jolly mood in the land-rover, with the bad news from the 48th Battalion in Lebanon forgotten for the moment. We pass Goffs and The Red Cow Inn. We know the landmarks on the road to Dublin as well as we know the respective ceilings we sleep under. We glide through the southern approaches to Dublin like ghosts.

The driver could drive through these streets in his sleep. He drives as self-assuredly as a taxi-driver who uses this route every day. He's been up and down to Dublin countless times, sometimes driving heavy Bedford trucks. Expertly he scans the streets as he drives, watching out for shapely young women. He's the first to point out any female worth a second look. At Inchicore a young lad cycling on the pavement gives us the middle finger. Fu Manchu takes the trouble to acknowledge the lad with a brief wave. It'd take a lot more than a jutting middle finger from a passing civilian to raise the hackles of the average Irish soldier.

There are those innocent enough to believe we should be in our trucks and armoured cars and on our way to the border. They are probably not students of the action at Pettigo-Belleek in 1922 when London rushed battalions of their best soldiers to reinforce their side of the border. Everyone knows our chain-smoking, beer-loving militia-like army are no match for the frontline infantry of the British Army. We only laugh at the occasional middle-finger gesture or shout of Free State bastard. Our daring general is a long time dead. Everyone knows we're going home for our tea.

Yet in the ranks of the Irish army of the eighties are men who if picked for special training and given the correct leadership and context could trouble any military outfit on the planet. Men with supernatural strength who hardly blink when hurling sticks are broken on their bones. Men with violent, psychopathic natures who'd kill, maim and destroy if given any encouragement at all to do so. In a few units based on the Curragh Camp are a dozen or two of such men. There's another dozen or so in the newly formed Army Ranger Wing and a few more in the Military Police. In the ranks of perhaps the army's best battalion, the 6th Battalion based in Athlone, are others who'd take human life in the name of the Irish nation without asking a single question. They'd ram a bayonet into the guts of an enemy or kill with their bare hands if they had to.

Perhaps if pooled together these men could make up a battalion or maybe even a brigade at a push if they were padded out by new blood. They'd be a match for any similar unit anywhere on the planet, more than capable of whatever's needed from the killing infantry. But Ireland has no need for such a unit of killers. The individuals who by nature and inclination would populate such a unit are scattered about the various barracks, kept busy with the banality of peace-time duties and long tedious hours guarding the walls of Portlaoise prison and the grim forts and barracks inherited from the old British regiments. Their beer is subsidised in enlisted men's canteens and NCO's messes. We're an army with no need for killers.

In the back of the land-rover I'm absorbed by the passing images of Dublin. For the mentally oppressed and for dreamers the sights and smells of a city are an elixir. How much of an illusion is it? Can people caught up in the lives and fantasies of Western pop culture really find an answer in cities? I'm hung up high in the breezes somewhere between an unformed mind and a demoralised spirit.

Surely somewhere in this city there's an art college or a place where people can learn to draw cartoons and illustrate. And libraries and bookshops too, maybe a coffee shop where a citizen can sit peacefully with a book for a full blessed hour. Surely there's another way of living, another way of travelling through Dublin other than in the back of an Irish army land-rover. The city streets are a pained reminder of one too many inadequacies and the societal boxes so many of us are squeezed into from the very first moments we emerge from the womb.

There's an ache at the base of my stomach and palpitations in my chest. My mouth and throat are dry and a sadness weighs on me with the dead-weight of a thousand gloomy ancestors. The back of the military land-rover is a dungeon for the human spirit. Just then the everyday streets of southwest Dublin are the lights of a distant Christchurch as viewed by the idealistic Jude. This is fate. This is how life pans out.

Fu Manchu has turned around and is speaking to me. At first, I can't hear his words as if he's miles away or as if his voice is distorted by a long tunnel. I shake my head from side to side, shaking off a crown of useless thoughts. He's asking a routine question, something to do with what the company sergeant of our home unit said the week before. I mumble a disinterested 'yeah I think so'. He looks at me for a second or two longer than necessary. Has he noticed a stranger madness in my eyes? Then he turns around in his seat and I'm forgotten about again, left in peace with my silent longings for a different life.

At this very moment there are many other eighteen-year-old soldiers in many parts of the world, French and Italian conscripts and others in the ranks of a million-man army of Communists. Albanian and Romanian border-guards are watching the skies for signs of a NATO attack. Russian lads in Siberian outposts are dreaming of whatever Russian lads dream of. Hundreds of thousands of Cold War soldiers are sitting at the controls of battle-tanks and in Warsaw Pact and NATO billets, waiting for the beginning of another war to end all wars.

At certain moments they must feel like this too, feel like life is passing them by. Out of all the situations in the world to find themselves in they are lowly, unimportant conscripts or volunteers of necessity in an army with designs and purposes opposed to the spirit of the young. They wait, just like I'm waiting, for another door to open.

The mendacity of humankind has check-mated itself, turned nuclear warheads into a loaded revolver with the barrel aimed at humanity's own forehead. Mutually assured destruction. The humble solder with his rifle and tin-hat is almost redundant, reduced to guard duties and a bit-part in an occasional war-game. The universal soldier is trapped in the prison of lonely military service, waiting for the nuclear holocaust to black out the very light from the sun.

The tensions and proxy wars between the USSR and the U.S decide everything and shadow every U.N debate and foreign policy decision globally. We're on our way to Lebanon with our helmets painted blue to help avert the next world war as much as anything else. Nixon was a whisker away from sending in U.S paratroopers to fight alongside the Israelis in 1973. If he had gone ahead and done so historians tell us the opening shots of WWIII would have been heard shortly afterwards. History whispers that if there is going to be another world war it's likely to begin in these Middle Eastern lands. In Lebanon we'll shelter behind sandbags and watch the Israeli border through binoculars, waiting like a global brotherhood of sentries. We are the midnight watch, dreaming of home and hoping to never see a mushroom cloud on the horizon.

At this very moment there are eighteen-year-olds practising guitar chords in their bedrooms or showing up to track and field events or chess clubs, going through the transformations they are meant to go through to take them to the next stage of their development. Random throws of cosmic dice decide so much. I'm here in the back of a land-rover and we're not far from Collins Barracks. My consciousness is hammered into submission by negativity from a number of directions. This is probably as good as it'll get for now. Aspiration is not an actual word people use around here.

I'm seriously wondering if there's any way out of this mental dungeon conjoining my personal beliefs with the fate of so many who seem to like the role of peacetime soldier in a small neutral country. Then Collins Barracks comes into view. There's a little hope Lebanon might be a revelation, an escape from the psychic hell of a teenage existence in our odd peacetime army. I sit up straighter in the backseats of the land-rover. This is the day before Lebanon after all, and we have things to do. We have lives to live, or a valuable life not to live, depending on how we see things.

Post Oct 7ᵗʰ 2023 attack on Israel. London.

From the perspective of a Londoner the attack on October 7ᵗʰ can seem part of the culture wars. But the cultures at war are drawn from certain forces from the Muslim world set against an increasingly secular West. Protests bear this out, with columns of displaced persons from the Muslim nations marching angrily through the centre of London every weekend, shoulder to shoulder with homegrown protesters who only ever seem obsessed with one particular overseas conflict. Keffiyehs and clenched fists. Palestinian flags. From the river to the sea. Eventually the Metropolitan police commissioner will complain about the cost of policing such marches.

Anyone who lives or has lived in London can tell you about the cost in sleepless hours and psychological well-being from anti-social behaviour. The tepid, often useless response from the police to such things belies the torpor of a nation ill at ease with itself. The bleary-eyed early-shift worker rings the police at 2am to complain that the neighbours are having another party and the bedroom walls are literally vibrating from the sound of loud music. How can someone get up at 5.30am and go to work after such a disturbance? The operator is sympathetic but there's nothing they can do about it. You'd have to ring the council after-hours number. If the sleepless citizen manages to focus enough to get through to the emergency number they'll be told there's nothing they can do about it either. If they like they can fill in an online complaint form or ring environmental health during working hours.

In more civilised parts of the world the police would show up. The music would end. The party would be over. In London as in much of the U.K the police have simply given up on key aspects of their accepted policing role. Those with insights into such things will say it's got to do with resources. Maybe they're just too busy policing protests in favour of the Palestinian cause in the centre of London to worry about such things. Displaced migrants from Muslim nations and their families are joined on the Free Palestine marches by people from what could be euphemistically called the Left in British politics. Leaders of the British Left refused to condemn Hamas in the days after the attack. One famous doyen of the popular Left said-

...ending the occupation is the only means of achieving a just and lasting peace.

As the Israelis left Gaza in 2008 it's not quite clear what occupation is referred to. Do they mean the occupation of Gaza by the Iranian-sponsored terrorist group Hamas? What other occupation could be meant? Surely a country can't occupy a neighbouring land from a distance. As in much of human affairs language is often used in ambiguous, far from lucid ways in relation to the Middle East. The doyen in question remains a kind of secularised saint of the radical Left for he abandoned what could be called the mainstream Left some time ago. He can creep into the more peaceful thoughts of those who generally see themselves as supporters of the Labour party, appearing as a Goldstein-type figure from Orwell's dystopia.

As we'd expect the Irish Left join in with the pro-Palestinian protests, often unclear as to whether they're in support of Hamas' terror or not. Clips on social media are viewed millions of times. The anger is so charged it's as if they just want to get it off their chests. Spit it out. Feel the deep relief of just spitting it out. Kill the Jews! The lack of sensitivity from Irish commentators and politicians in the days and weeks after the October 7th attacks invite another title of shame for a country that has struggled to find a place for itself in the world outside the tired old stereotypes. The most anti-Semitic country in Europe.

Weren't we despised too for wanting a homeland for the Irish people, a land independent and free from outside influence? A number of our forefathers were willing to fight and lay down their lives for it. Irish national hero Tom Barry's 'Guerilla Days in Ireland' was studied by the Jewish nationalists of Hagenah and Irgun and much respected as a template for national insurrection through guerrilla warfare. It was okay for us but not okay for them. It was okay for us to have part of our constitution dedicated to taking land from another sovereign state, by force if necessary, as we believed it was part of our ancestral land. It's not okay for Jewish nationalists to regard the West Bank/Judea/Samaria as part of their ancestral lands. Arab propaganda has joined forces with a post-Marxian view of the world to create a formidable critique of Israel. It's a critique that can harden the hearts of the young against a country fighting for its very existence against hostile forces on several fronts.

This seems a logical analysis of the facts to hand, insofar as anything to do with the affairs of human beings can fit into to a logical analysis. But turn on the main evening news or buy a newspaper and doubts creep in. Israel again. Hitting out with its military. Targeting enemies. Cast in Western liberal eyes as a malignant Leviathan, sucking the blood from gentile children as once it sucked the blood from gentile children in the Old Pale of Settlement and in the ghettoes of Krakow and Lviv.

The displaced Arabs are Clongorey's poor and evicted, sitting on ruined roads, their belongings scattered about them. There's a lament among the nations and the ghost of O'Casey can be heard on Abbey Street.

Sacred Heart of Jesus take away our hearts of stone and give us hearts of flesh.

April. 1981. Dublin.

Anyone familiar with Collins Barracks in the days when it functioned as a military garrison will remember its small, quaint, stone-arched entrance. Such a vast barracks, such a small entrance gate. Drivers of Leyland, Man Diesel and Bedford trucks as well as Panhard APCs had to get the angle right before swinging through the tight gateway. Our driver has driven through the gate of the barracks so many times he's got a fair chance of driving through it blindfolded. The guard sergeant at the gate is lively and welcoming, waving us through as if waving through his own fond brothers.

The barracks is a mute post-colonial sentry, an impassive stone ogre from history. It speaks of another Ireland, an Ireland where the boldest sons of Presbyterian, Catholic and Anglican families alike took the King's shilling. It speaks of the Royal Dublin Fusiliers and older regiments of foot and horse. It's a sullen reminder of when Dublin was the second city of the Empire, a city vouchsafed by a Governor General with the seal of the Royal Houses of England stamped on his communiqués.

The driver knows the barracks intimately and drives us exactly to where the rest of our chalk is forming up. He doesn't hang about. As soon as we climb from the land-rover he revs up and is on his way, shouting out a final word or two of encouragement as he goes. Hopefully he'll see us in six months' time if all goes well. The vast square of the barracks is daunting, meant for another era and a different body of men. As cigarettes are stubbed out and berets straightened a Transport Corps company sergeant exits from one of the many doorways of the barracks. He must have seen our land-rover drive away with its command emblem as he knows exactly who we are. He fires off a series of quick orders. His orders and gestures are not bossy or bullying but rather sharp and correct.

Basically, we'll be in a barrack-room all day except when the Transport company sergeant marches us around the square for exercise. We'll form up as a chalk throughout the day until trucks take us to Dublin airport where we'll be flown to Lebanon. As the senior NCO on the chalk the Transport company sergeant is responsible for us until we get to the airport. He's switched on, keen to make sure nothing goes wrong.

We're part of H.Q Company of the 49th Battalion UNIFIL. There's less expected of us as regards to having much interest in marching up and down the square. We're mostly signals, transport, engineers and medics. In the barrack-room where we'll hang around for most of the day the mood is subdued. There are bunks to sit on and lie on if we feel like sitting or lying. There's a long timber table with the obligatory iron-legged solid benches which furnish every billet and guardhouse in the land.

Most of the men are a little on edge, slowly getting used to the idea of an absence from wives and girlfriends, from young children and from the close family ties common back then. We sprawl on bunks and several soldiers are already dozing off. A sergeant is reading The Irish Independent with admirable concentration, carefully tapping the ash from a cigarette into an opened cigarette-box. Somebody suggests a game of cards but nobody else is interested. It's too early in the days for cards. And besides, people here have things on their mind.

I stretch out on a bunk and tip my beret forward so as it covers my eyes. I'm not tired but there's nothing else to do but doze. Fu Manchu and the other corporal have met up with an Eastern Command corporal they know from some earlier shared moment in the life of the army. The three men are wringing their hands and talking together in grave concord. They are talking too cautiously for their words to carry to my bunk. There are quite a few NCOs and married soldiers in the billet, so the mood is more civilised. A billet filled with teenage soldiers is a chaotic and violent place. The men waiting here are quieter and more upstanding, for the most part speaking peacefully to each other when they do speak.

Looking back, it's easier to see the nature of the malaise, to break down the parts of what was perhaps some kind of clinical depression. At the time I just got on with it as people in the Ireland of the eighties were expected to get on with so many maladies, suicidal moods, ups, downs and undiagnosed conditions. Maybe as the philosopher once said anxiety is a response to the possibilities of freedom. I was both anxious and depressed, hoping Lebanon would be a distraction at least from an obstinate darkness of mind and from a society that offered little if anything of interest to the likes of us.

On a higher level of thought there was always the possibility that the Irish army was cursed, with its movements shadowed by energies not from here. Maybe idealistic Republicans executed by Free State army firing squads or shot out of hand had not forgotten us. From a view set in the public imagination by the martyrs of 1916 we'd settled for very little, even though we were given a lot. It felt as if they'd damned us from their martyred graves, Ireland unfree shall never be at peace. The fanaticism of men like Tom Clarke, Erskine Childers and Cathal Brugha can't be extinguished by physical death. Such war-spirits live on somewhere. They leave a legacy.

I doze off for a little while. As ever sleep is a mercy cure for the ailment of too much reality. Someone is shouting in the barking voice of an NCO with something urgent on his mind. It's the Transport company sergeant. He wants everyone out on the square for a rollcall. There's the usual confusion as men stumble from sleep and from thoughts filled with loved ones. The Transport company sergeant's face is a mask of worry. Apparently senior officers have complained about soldiers drinking on the day before Lebanon, with a few showing up clearly drunk at Dublin airport.

The Transport company sergeant's been briefed and instructed to keep a closer eye on all men forming up for Lebanon. It's probably why they've called us up to Collins Barracks so early, to prevent the parting glass developing into the parting dozen or two glasses.

Out on the square the Transport company sergeant calls out our names and we answer in turn with a yell. It's a dry day but overcast. There must be a sun up there somewhere. The company sergeant is unhappy with us and marches us briskly up and down the square. He marches us back to the front of the billets and goes through the rollcall again. Names from the list he reads from are unanswered. Three privates from the Engineers haven't yet showed up. The company sergeant is annoyed at the gaps in his roster, and it looks like he's going to take it out on us by marching us around the vast square a few more times. But then he finds a red-faced, diminutive corporal from the Engineers and takes it out on him.

We're dismissed and back in the barrack-room most of us hit the bunks again. I've never experienced this before, forming up for Lebanon so I don't know if there's more tension around than usual or not. The

Transport company sergeant looks tense, but I've not seen him before so maybe he always looks tense. There's some discussion about the deaths of the two soldiers at Deir Ntar.

Even though one of the bodies is missing nobody believes militiamen in Lebanon are going to try and extract a living Irish soldier from UNIFIL's area of operations and take him to Tyre or Beirut. It wouldn't make sense. Intuitively we know both men are dead, with one body found and one missing. It's a U.N mission so there's nothing we can do about it. It's not like we're already marking the PLO out for retaliation.

The boredom of hanging around army billets is a shocking reminder of just how much boredom an average life entails. The German philosopher Arthur Schopenhauer understood the sensation of boredom as proof of the meaninglessness of human existence. From the middle of the nineteenth Century he writes:

... boredom is a direct proof that existence is in itself valueless, for boredom is nothing other than the sensation of the emptiness of existence. For if life, in the desire for which our essence and existence consists, possessed in itself a positive value and real content,

there would be no such thing as boredom: mere existence would fulfil and satisfy us.

The ideas were influential at the time and Friedrich Nietzsche shaped many of Schopenhauer's conclusions into his own rousing realm of thought. Equating boredom with a perceived meaninglessness of existence is not so unreasonable for anyone who has outlived the dramas of adolescence. Most of us can understand all this at a deeper level of consciousness. If Western modernity is anything at all it is a demented drive to do away with boredom. For Schopenhauer existence at its core and in its starkest terms is intolerable.

Is it this horrible void of fear and meaninglessness the modernist trapped in the town or city is trying to avoid through exhaustive working hours, the usual old addictions and endless activities? Lazing about the billets of the Irish army is one way of fully embracing the boredom Schopenhauer writes of. The hours of tedium are crushing and demoralising. If boredom is proof that existence is valueless then hanging around the billets of small peacetime armies presses the meaninglessness of existence home with all the subtlety of an army boot pressed on an innocent face. If Debbie Goes To Dallas is not playing yet again on a nearby VHS recorder or if some lout is not shouting abuse from one end of the billets to the other the mind of the depot soldier slews into a great torpid void. Sleep is a great mercy when there's a spare bunk around.

The modern world with its technological wonders has given us more time to reflect on Schopenhauer's gloomier thoughts. Generations of philosophers and psychologists have since offered millions of words on what we know as boredom and its associated mental states. The secular Western consensus tends towards the idea that Schopenhauer was probably right and that consciousness is often intolerable. It has no meaning other than the meaning that can be shaped from it. Meaning and meaningfulness are constructed rather than natural values of human life. Boredom can just about be tolerated by whatever meaningfulness we can bring into our lives.

As a seventeen-year-old I swore on the bible and the tricolour, pledging my life to the Republic. That was a source of meaningfulness. For days and weeks afterwards, the ritual fired my imagination, gave me new and real meaning in life. It was a significant ritual in a culture and age when ritual is often underplayed. But as the impact of the ritual faded under the beastly reality of life as a recruit a malaise was to be expected. A symbol of this malaise was seeing the infantry captain who swore me in on the bible and the flag drunk out of his mind on the square in the middle of the day. He was tossing his service cap high in the air until the barracks' sergeant-major led him to the officer's quarters. It was a demoralizing sight for young recruits looking on.

Not everyone is at odds with the monotony of hanging around army billets like players in a degraded distortion of a Beckett play. Over three hundred years before Arthur Schopenhauer dissected the nature of existence Erasmus recommended the simple life, reminding us how naive ignorance is a central part of being human. Knowledge is a burden and brings needless complications. Most of the soldiers crashed out on the bunks are in blissful concord with the reasoning of Erasmus. The very sight of a book is an insult in itself.

Collins Barracks was built in 1702 and was continually used as a military barracks until the Eastern Command's 5th Battalion marched out its main gate in 1997. The barracks was then transformed into a National Museum of Ireland site. Its main building is faced with granite and arcaded colonnades front the east and west sides of its vast square. It was commissioned during the reign of Queen Anne and designed by the architect Thomas de Burgh. One of Dublin's most famous buildings, the library at Trinity College Dublin, was also designed by de Burgh.

Among the National Museum's exhibits are the gauntlets worn by King Billy at the Battle of the Boyne and one of Wolfe Tone's pocketbooks. Wolfe Tone was held at the Royal Barracks after the failed rebellion of 1798. There's no clear evidence as to whether he committed suicide in his cell after he'd been sentenced to death or if the British soldiers guarding him tortured him to death. A popular story has the great rebel severely wounded and advised that if he removed the bandage to his wound he would bleed to death. Wolfe Tone is said to have replied-

I can't find words to thank you sir. It is the most welcome news you could give me. What should I wish to live for?

The soldiering deeds of Wolfe Tone and his comrades in the United Irishmen are an eternity away from our surly day in a billet at Collins Barracks, on a day before Lebanon. Tone's son William fought at the battles of Aachen, Leipzig, Bauthen, Muhlberg, Goldberg and Dresden as a lieutenant in Napoleon's 8th Regt of Chasseurs. He took lance wounds at Leipzig and was decorated with the Legion of Honour. After the defeat at Waterloo the young Tone immigrated to the U.S where he was commissioned a captain in the U.S army, dying at the age of 37. History and the doings of fearless fighting men are long shadows across the peacetime soldier's soul. What can we do when we read or hear about the sacrifices of the long-ago dead but pretend it's got nothing to do with us?

Post October 7th attacks on Israel. London.

My thoughts are with those suffering in Gaza, badly led and fooled into an endless mindset of war ever since the nineteen sixties when an ambitious Egyptian took the star off the Jordanian flag and declared it as the flag of Palestine. My thoughts are also with the hostages held in Gaza by Hamas. I find the words of one of the hostages' mothers and repeat them like a mantra.

Real repentance is when you find yourself in the exact situation where you did the thing that was wrong, and you choose differently.

Meanwhile the Free Palestine marches are upping the tempo. On weekends they soak up yet more police resources in the centre of London. I came across them one Saturday in Victoria. The number of police officers shepherding them along Victoria Street was incredible. The average Londoner has no idea how many police officers we actually have until they stumble across a pro-Palestinian march in the centre of London. There's quite a bit of anger among the marchers. Flags of various design bearing Arabic lettering and the Palestinian flag flutter high among the chanting columns. There are no union flags in sight, as if those in sympathy with the union flag are enemies too. Most of the slogans carried on placards and banners could be read as antisemitic. From the river to the sea after all is a call for the purging of all Jews from the River Jordan to the Med.

As Londoners we are used to such things, used to hate marches of one kind or other. If a person stays here long enough they'd probably get used to anything.

April 1981. Dublin

Sadly in 1981, after just over twenty years of sending soldiers to the U.N in Congo, Cyprus and Lebanon, the Irish military hadn't learnt a lot. Much like the Irish soldiers of 1960 who'd stepped into the tropical heat of Africa wearing bulls-wool uniforms meant for bitterly cold and wet Irish winters we stepped into the heat of Ben Gurion airport in Tel Aviv wearing even heavier uniforms than bulls-wool. After twenty one years of continuous U.N service our senior officers and civil servants hadn't yet worked out the logistics. Our sense of national consciousness and esteem as a nation needed yet more time to mature.

We arrived in Israel wearing heavy green uniforms and our black berets with Oglaigh Na Eireann cap-badges. An earlier flight arrived at Ben Gurion airport not only in their national uniforms but carrying F.N rifles, Carl Gustav machine-pistols and general-purpose machine-guns. An armed group of men in foreign uniforms almost caused an international incident. Luckily a quick-thinking Israeli official ushered the heavy-armed men into an airport annex out of the sight of civilians until the matter could be sorted out.

Such embarrassments were hushed up as Israeli officials were as diplomatically minded as all those concerned with the bigger picture tend to be. But by 1981 the Irish army was in existence for sixty years or so and had taken part in U.N missions for over twenty years. It could not just send its men to Lebanon wearing heavy uniforms intended for Irish winters and wearing black berets and be taken seriously. All the other contingents ensured their soldiers arrived in the Middle East wearing the correct uniforms, insignia and blue berets of the U.N. We however arrived confused and embarrassed, sweating in heavy jumpers and uniforms which enclosed our bodies like shrouds. Yes, as a nation we were maturing, but slowly.

Our flight was supervised by a skittish commandant who was way out of his depth. He looked like he was forever on the edge of a panic attack. As we trooped out of the Aer Lingus jet at Ben Gurion airport the commandant waited at the door, shouting at us for loosening our top shirt buttons and panicking over details of our dress. The guy obviously wasn't cut out for this line of work. I felt sorry for him. He should have been back home in Blackrock or Castleknock pruning his rosebushes or talking to teenage kids about exam-prepping or getting ready for a nice round of golf.

We stood blinking in the mid-day sun, waiting for orders from our disorientated and out-of-his-depth commandant. The Aer Lingus plane had been guided to the most distant runway in Ben Gurion airport. From where we sheltered in its shade it seemed like we were miles away from anywhere. The commandant had meanwhile commandeered a small electric-powered buggy driven by a bemused airport-worker and ordered it to be driven to the main airport buildings.

Just then a U.S type jeep arrived, driven by an Israeli military officer wearing a peaked forage cap, sunglasses and Rav Seren insignia on his short-sleeved shirt. He calmly reminded us waiting soldiers that we were on Israeli ground and could not wear our national army uniforms. We were here as U.N soldiers after all and not as Irish national soldiers. They could not expect one hundred and twenty or so men to strip to our underwear, although considering the heat and the stifling confinement of our Irish winter uniforms it wasn't such a bad idea. As a compromise we were told to at least remove our black berets and stick them in a convenient pocket. We removed our berets and neckties and loosened the top buttons of our shirts just as our commandant came skidding to a halt in his commandeered buggy. He ordered us to put our berets back on and button up our shirts and put our neck-ties on and then he began arguing with the Israeli officer. The commandant was losing it, panicking when there was no reason under the sun to panic. He'd pushed his own beret back onto his head in such a hurry it perched at a silly angle, giving him the look of an old Vaudeville stager. The Israeli officer shrugged and walked away, coolly jumping back into his jeep and driving off. Our commandant had showed himself up in front of his own men and others too, with his rage at having to take orders from an Israeli clear for all to see.

From the longer view it's more obvious how the nationality of the Israeli officer bugged our nervous commandant more than any actual words said. At the time the Israelis were excoriated in the Western press, frequently condemned by a politically liberal European perspective which damned them as hapless victims of Hitler's Holocaust who had internalised the killing techniques of their old persecutors. Ireland's foreign affairs minister Brian Lenihan had already made his position clear. There was no Israeli ambassador in Dublin to balance the argument, only a young articulate Chief Rabbi.

In the ranks of the Irish army when any consideration was given to it the Israelis were very much the bogeymen, oppressors of an entire geo-political region. The sense of victimhood in the re-constructed constitutional Irish nationalism of the time was in sympathy with the Palestinians and the Arab populations of the countries neighbouring the central conflict. In a simplified analysis Israel was seen as an outpost of the Cold War, protected by Washington despite a lamentable human rights record.

To be fair to our skittish commandant there's a middling chance that he'd not been very well briefed on the complexities of this Holy Land we're entering. He's a conservative and practising Catholic as nearly all the officers of his rank are. It's a prerequisite in a state so faithfully created in the ethos of the Catholic mindset and in deference to the wealth, traditions and privilege of Irish Catholicism. Haunting the darker regions of the Christian psyche are grave reservations about the Jewish faith, the Jewish people and the role of the biblical Jews in Christianity's central narratives. Can our commandant be forgiven for remembering ancient misunderstandings between Christians and Jews? He's a ruddy alumnus of the Christian Brothers, a mere human with human weaknesses. He'd have overheard drunken rants or whispered intimations as a boy, the re-workings of blame heaped on the biblical Jews for the crime of denying the Messiah.

Like most Irish people our commandant would have had little if any contact with or personal experience of actual Jews. The Jewish population in Ireland was too tiny for most people to reference it in everyday life. Irish Jews Estella Solomons and Bob Briscoe became a part of Irish revolutionary history, heroes at the birth of a nation. Briscoe was honoured with the Lord Mayor of Dublin's chain of office and another Irish Jew Gerald Goldman was made Lord Mayor of Cork. June Levine emerged from Dublin's small Jewish congregation to become one of Ireland's leading feminists in the nineteen seventies.

As the son of Lithuanian-Jewish emigrants to Ireland Robert Briscoe was not the likeliest convert to Irish revolutionary politics. He joined the IRA during their struggles against

British Rule and was so trusted by Collins he was sent to Germany in 1919 as the IRA's chief procurer of arms. Having served in Dail Eireann for thirty eight years, elected twelve times in Dublin South and from 1948 in Dublin Southwest he retired in 1965, succeeded by his son Ben who served in the Dail for 37 years. In 1956 Robert Briscoe became Dublin's first Jewish Lord Mayor.

Briscoe's loyalty to revolutionary Ireland was not as rewarded as it might have been, especially when it came to the question of his Jewish co-religionists under threat in Nazi Germany. In the nineteen thirties Briscoe lobbied for those in fear of their lives to be given political asylum in Ireland but the Irish state threw a lifeline to less than a hundred or so German Jews. Out of that hundred perhaps nine or ten stayed on for any length of time in Ireland. The Quaker turned Catholic Charles Bewley from the well-known Bewley Coffee shops family was Briscoe's most vocal enemy at the time.

Bewley's appointment was extraordinary because of his religious bigotry, particularly his bigotry towards Jews and all things Jewish. He redefined his appointment to Berlin as that of a pro-Nazi lobbyist and anti-Jewish demagogue. Naturally he clashed with Briscoe who was lobbying for the Irish state to resettle Jews from Nazi Germany. History records how Bewley's views won through as a mere handful of Jews were issued with documents for to travel to Ireland.

The xenophobic anxieties and anti-Jewish bile of Charles Bewley's arguments were as absurd as so much of what passes today for public debate. Often it can seem like entire populations are brow-beaten, lied to or seduced by pseudo-hypnotic suggestion rather than given a factual analysis of events as they stand. The more educated, discerning and informed citizens become the more difficult it is for liberal democracies to perpetuate the illusion of impartiality in debate, parliamentary affairs and general information.

The kinder view is to view the ordinary people of Ireland in the nineteen thirties as intentionally cut off from independent news and information. The potential at the time for brainwashing entire populations was immense. Bewley's reports sent from Berlin back to Dublin were little more than regurgitated newssheets written by Joseph Goebbels. In fact, Goebbels gave Bewley a job after the Irish government had enough of his anti-British and anti-Jewish rhetoric and sacked him in 1940.

The majority of German Jews the Irish state had an opportunity to throw a lifeline to in the nineteen thirties would have most likely relocated to America or later to Israel as soon as it was established as a state. The rainy melancholy of a darkly Catholic land on the edge of the Atlantic would hardly have pleased them as a permanent home. As a nation we lost this chance to raise our humanitarian profile among the progressive nations. This lapse of humanity was considerably aided by the bigotry and spiteful misinformation of Charles Bewley and his friends. It was if a Quaker education was wholly wasted on Bewley.

To this day enemies of Ireland and the Irish people trawl the well-thumbed pages of history to dig up isolated facts with which to drag Ireland's name through the gutters. One of our gifted writers Frances Stuart broadcast Nazi propaganda from Berlin during the war. Charles Bewley was a rabid Jew-hating lackey of Goebbels when he was our man in Berlin. De Valera signed the book of condolences at the German Embassy in Dublin when Hitler died. And so on and so forth. Our neutrality in the Second World

War comes up a lot too. It's hard to shake off the idea that the only reason Lord Haw Haw, one William Joyce from Mayo, was not relegated to the category of Irishman was that to do so meant he could not have been hung as a traitor to England. Selected readings and a misreading of the past are trotted out as justifications for the pretentiousness of today's nation states. How humdrum the whole thing is.

Briscoe and Bewley's clashes over the question of whether to accept Jews from Nazi Germany tell us more about the interconnectedness of people's lives and destinies. The outcome is another causal factor in the arrangement whereby we are bound for Lebanon as part of a U.N mission. It's another small part of how we see ourselves in relation to the Middle East and to racial and national questions to do with Arabs.

Robert Briscoe's son Joe is a more direct link to Irish soldiers bound for Lebanon. He joined the FCA, the Irish army reserve, in the nineteen forties and served in it loyally until the early nineteen nineties. Joe Briscoe joined the reserves as a private and retired as a commandant, a Jewish officer in a Catholic army. For Charles Bewley and his fellow travellers in human affairs Joe Briscoe's commission would have stuck in their craws.

Religious quarrels in the Ireland which influenced our commandant may not have involved any suspicions or venial thoughts concerning the Jewish people or their faith. But people claiming to be Christians and who are literalist in thinking have always found novel ways of re-introducing the gripes and chauvinism from the very origins of Christianity. Maybe our commandant at Ben Gurion airport was troubled enough to default to an ancient prejudice buried in deeper mind.

The Jesus of Paul's visions and of the Gospels was rejected by the biblical Jews as their Messiah in keeping with their scriptures, their customs, their culture and the guidance of elders. The Psalms of Solomon from the 1st Century B.C are a general guide to what was expected of the Jewish Messiah. The Messiah would drive foreign armies from the blessed land of Israel and re-establish the kingdom on its original model. The Messiah would unite the tribes of Israel, re-instate Mosaic Law, isolate sinners from the people of Israel and in the end rule over all nations. To claim an itinerant rabbi largely viewed as a magic-worker who'd learnt his diabolical ways in Egypt as the Messiah was a sharp insult to the biblical Jews. The weight of this insult is referenced in Deuteronomy where *anyone who is hung on a pole is under God's curse.* Why would the biblical Jews see anything but insult and impertinence in the Messianic claims of a crucified and publicly shamed rabbi who fulfilled none of their scriptural prophecies?

Only after Paul's visions, the work of 1st and 2th Century annalists and the protection of Christianity under Constantine did a Christian history recognisable to the modern Christian appear. It quickly grew into a bulwark of faith which damned the biblical Jews as heretics and left their descendants exposed to racial and religious hatred. The biblical Jews were correct in their responses to what we know about Jesus, for only an act of collective insanity could have persuaded a people to cast off their entire cultural wisdom and revelation for to accept as their Messiah someone who fulfilled none of the criteria for the Messiah.

Jewishness as we understand it was re-created on the wrong side of history. Paul, Jewish by blood and born into the Tribe of Benjamin, rewrote the tenets of Christianity in the spirit of the fanatic and with reference to his visions rather than actual fact. It was the beginning of a long tale of pogroms, exile, suspicion, humiliation, conversion and inquisition but also of mutuality and cultural solidarity. It's a story which informs the interaction between our nervous commandant and the Israeli military officer at Ben Gurion airport.

It's impossible to untangle Christian and European guilt from the origins and legitimacy of the Jewish state. The more thoughtful officers and NCOs I happened to overhear in conversation tended towards the less generous view of Israel and those from the Jewish Diaspora who were in the public eye. It's not an uncommon view, reclassifying the arrival of Israel as a nation among the nations as an opportunistic land-grab by international Zionists quick to take advantage of allied post-war guilt.

The millions killed in WWII were stratified into Jewish and non-Jewish dead the narrative runs, with the numbers of Jewish dead overstated and their horrors at the hands of the Nazis overemphasized. The Jewish dead were then exploited and monetised by a proliferation of organisations and charities dedicated to

Jewish victims. A Holocaust industry mushroomed, fertilised by reparations from Germany and later Austria and from the state-funds of other participating nations. Thus, Israel is reinvented as a recipient state dependent on public handouts, much like Northern Ireland as it happens. It's hard to fully escape these concepts of the Israelis and their co-religionists outside Israel and concentrate on the impartial policies and rules of engagements of UNIFIL. Such things weight on a U.N soldier's mind to one extent or other.

Were we too somehow complicit in Hitler's atrocities against the Jews? We're European Christians after all, an outpost of Constantine's old empire. How far to any one side of this globally divisive question are we? Or in a world of deceit and shifting allegiances is it more about how actions and words are weighted in the sanctuary of mind? In accord with the higher principles of the U.N the Irish soldiers on the ground were committed to protecting civilians and doing everything in their power to restore normality to the South of Lebanon. The threat to peace was very much seen to come from Israel. Irish UNIFIL soldiers in Lebanon unconsciously at least cast the Israelis and their South Lebanese militias in the same light as Commandant Pat Quinlan and his tough Athlone soldiers cast the rebels and mercenaries of Katanga a generation before.

Our commandant panicking on the most isolated runway at Ben Gurion airport was simply caught up in a series of causal factors extending back in time. It probably wasn't his fault. In our briefings it was always the Israelis or their Christian-Arab allies who were mentioned as sinister characters pulling all the wrong levers in the background. The sufferings of our national heroes were paralleled with the sufferings of the Shiite Arabs of South Lebanon. Our government had officially taken the side of the Palestinians and embraced Yasser Arafat as the hero of the day. The Syrian army had surrounded Beirut airport and the airport was closed temporarily to all flights, hence our detour to Tel Aviv. Given these causal factors our commandant's impersonation of a man just about to have a serious panic attack was almost understandable. It was his first time in this strange land and he seemed to have suffered a kind of allergic reaction on seeing an Israeli military officer.

After more time sweating in the shade of the Aer Lingus jet we're relieved to see a detachment of French paratroopers show up. Their job is to drive us from Tel Aviv to our base at Camp Shamrock in Tibnine. At the sight of the French paratroopers our commandant recovers from his allergic reaction at seeing an Israeli officer for the first time. A French paratrooper chef-corporal gestures that we should remove our berets and keep them removed. Then he orders us onto French army trucks and we move quickly. Inside a minute or two we are on our way to South Lebanon. Our commandant in his confusion salutes the French chef-corporal, delighted not to have any further face-to-face dealings with the Israeli major. He jumps into the front of one of the French trucks like a schoolboy on a daytrip and we hear no more from him for the remainder of the journey.

Perversely only the day before our commandant was breaking out in a nervous rash caused by contact with an Israeli official two Irish soldiers were killed in Lebanon. They were not killed accidently by an Israeli shell, or by the Israeli-backed militia known as the South Lebanese Army, also known as the De Facto Forces when referenced by UNIFIL. They were killed wilfully and without mercy by the PLO. Such is the way with human affairs. A narrative rarely unfolds as it is intended to unfold.

Post Oct 7th 2023 terror attacks on Israel. London.

They've closed the Israeli embassy in Dublin. Ireland waited until the nineteen nineties for to invite Israel to open an embassy, the last Western European country to do so. Now they've closed it. Ireland's leading politicians can't seem to get past a cerebral mist of antagonism against Israel that's been around for a long time. In fact, before the state of Israel even existed the hum of antisemitism could be heard in the walkways of Irish political life, personified by the diplomat Charles Bewley.

The Israeli foreign minister Gideon Sa'ar announced the Dublin embassy's closure because of 'extreme anti-Israel policy' promoted by the Irish government. A few months ago the Israeli ambassador to Dublin was withdrawn after Ireland along with Spain and Norway unilaterally recognised a Palestinian state. Gideon Sa'ar also mentioned the Irish government's decision to involve itself in the South African lawsuit against Israel at the International Court of Justice.

The exchanges between Israeli and Irish governmental agencies and individuals don't do much to further the cause of international diplomacy. How put upon the Israelis must be when surrounded by hostility and endless threats of annihilation they look to the Western democracies for support and find instead the cold eye of Ireland, Spain and Norway. The antagonism of the ANC in South Africa towards Israel might be viewed in the light of a country that doesn't see a problem with its elected representatives calling for the killing of white South Africans. But why is there so much hostility in Ireland towards Israel?

The evicted of Clongorey linger in the national consciousness of a people whose identity is very much set on resistance to British political dominance over several centuries punctuated by hardship, war, famine and discrimination. The fact that the emerging Jewish state also fought the British empire is lost amid the endless television news coverage of Palestinians mourning their dead in the chaos of another explosion. Pathe newsreels of the Stern Gang using tactics against British forces in Palestine that they learnt from the tactics of Tom Barry in West Cork in 1920 and 1921 are overlooked. Who can even remember when there was solidarity between Irish nationalists and Jewish nationalists as they struggled to break free from the political control of one of history's great empires?

The photograph of Mrs Kelly sitting with such dignity among her belongings after she'd been evicted at Clongorey is frozen in time, imprinted along with numerous such impressions in the Irish national psyche. It's regurgitated when the age-old tensions of a pan-British consciousness brushes up against Irish nationalist sensitivities and yet again the evictions at Clongorey and many other similar places resound deep in the Irish heart. Over time Israel has found itself shunted from its place in Irish nationalist consciousness as a small nation struggling against British imperialism and hostile neighbours to a pariah state linked in principle to that great evil of the modern liberal mind, the settle-colonial-oppressor.

Charles Bewley was sent to Berlin as its 'Irish Minister Plenipotentiary and Envoy Extraordinary'. Bewley admired the writings of Fr. Denis Fahey, a Holy Ghost father from Tipperary who wrote a lot about social and religious matters and who was even criticised by the conservative Archbishop of Dublin John Charles McQuaid for his reckless antisemitism. Fahey once wrote that 'every sane thinker should be an anti-

Semite'. Fahey founded a Catholic order, Maria Duce, which was staunchly anti-communism and antisemitic. IRA volunteer Sean South, immortalised in the popular republican ballad 'Sean South of Carryowen' founded a branch of Maria Duce before he was martyred for the Irish cause after a shoot-out with British forces on the Irish border.

Almost as soon as Bewley got to Berlin he began sending reports back to Dublin describing Jews as pornographers, abortionists and involved in the 'white slave trade'. It is hard to believe now but this was the man with the job of administering visa applications from Jews desperate to leave Germany for the sanctuary of any country that wasn't planning to frogmarch them to death-camps. In over six years Bewley allowed less than a hundred applications to be processed to the point where the applicants were allowed to leave Germany.

That's about one person a month during the years before what's been described by German historian Wolfgang Benz as the 'singularly most monstrous crime committed in the history of mankind'. And even at that Bewley criticised Ireland's policy for refugees as '... inordinately liberal and facilitating the entry of the wrong class of people'. By the wrong class of people he meant Jews. At the end of the war Bewley was arrested in Northern Italy but he was carrying Irish diplomatic papers that were in effect a 'get out of jail' card. He lived out the remainder of his life in Rome.

Distrust of Jews was referenced by Joyce in Ulysses when Bloom was questioned in Cyclops.

What is your nation, if I may ask?

In Nestor Mr. Deasy gives credibility to the usual old slurs that Jews control England's finances and media. For a small country with only ever a tiny Jewish population one might fairly ask where did all the anti-Jewish fear, distrust and hostility come from? Any honest answer to that must venture very close to the Irish heart.

Ireland's Chief Rabbi Yoni Wieder adds his voice to the controversy, understandably saddened at news of the loss of the embassy. What the rabbi has to say isn't uplifting from an Irish perspective.

Ireland has not engaged constructively with Israel over the past year, instead preferring to vilify and roundly criticise Israel without any recognition of the complexities of the situations in Gaza and Lebanon. Irish political leaders have routinely failed to acknowledge that Israel is waging war against jihadist terrorist organisations intent on its destruction. The anti-Israel narrative in Ireland has become extremely hateful, and full of disinformation and distortions. And already in the immediate aftermath of the Oct 7th massacre, whilst many other European countries flew Israeli flags above government or public buildings – no such solidarity was shown in Ireland.

As I read the Chief Rabbi's words I have a horrible vision of Charles Bewley, Simon Harris, Michael D O'Higgins and Fr. Denis Fahey laughing and wagging fingers at the Chief Rabbi, obviously finding it all hugely entertaining. I'm left with a bad feeling deep in my guts. Is that what we are now when we leave Ireland's shores, citizens of Europe's most antisemitic country? There are days when I'm convinced I was born and brought up in a dysfunctional and hopelessly irrational country. This is one of those days.

April. 1981. Ireland.

In Collins Barracks the Transport company sergeant has barged into the barrack-room and is shouting for another rollcall. He's now more annoyed at the absence of the three Engineer privates. After the rollcall the pintsized, red-faced Engineer corporal helpfully suggests the three privates might be absent due to a communication problem. They may have been told to report to Collins Barracks later than everyone else. This is not what the company sergeant wants to hear. He swears like a Saturday night drunk and orders the corporal to go to the 5th Battalion's orderly office and ring every number he can think of ringing. The company sergeant's face says it all. It's the day before Lebanon and the tricolour is flying at half-mast in honour of two fallen comrades and three privates from the Engineers haven't even bothered to show up.

The men of the 5th Infantry Battalion have been based at Collins Barracks since 1959, so they are comfortable here. It will hurt when the government decides the battalion must leave and the barracks is transformed into a museum. The battalion will move up the road a mile or two to McKee Barracks before finally disappearing from the army's organisation, disbanded forever as a unit.

It's hard not to sense the history of Collins Barracks, to grasp the sadness and solemnity of the place at a level beyond words. Out the back of the barracks is Arbour Hill Cemetery where martyrs from the 1916 insurrection are buried. This place is stamped with the indelible mark of history, anchored in sombre moods. I stayed in Collins Barracks for about a week as part of the drill of forming up for Lebanon. I didn't actually see or sense a supernatural presence or hear horse-hooves out on the square at the witching-hour. But there was a kind of vibe not exactly of this world, a stifled aether in places or a sense of pressure in the air. It's hard to pin it down. Maybe the actual granite and concrete blocks of the physical barracks held onto a fraction of the presence of long-dead soldiers who once billeted here and who were once young. It sounds fanciful when weighted with the rational mind but in the darkness of an Arbour Hill night it's not fanciful at all.

Post Oct 7th 2023 attacks on Israel. London.

Hatred of Jews is at the core of exoteric Christianity, so much so that an apology to the Jewish people should be part of every Christian service. If we class ourselves as Christians or cultural Christians in some way part of Western civilisation we are indebted to those who kept alive the Christian message through the centuries. The hands of so many Christian leaders from the past were stained in the blood of innocent Jews. Of all the varying kinds of Jew hatred manifesting in the Christian lands the strains of Jew hatred coming from the direction of the Vatican were the most egregious. Only through the centuries as Western societies tired of Christian political interfering and religious extremism did the worm begin to turn and entire populations became secular.

After a human rights revolution that's only really been felt and put into action by state power since the nineteen sixties has the autonomy and spiritual freedom of the individual been given protection against religious and moral extremism. Finally, after two thousand years or so of Christian faith the Church has found its rightful place in Western societies. Or, it might be argued, the Church was assigned its rightful place by men and women of conscience.

I say that because anyone who sees themselves as part of Western Christian culture long-since forfeited a natural right to freely criticise how Israel defends itself against forces intent on wiping it off the face of the earth. Christian authority persecuted, stigmatised, ghettoised, judicially murdered, tortured, humiliated and insulted Jewish people over many centuries simply because they were Jewish. Yet the average citizen who has imbibed a certain dollop of media content about the Middle East feels they have a God-given right to take to the streets and chant anti-Israel slogans as if the great Jew-hater Pope Paul IV was still in situ in Rome.

The ranting against Israel is nearly always qualified by differentiating Israelis from Jews. It goes something like-

I've got nothing against Jews. I'm not antisemitic. It's just Israel I hate. And Zionism too.

But at the International Holocaust Remembrance Alliance in Jerusalem Britain's Chief Rabbi Sir Ephraim Mirvis had this to say-

Israel is not just a geopolitical reality for the Jewish people. It is far more than that. It is the centre of our Jewish religion. So therefore, if you are anti-Zionist, you are also anti-Jewish. But more than that, you're anti-Judaism, and your animosity affects the very well-being of Jews right around the world.

Those on the side-lines who rant, shout and wag fingers at Israel might benefit from heeding the chief rabbi's words. Personally, as a son of Ireland, Europe's most antisemitic nation, I'm careful when it comes to voicing opinions on very complex matters in the Middle East, mindful of the motivations of the people behind the slogans that are synonymous with protest movements.

April. 1981. Dublin.

Fu Manchu surprises me by asking me if I am all right. I'm lying on a bunk with my beret tipped in front of my eyes and my thoughts are a million light-years away from the boredom of the barracks. I'm preoccupied with my own ideas, mildly looking forward to this jaunt in Lebanon, hoping that whatever happens out there will be a distraction from the general morbidity of my thought-life. I'm relaxed and dozing, drifting in and out of a light sleep. Why wouldn't I be all right? I tell Fu Manchu I'm all right and that I'm just lying on the bunk dozing as there's nothing else to do. Most of the other solders waiting in the billet are lying on bunks dozing too. There's an old spiel repeated now and then in the barrack-rooms.

Why stand up if you can sit down? Why sit down if you can lie down?

Fu Manchu is okay. He's the senior man of the small party of three who travelled up from the Curragh this morning. He's asking if I'm okay from a sense of responsibility. Later when I get to know him in Lebanon and back in our home unit on the Curragh I'll realise he's one of the good guys in life.

He's a humane, hard-working and thoughtful man with a tendency to over-worry. On a human level does he even want to be here? He's a married man with young children, a man who truly loves his family.

For Fu Manchu and most of the others this is not just about duty, but money too. A stint in the Lebanon is money in the bank. For a husband and father of young children on the modest wage of an Irish army corporal a few grand is a godsend. The disruption of six months' absence from family life is almost worth it. It's the Ireland of the early nineteen eighties after all and as our politicians are quick to remind us money doesn't grow on trees. Fu Manchu is troubled by family life and the money needed to keep a young family well and thriving. He carries the weight of his troubles in deep furrows on his forehead. His heavy smoking can easily switch to chain-smoking. He can go into long moody silences and rotten tempers that in all fairness don't last long.

Soldiers are masters of half-truths, rumours and lies, especially under-employed garrison soldiers from a restless peacetime army. There are rumours about Fu Manchu's private life. Maybe it's his nature. Maybe he's just naturally inclined to over-worry. On the Curragh Fu Manchu was industrious among men who were often not industrious at all. He was a grafter who volunteered for everything rather than sitting around drinking strong sweet tea, smoking and skiving like so many depot soldiers. He drives vehicles from one end of the command area to the other, assembles and disassembles radio kit and dipole aerials from the top of Mount Leinster to the glens of Wicklow.

He sounds different to most of the rest of us as he carries the tones of Southern England in his voice. He worked for a decade or so in an English factory before returning to Ireland and joining the Irish army. Irish people are known to spend fifty or sixty years in England and hardly change their native speech but Fu Manchu's voice is strongly shaped by England. People often mistake him for an Englishman. We had more than a few soldiers in the Curragh who spoke with English voices, usually the children of Irish families born in Manchester, Birmingham and London. Somehow Fu Manchu could sound more English than them.

We had a Scotsman and Englishmen with Irish mothers and English fathers who'd ended up in Ireland for family reasons. We had a black soldier from the English West Midlands who'd no blood connection to Ireland but had an Irish girlfriend. The English voices in our ranks confirmed the idealistic Republican's worst projections of the Irish army as a construct of England, an unholy beast of Free State compromise.

Considering the levels of unemployment and the necessity for so many Irish people to live and work in England it was almost delusional for Fu Manchu to expect to live and work in the County Kildare town he was born and brought up in. Due to family bonds returning to England was not an option for a man of his character and sense of loyalty to others. He had to remain at home and find some kind of regular work. The Irish army enabled him to do this. He was stubborn in how he carried himself, a working man who insisted on now ignoring the exodus from Ireland to the cities of England he was once a part of.

A salient impression of Fu Manchu was of a man who'd overcome the forces of necessity compelling so many Irish people to leave Ireland as disposable labour for the work markets of England and beyond. He insisted on returning to his hometown only a few miles from the Curragh camp and living close to kin, raising his children in the same environment, social codes and traditions he himself was raised in. With the social conditions in Ireland in the nineteen eighties in mind Fu Manchu's determination to live and work at home verged on the revolutionary.

I push my beret over my eyes and try to doze off again as there's nothing much else to do. Peacetime soldiers of small neutral countries become experts at killing time. It's really what we are doing the day before Lebanon, killing time. A few of the others are fast asleep, snoring from the depths of heavy somnolence. Others are coming and going, making calls from pay-phones and from the 5th Battalion's orderly office. We don't know any Jews or Arabs. To allow such strangers from faraway shores to take up any space in our thoughts would seem like an insane thing to do.

From nearby bunks two soldiers are discussing the Artane Stardust fire from a couple of months earlier when forty eight young people died and hundreds more were injured. The soldiers are from Dublin's Northside and know the families of some of the dead. The Ireland of the time is interconnected - everyone knows or knows of almost everyone else. There actually are real communities with individuals and families bonded by shared experience and bloodline, mythology, a national history and communal lives. The deaths of so many young people on one nightmarish evening of dancing are an appalling intrusion on the life of the country. The soldiers mention chained fire exits in disbelieving voices.

Years later in London I met an Irish Traveller couple who were teenagers and living not far from Artane. Like other teenagers in the area they went along to the Saturday night disco at the Stardust. They were turned away from the door because they were Travellers. They accepted it as it happened almost every day of their lives. Casual discrimination against Travellers was routine in the Ireland of the time.

For the young couple the Stardust tragedy was a defining moment in their harsh lives. They interpreted it as an omen, a Marian sign of holy intervention for they had a special devotion to Mary. A moment of casual discrimination was lifted to transcendent significance. Not long after they took the boat to England where they had a slightly better life than what they knew in North Dublin. For probably the only time in the years they'd lived in their native country being members of a hated minority worked in their favour. Maybe the art of living is in its interpretation as much as in its daily trials.

Something is happening in the barracks where we're forming up for Lebanon. Someone with a strong voice is shouting out on the square. I swing my boots from the bunk to the floor and straighten my beret. Then the Transport company sergeant's voice is more distinct. It sounds like he's bawling somebody out. An NCO hurries through the billets, others are stirring at the sound of the raised voice and general hubbub. The three absent Engineer privates have finally showed up. They are sturdy lads and the sturdiest is flushed in the face and is crunching on a mouthful of polo-mints. They don't seem at all bothered and explain they were ordered to show up at Collins Barracks at the exact time they showed up. One of them shrugs as he says-

What's the problem? We're here now aren't we.

It's a communication glitch it seems, with the engineer privates working on different orders than the rest of us. It happens. The Transport company sergeant is still annoyed and studies the flushed face of the sturdiest engineer soldier with the practised eye of an old barrack-square hawk. He stands close enough to smell any trace of alcohol from the private's breath but can only smell polo-mints. The private looks like he's had a good drink but is managing to keep a straight face. He stands to attention with ludicrous exaggeration. The transport company sergeant's roster is now complete so he's plainly less tense. Whether or not the engineers were drinking is not really the question. For the company sergeant it's about getting us all to Dublin airport without incident. If soldiers don't look or act drunk, then nothing is lost.

Pleased with the new numbers the company sergeant has us out on the square again, marching in formation. The day is overcast but the rain is holding off. We march up the square and then down the square. We march around the square and then about-turn and march in the other direction. The Transport company sergeant orders one of the sergeants on parade to fall out and take his place shouting out the marching orders. We march a little more. In the greater scheme of things it's not such a bad deal, marching around Collins Barracks on a day before Lebanon.

Cold War soldiers across the globe are guarding nuclear installations and waiting, watching the skies for strange lights. Nuclear war between the USA and the USSR almost happened during the Cuban Crisis of 1962 and later during the Yom Kippur war in 1973. There were several other near-misses including communication errors, accidents, blips on radar-screens and air-crashes where nuclear weapons were almost detonated. How we've gotten as far as the nineteen eighties without a nuclear war between the global powers is due not merely to one miracle but to a series of miracles.

We're marched back to the billets and to the torpor of the bunks. The engineer privates are laughing and horse-playing in the corridors of the barracks-room, not taking the forming-up process very seriously. The little engineer corporal avoids the engineer privates as if they have nothing to do with him. They're from the same unit so he'd know them well. Probably that's why he is steering clear of them.

One of the engineer privates is bawling out a joke from one end of the billets to the other.

What'd call a virgin from Kildare?

Not yer sister anyhow!

A sheep who hasn't strayed onto the Curragh!

The red-faced engineer corporal is a game little fellow, a deadpan Leinsterman with the most honest face in Christendom. He certainly wouldn't be mistaken for a guardsman but he's a grafter. Many of the engineers are tradesmen with civilian qualifications and can put in a proper shift. They are the army's pragmatists, and their skills are needed in somewhere like the hills of South Lebanon.

A day or two after we'd arrived in Lebanon, I happened to pass the checkpoint outside Tibnine, close to Camp Shamrock. I was in the back of a truck and recognised the red-faced engineer corporal manning the checkpoint. It wasn't his fault but he'd been only issued with the standard Irish army combat trousers and ordinary cream-coloured shirt. These he wore along with a flak-jacket and a brand-new blue U.N forage cap. The army combat trousers when first handed out by quartermasters were an atrociously baggy affair which looked like something more suited to a circus clown

than a soldier. Whoever designed it must
have had a hell of a sense of humour.

They were so heavy it felt like how it must
feel to wear several pairs of trousers one
over the other. The soldier was expected to
go and find a tailor and have the eyesore
altered at his own expense. Some soldiers
didn't bother and just wore the hideous
combat trousers as they were issued. In their
unaltered state they looked ridiculous. Why
the Quartermaster General hadn't found a
clothing source to offer a more normal
combat trousers rather than a baggy
monstrosity which required serious
tailoring is one of those questions that will
forever remain unanswered. All these small
embarrassments added up. We could only
guess what the other contingents and locals
thought about us.

Maybe the engineer corporal had been
issued with the monstrous trousers too close
to our departure for Lebanon and didn't
have the time to find a tailor. He might have
thought he'd be issued with the light-wear
uniform of Irishbatt on the day he arrived in
the area of operations. The production and
supply of uniforms were not his
responsibility. He could only wear what he'd
been issued by the quartermaster to wear.

He stood at the checkpoint with the crotch of his heavy Irish winter combat trousers hanging to his knees and wearing the cream-coloured shirt which served as a ceremonial shirt, a workaday shirt and a shirt for security and training duties back home in Ireland. A Swedish-made Carl Gustav 9mm machine-pistol dangled from his neck on a thick brown leather strap and his red face was further reddened by the sun and layered in sweat.

The engineer corporal had a naturally comedic look. If he'd ever decided to forget all about the Irish army he'd have made a great clown or funny guy in a cabaret troupe. As he stood at Tibnine checkpoint he was the perfect candidate for the anti-soldiering role of the U.N peacekeeper. He was anything but war-like or arrogant, unlike the French paratroopers who worked logistics for UNIFIL or the strutting Italian pilots who flew helicopters out of UNIFIL HQ at Naqoura. He was a fascinating sight, a five foot two epitome of endurance, absurdity and innocence. His baggy army trousers hung so low between his knees they'd be mistaken as a prop for the beginning of a panto or outbreak of clowning.

By coincidence I happened to be in the battalion's comcen, or communications' centre a bit later on that day, when a captain with a reputation as a bully was ranting about the engineer corporal at the Tibnine checkpoint. The captain was really angry, which was not surprising as anger was more or less his constant condition. He raged against the engineer corporal's baggy, ridiculous trousers, furious that an Irish soldier could present himself in full view of Lebanese civilians and other UNIFIL soldiers dressed like that. By the sound of the angry captain, who went on in time to achieve high rank, it was if the engineer corporal was guilty of an unforgivable crime. Yet what had he done but wear the army gear given to him by his quartermaster to wear.

The raging captain should have aimed his anger at whoever signed the contract with the clothing outfit which provided the clownishly baggy trousers to the Irish army. Or he could have had a good rant against the incompetent quartermaster and the civil servants who ran the army who hadn't yet worked out a system whereby soldiers bound for Lebanon were dressed correctly before arriving at Beirut airport, or in our case at Tel Aviv airport. Were they doing this to us deliberately? Keeping us in our place?

Making sure we didn't get any ideas above our station?

It's always easier for middle-management to blame the frontline staff for organisational cockups which begin higher up the food-chain. People can feel so much better when they have some harmless little guy like the engineer corporal to blame. The angry captain insisted the engineer corporal be stood down from duty at the Tibnine checkpoint.

Eventually a quartermaster sergeant would get around to issuing the red-faced engineer corporal with light-weight green combat trousers and green shirt which was the standard Irishbatt uniform in Lebanon. Not that there was any rush about it. The angry captain could rant all he liked but quartermasters on the ground could never correct the organisational shambles at the beating heart of the Irish army at the time. We were not going to Pettigo-Belleek or to England's colonial wars. Often, we were going around in circles.

Male pride put to one side for the moment the red-faced engineer corporal with the baggy trousers standing at the Tibnine checkpoint was the ideal soldier for

Lebanon. He was the anti-soldier whose appearance and attitude were well-suited in a situation where there was no shortage of hotheads ready to kick off at the first minor provocation. In fact, if male ego and human pride and all the macho pretensions of military organisations were taken out of the equation a brigade of soldiers inspired by the engineer corporal at the Tibnine checkpoint would be the ideal peacekeepers for the world's warzones. They could wear clown's red noses and hand out balloons to children. It'd be easier for them to then stand aside when the next wave of fighting begins.

Our camps and billets were among the Shiite Arab villages close to Lebanon's border with Israel. As such we were viewed by Israel and their Christian Arab allies as too compromised to carry out U.N resolutions. Outside our area of operations, the PLO fired Russian-made rockets into Israel from their bases. PLO and Amal fighters crept through our positions at night to attack Major Saad Haadad's Christian militia with AK47s, machine-guns and RPGs. We were seen as too sympathetic to the local Arab population and militias to stop them attacking the buffer zone between Israel and Lebanon controlled by Haadad's militia.

Although many Irish soldiers in UNIFIL didn't much like the local Arabs our officers and our government and civil servants back home did, siding with them instinctively and going way beyond the impartiality that was needed to carry out ambitious U.N missions. No wonder the leaders of the local Shiite communities liked the idea of having Irish peacekeepers among them and supported the Irish battalion in UNIFIL over many years. After all we were on their side and our government and civil service back home were more than pleased to promote the idea that we were on their side.

Locals were caught in an aerial war between Israel and the PLO, sheltering where they could and watching the skies as PLO rockets thundered towards Israel and IDF jets responded in kind. Their livestock were maimed and killed, their children too. They were victims of a most terrible conflict, their national boundaries violated and their proximity to the ancient land of Israel their most abiding curse. From an Irish perspective they were linked eternally to the evictions at Clongorey, to the trail of tears the coffin ships sailing from famine to the new world left in their wake. They spoke of martyrs and of a great reckoning that Allah would one day bring about in their favour.

They watched television shows beamed from Damascus that consisted for the most part of hour after hour of mesmeric Dabke and Ardah dancing, punctuated by dour news' broadcasts from Assad's regime.

The red-faced engineer corporal with his clownishly ill-fitted combat trousers and all the rest of us too had stepped onto a stage of great tragedy, witnesses to the unfolding of another scene in a drama without end. Of course, we couldn't stop the PLO doing pretty much what they wished to do in a country they'd occupied as effectively as any other presumed occupation in that part of the world. In a year or so the Israelis will lose patience and send in their military. They'll purge Lebanon of the PLO and lose yet more young soldiers in defence of their national territory and population. UNIFIL peacekeepers will open their checkpoint barriers and wave at the soldiers of the IDF as they pass in their armoured vehicles.

In one humorous moment several UNIFIL peacekeepers were sunbathing in skimpy swimming trunks when the Israeli armoured vehicles passed. Men of war going into the teeth of battle waved good-humorously and the sunbathers waved and laughed in response. In the overall scheme of things what else could they do?

Post October 7th attacks on Israel. London.

German-born French documentary film-maker Marcel Ophuls has died at the age of 97. The self-serving narrative of post-war France was constructed on the myth of the French Resistance, claimed by both Gaullists and communists to have had the support of almost the entire French population. Research centred on the city of Clermont-Ferrand by Ophuls and his producer Andre Harris revealed a very different story.

In his film 'The Choice' we see Jewish businesses and properties stolen by locals once the Jews in question had fled Nazi terror or were arrested and sent to deathcamps. Ophuls' truthful but inconvenient truth of a French public as much supportive or quick to exploit the persecution of French Jews brought much anger and denial when it was first released. The film was shown on French television and during France's political crisis of 1968 Ophuls' veracity in bringing France's wartime attitudes towards Jews to light was finally acknowledged.

There's an Irish connection as Marcel Ophuls 1972 film 'A Sense of Loss' set in Northern Ireland was rejected by the BBC who judged it as too sympathetic to the IRA. Ophuls was also involved in documentaries critical of Zionism and Israel. We hate the truth-bringers as the truth needs a lot of dressing before it can be properly digested. In Marcel Ophul's work we find the British state's difficulty in recognising the fuller humanity of the IRA in the early seventies and the French people's difficulty in accepting the fuller humanity and property rights of French Jews in German-occupied France. There are lessons there for all of us.

April 1981. Dublin.

In Collins Barracks we've barely laid our
heads on the bunks when someone is
shouting for us to form up again on the
square. It's time to eat. Army food is not
great. Often, it's so poor soldiers ignore it
and find something else to eat. Army cooks
are often either cranky or alcohol-
dependent, or both. One morning on the
Curragh the soldier in front of me in the
breakfast queue complained the food wasn't
cooked right. Without a second's hesitation
the cook picked up a large carving-knife and
flung it at the soldier. Luckily the knife spun
in the air and the handle rather than the
blade hit the guy in the chest. It was quickly
forgotten and nobody reported it. In the day-
to-day life of the depot soldier such
spontaneous little moments of madness were
for the most part accepted.

I skipped what the cookhouse in Collins
Barracks had to offer and settled instead for
a Mars bar and packet of crisps. This was a
mistake which nearly cost me dearly on the
following day. There was little by way of
food or drink during our confinement in
Collins Barracks on the day before Lebanon.
The meals of sloppy potatoes and dodgy cuts
of meat were ignored by many of the chalk.

Not that I was aware of it, but I wasn't hydrating properly. It wasn't the culture at the time for a section NCO or medic to remind soldiers to hydrate. In a macho world of crudity and ignorance the cruder and more ignorant the soldier the more favoured he was.

I guessed there'd be something to drink when we arrived at Ben Gurion airport but there wasn't. We baked on the runway for hours in our heavy winter uniforms before jumping in the French paratroopers' trucks. We travelled in the trucks for a dozen hours or so before arriving late at night at the Irish Battalion's headquarters at Camp Shamrock in Tibnine. By then I was very thirsty but predictably there was no provision made for us. The cooks had decided it was past their bedtime and had locked up the cookhouse and gone to bed.

A bad-tempered little runt of a company sergeant with a full head of grey-white hair greeted us at Camp Shamrock. When one of our NCOs asked for a few sandwiches and an urn of tea as we'd been travelling all day without so much as a glass of water the striped runt was even more bad-tempered. The cookhouse was locked up, he said. He then ordered us to find whatever space in the billets we could and bed down for the night.

In the morning there'd be breakfast we were told, or at least water or tea to wet our lips. I found a fold-up bed in one of the Nissan huts used by enlisted men. It'd been a long day, so I bedded down quickly. I slept for about ten minutes or so before three soldiers from Lifford Barracks in Donegal barged into the billet with drunken belches and shouts. They sat on their bunks to continue their drinking, talking in the wild voices of the inebriated.

It was impossible to sleep. The Donegalmen began singing and arguing, voices rising and falling in harmony with the logic of John Barleycorn. Now and then one of them reminded the others to keep their voices down as men were trying to sleep in the billets. They'd lower their voices for a minute or two before forgetting all about the sleeping soldiers in the billet and in nearby billets and raise their voices again.

They were from the 48th Battalion and had just got to the end of their tour of duty in Lebanon. They were going home the next day. The sergeant-major of the 49th Battalion came into the billet after about an hour or so as the racket caused by the Donegalmen must have resounded throughout the camp. In any army the rank of sergeant-major is a serious rank, the mark of a serviceman who'd once walloped dixies and stood for tedious hours of guard-duty as a private soldier. It's not the class-defined rank of an officer but the rank of sweat, blood and experience. It's a rank universally respected.

The drunken soldiers respected our gentlemanly sergeant-major and promised to drink up their beer and hit the bunks. No sooner had the sergeant-major left the billet than the Donegal privates pulled out yet more crates of beer from under their bunks. The boozing and drunken singing went on all night. I hardly slept, maybe dozing for a few minutes at a time. At about 5.30am the boozing soldiers from the 48th finally passed out on their bunks and I must have fallen asleep. I was woken at 6am by the beery breath of the runty company sergeant with the shock of grey-white hair. He was panicking and ordering me to get up and go to the guardroom to be issued with a rifle and flak-jacket.

There was time for a quick visit to the latrines before rushing to the guardroom to sign out one of the army's trusted old servants, a Fabrique National 7.62mm assault rifle. For strange reasons known to only a select few at the top of the food-chain Irish soldiers in Lebanon were issued with only one spare magazine. This meant we carried a mere forty rounds of ammunition each, a miserly effort for soldiers in the middle of a warzone. The dead soldiers at Deir Ntar would have carried the same forty rounds and experienced the same vulnerability as the rest of us, knowing that if they had to fight for their lives they were pretty much screwed.

I'd no sooner stepped from the guardroom when the runtish company sergeant was on my heels. An old truck that once belonged to the U.S army and was now painted in the U.N colours waited at the gates of Camp Shamrock. About a dozen soldiers with rifles waited on the back of the truck and the truck's engine was ticking over. The white-haired runt with the stripes of a company sergeant on his sleeves jogged alongside me to ensure I jumped into the truck as quickly as possible. I just about had time to ask if there was breakfast or even a mouthful of tea. As expected, the company sergeant said there was no time for breakfast or tea. And anyhow the cooks hadn't yet opened the cookhouse for business. We were on our way to Deir Ntar to search for the body of a missing soldier.

About half of us on the truck were from the newly arrived 49th Battalion, so we wore the heavily lined winter uniforms designed for the worst of the Irish winter along with cumbersome flak jackets. We were without U.N insignia or the distinctive blue berets, helmets or forage caps of the U.N. I was dehydrated but there wasn't any hope of finding drinkable water or filling a water-bottle. As the truck took off from Camp Shamrock I looked out on the rolling hills and wadis of South Lebanon for the first time, fascinated by the terrain to the point where I mostly forgot my thirst. At least we were doing something that felt useful, searching for the body of a dead soldier. It was probably as useful as we could be to anyone.

Post October 7th terror attacks on Israel. London.

The angry denunciations of Israel sent forth into the world from public figures in Ireland and by leading Irish politicians is relentless. All matters of sensitivity and historical nuance are ignored in the rush to portray the modern state of Israel as the devil incarnate. The antisemitic murders in the U.S of Yaron Lischinsky and Sarah Milgrim are unmentioned. The death of Tzeela Gez's baby is also not worthy of mention. Tzeela Gez was a heavily pregnant mother killed in a West Bank terror shooting. Medics removed the baby from Tzeela's dying body and the infant boy was named Ravid. He died on the day Irish politicians were calling for more sanctions against Israel.

In the denunciations of Israel there's little humility or self-awareness on show. As Irish people are we even in a moral position to criticise Israel? Is it really helpful to superimpose the suffering at Clongorey and so many other sites of eviction and hardship onto the televised images of suffering from a warzone a very long way away from Ireland? Again, my thoughts turn to Irish diplomat and antisemite Charles Bewley and his malevolence in nineteen thirties Berlin.

Bewley could have saved thousands if not tens of thousands of innocent German Jews from Hitler's deathcamps if he wasn't so consumed by an ancient hatred of Jews that infected mainstream Christian thought since the origins of the faith. He was spoon-fed a lie like millions of Christians, deceived into believing that the Jews were Christ-killers. Modern historians are now more informed about Roman rule in what without irony we refer to as the Holy Land. Crucifixion was a Roman punishment reserved for political rebels and could not have been used against someone considered to be a false messiah or a heretic.

Early Christians in trying to avoid censure from Roman authorities couldn't admit that the leader of their faith had been killed by the very same authorities they were trying to curry favour with. So, they blamed the Jewish leaders in Jerusalem who were already viewed with suspicion by Rome. It was a winning move, to exonerate those who did actually kill Jesus and then to blame the Jews. It's a lie that reverberates through the centuries and found expression in Tsarist pogroms, Hitler's deathcamps and in political administrators like Charles Bewley's contempt for the almost certainly doomed German Jews he took such trouble not to help.

So, do the modern-day Irish have Jewish blood on our hands? Of course we do. Our appointed diplomat in Berlin in the critical years before the start of WWII was a Nazi sympathiser who went on to become an active Nazi under the tutelage of Hitler's propaganda chief. He did all he could to block legitimate visa applications from German Jews who would not have been a burden to Ireland. In truth most if not all of them would have moved onto the U.S or a little later to the emergent state of Israel. Much like the vile and destructive lies at the roots of our Christian faith are hidden by obscurantism, religious semantics and the self-righteousness of an entire civilisation the Jew hatred of the Irish state is hidden behind faux virtue and an indignant refusal to acknowledge the darkest secrets lurking in the Irish national consciousness. Deep down are we antisemitic? Of course we are. Why wouldn't we be?

Lebanon. 1981

Tibnine is built on hills and is identified as the town of Tafnis in the Jerusalem Talmud, a border town in the kingdom of Judah. The people of Tibnine are often fair-haired and fair-skinned as they have Phoenician and European as much as Arabic ancestry. Stone-age megaliths from the region are preserved at the Institut de Paleontologie Humaine in Paris. This is an ancient, solemn land.

The governor of Tyre Izz Al-Mulk raided Tibnine in 1107 and massacred the town's population. The occasional shells and rockets falling short from Israeli positions to the south and from PLO positions at Beaufort Castle are part of a continuum of conflict with roots buried deep in time. Maronite Christian churches in the surrounding hills and villages have a lineage extending back to Innocent II's Crusades. In 1981 the Maronites are yet joined with the Holy Sea of Rome. This is an unusual land of ancient inter-connections and secrets.

The old American truck just about gets us to Deir Ntar where we join other soldiers in searching the wadis for our missing comrade. We can only hope he died quickly.

A contrary-looking captain with thick spectacles orders me to strap a 77 radio-set to my back and follow on after him. The 77 set was used by the U.S army in Vietnam and is a reliable piece of kit. For hours the grouchy captain runs me up and down the wadis, holding the handset of the radio and leading me along as a beast of burden, a living symbol of a class divide humanity hasn't made much progress with. Dozens of soldiers pan out on either side of us, both from the 48th and newly arrived 49th battalion. There's no water anywhere and by now I'm more aware of dehydration, my dry tongue sticking to the top of my even drier mouth.

Eventually the captain tires of running up and down the wadis leading me behind him like his own personal two-legged mule. He takes the 77 set from me and retires to the shade where he begins the officer in the field's favourite past-time, studying a map. I'm ordered along with about twenty others to search yet another wadi. At this point I'm seriously dehydrated and about a minute or two away from passing out. There's no medic with us or anyone who might have water. And I don't know any of these soldiers. Even if they had water why would they share it with me? I pick a terrapin up from the ground and carry him with me as a distraction from thirst and boredom.

A passing soldier notices the terrapin and asks me about it. He's obviously a pet-lover. He stops to peel an orange, a little intrigued by the animal I've picked up from the brush of the wadi. I barter the terrapin for half an orange. The juice from the orange saves me from the embarrassment of collapsing from dehydration on my first day in Lebanon. I devour the orange-skin like a savage. It's typical of armies worldwide I guess, a carelessness and barely hidden contempt for the common soldier. Maybe it reflects a wider human disinterest in others, a revelation to do with selfishness and the unavoidability of selfishness.

In the Irish army of the time a macho disregard for the sensitivities of others was as much a part of day-to-day life as were profanity, alcohol abuse, heavy porn played on VHS and chain smoking. Often this contempt for the well-being of others was disguised by military procedure and the abuses of rank. Men were left without food and water or ordered into dangerous situations where injury or even death was more likely than not. The deaths of the two soldiers at Deir Ntar might be included in this overall thoughtlessness for others.

Post October 7th attacks on Israel. London.

The conflict in Gaza brought on by Hamas and Palestinian Jihad's October 7th attack, brings to the public conscience a raft of names, most of them already known to us to one degree or other. Celebrities who are nearly always on television ally their name and brand with the plight of the Palestinians caught up in yet another nightmare of war. Social media is spitting with indignation. Those who are only known a little to the public really go for it, sending their best messages of indignation into cyberspace. Others who are household names solemnly take on a whole new aspect to their public persona by association with the Palestinian cause.

Commentators and news' presenters are also quick to add whatever gravitas they can to the situation. Other equally serious or more serious conflicts in the world are ignored. When we think of the Gaza conflict there's an association with those who condemn Israel's actions for they are rarely off the large plasma-screened television sets networked throughout the land like a twenty first century version of Orwell's telescreens.

Death-faced BBC news reporters and commentators pronounce the lists of casualties provided by Hamas as if they're reading the gospel truth. Those of us who try to step back a bit from the more harmful effects of propaganda struggle with the cognitive dissonance at play. In our minds we're trying to hold in place two conflicting facts presented to us repeatedly. Firstly, Hamas is a murderous terror cult that attacked and slaughtered civilians in their homes in their hundreds on October 7th. Secondly, the casualty lists reported obsessively hour after hour, day after day, by BBC, ITV, Sky and the other mainstream media organisations are provided by the Hamas Health Authority.

By offering such casualty lists the liberal Western media are letting us know where they're coming from. They're not trying to hide it. We get our casualty figures from the terrorist death-cult that started the whole thing in the first place. That sets the tone for how the war is covered by the BBC and the other liberal news' channels. Now, when we think about Gaza the name of the death-faced BBC foreign correspondent forever on our television screens pops into our minds.

The names of radical leftists from the fringes of British politics resonate in our thoughts when that dreaded word is mentioned, stepping away from their chosen fields to add their voice to the outcry against Israel. Already a great many celebrities, internet influencers and political commentators have boosted their profiles, increased their subscriptions and added more followers as they bring forth from their psyches the saviour complex that's generally strong within them and repackage themselves to the world as almost saint-like in their concern for the victims of war. Their names come up again and again, linked in the common mind with the agonies of Gaza. At times it can seem as if their very names are synonymous with Gaza. In a broken world the wrong names are remembered.

In the documentary 'The Children of October 7th' the youngest survivor Ella Shan led the documentary maker to the attic where her father Yitzhak was murdered. Blood stains could still be seen on the floor. Ella was one of the thirty seven children killed on that day while hundreds more of the children that survived the terror of Hamas were left with lasting injuries. That's a name that needs to be remembered. Ellla Shan. Her father Yitzhak was murdered by the Iranian-backed terror group Hamas for the perceived crime of being Jewish. The fact that Ella Shan's name is left out of the media's take on the tragedy of Gaza tells us most of what we need to know about how affairs in that region of the world are covered. The fact that the names of the Palestinian and Israeli children no longer in the world are not as known to us as the commentators covering the war and the celebrities sympathetic to Hamas tell us more about sinister histories in the West than it does about actual events on the ground.

Dublin. 1981.

In the barrack-room where we're forming up for Lebanon Fu Manchu is telling a joke. He's trying to lighten the mood of the billet but doesn't have the skills or personality for telling jokes. The joke falls flat. Fu Manchu shrugs it off and pulls out his Carrolls' cigarette box and offers a ciggie to the nearest soldiers. He's really making an effort to lighten things up. As a senior corporal I guess he feels he must do something more than lie on a bunk, waiting.

Inevitably the Transport company sergeant shows up and rouses us from our torpor. Instead of falling us in on the square he shouts for us to form up in the billet. We fall in and are called to attention, then stood at ease. The company sergeant then goes through his favourite routine of calling out names from his roster. One of the engineer privates lets out a stage-whisper from the side of his mouth which can be easily overheard by the Transport Company Sergeant.

Jaaz dat man'd sicken yer hole with his roll-calls!

We snap to attention and answer *here company sergeant* as our names are called.

The engineer private with the flushed face bangs his boot to the floor like a deranged guardsman when his name is called. He shouts out in answer to his name loud enough for to be heard on the other side of Dublin. It's a funny interlude on a day of boredom and tension. The expression on the face of the Transport company sergeant as he again looks closely at the Engineer private is worth all the tedious hours hanging around the barrack-room. He's wise enough to ignore the engineer privates. The engineer is probably drunk but not drunk enough for him to have any problems travelling to Lebanon. Chances are he'll fall asleep on the plane and sleep off most of the effects of the alcohol by the time we get to Ben Gurion airport. The Transport company sergeant realises this and almost smiles as he continues calling out names from his roster.

In Lebanon the Irish battalion was situated close to the UNIFIL contingents from the Netherlands, Fiji, Norway and Ghana. We sometimes drank with soldiers from these contingents and bumped into them on the roads and crossroads of South Lebanon. They were generally like us, ordinary men with ordinary working-class lives back in their homelands. Some of our NCOs made friends with Norwegian NCOs as their maintenance camp at Camp Scorpion was close to Irish battalion HQ at Camp Shamrock.

The drinking sessions often ended with friendly invitations from the Norwegians for our NCOs and their wives to visit them in Norway when their tours of Lebanon ended. The Norwegians assured our NCOs they'd be more than welcome to stay with them at their Norwegian married quarters. Our NCOs went along with the banter but were coy on the question of the Norwegians visiting them in Ireland. Most of our NCOs lived in married quarters and were ashamed to invite NCOs and their wives from a progressive European nation to stay in the cold comfort of Irish army married quarters.

Married quarters at the time were often the old married quarters built by the Victorian and Edwardian British administration in Ireland. They had outside toilets and no bathrooms, a solid fuel fire in the living room and freezing bedrooms. Many of them had degenerated into structural slums and the army's Board of Works struggled to keep them habitable. Some were in a shocking state. There was no way the proud NCOs of our battalion were ready to invite

Norwegian soldiers from Camp Scorpion to such slums.

Yet the commissioned officers of the Irish army and members of An Garda Siochana did not live in bad conditions. In fact, the officer's houses I was in as a child growing up on the Curragh Camp belonged to a different world. They were spacious and arranged in the fashion of the upper middle-classes. Occasionally an officer's son from the neighbourhood invited us urchins into their gardens to teach us the rules of rugby. As soon as the boy's mother or father realised their child had invited the child of a poor family into their garden we were sent on our way. And we were not invited back. I'd never heard of custom officials, prison officers or any other employees of the state living in squalor. The old married quarters' slums were reserved for enlisted soldiers and their families. Maybe the thinking was that we were lucky to have anywhere at all to live.

People enjoy their comforts and privileges and protect them with both complex and blunt mechanisms. And it seems we've never really outgrown the old British class mentality or cultivated anything approaching the republican principles of the men and women of 1916. We were as differentiated by class and income as the brutalised workers in Plunkett's Strumpet City were differentiated from their betters. Equality in any make, shape or form was an abstract concept, an aspiration at best.

The human species can have very short and selective memories. The camaraderie and egalitarian spirit of Tom Barry and his men as they waited in a ditch for the Black and Tans can quickly become academic, the stuff of national legend consigned to books or to teary-eyed reminiscences in closing time pubs, rather than an actual goal that's worth aiming for. The dull routines of the depot soldier in the nineteen eighties blotted out all memories of the revolutionary ideals of 1916, or the national spirit of the battles at Pettigo-Belleek of 1922.

The significant difference between Irish national soldiers in Lebanon and Norwegian, Ghanaian, Fijian and Dutch troops serving under the same flag was that our national territory was annexed by another nation. In 1981 the national territory of Ireland according to our constitution included the entire island of Ireland. The partition of the country by force of arms and political power was nationalist

Ireland's most abiding humiliation. The Dutch, Ghanaians, Norwegians and Fijians did not have these unresolved issues back home. Patriots were not starving themselves to death in the Netherlands, Ghana, Norway or Fiji, protesting the partition of a district of their national territory by a far more powerful neighbouring state. People who met us had every right to be confused about who exactly we were.

Army advertising for recruits and RTE television news clips of soldiers at Dublin airport on their way to Lebanon could only do so much for army morale. Sooner or later, somebody was bound to ask why we didn't have a role in the crisis in the North in 1969. After Jack Lynch's televised address to the nation when he spoke of not standing by the people of the Falls Road in Belfast stood in the street waiting for the trucks and armoured cars of the Irish army to arrive. They are still waiting.

Even with the pathetic manpower and resources available in 1969 the national army could have taken the city of Derry and transformed it into a fortress. The infantry group serving with the U.N in Cyprus could have been withdrawn and deployed on the border along with every available officer from An Gardai. Civilians in the North could have been armed and incorporated into the FCA, the Irish army's reserve. The British response to such an incursion would probably have had devastating consequences politically, diplomatically and economically for all the people of Ireland. But the eyes of the world would have focused on the fortress city of Derry and its Irish army defenders.

Young lieutenants of the calibre of Dermot Earley and Michael Nestor were more than capable of leading men into action in the febrile summer of 1969. Before U.N or US diplomatic intervention hundreds of Irish soldiers, UDR and British soldiers and Northern civilians may have been killed or wounded in the fortress city of Derry and elsewhere. The blood sacrifice would have opened doors to the kind of international diplomacy and intervention which led to the signing of the Good Friday Agreement almost thirty years later. Whatever about inequality of opportunity and income disparity there was only one conflict of personal interest to Irish people in 1969 and twelve years later when we formed up for Lebanon. It was all about the national territory of Ireland and the partition of the island into two separate states.

Once the Irish army had withdrawn and the negotiations had begun, we could all be friends again. The problem really centred on the second-class status of the nationalist communities of the North and those inequalities could have been addressed in 1969 if the Irish army had the leadership, fighting spirit and daring to cross the border. It obviously hadn't. It took almost thirty years of violence, upheaval and conflict for the negotiations to begin in earnest.

Irish soldiers had sworn an oath on the tricolour and the bible to defend Ireland and the Irish people, so dying in battles to defend Derry or along the border would have made sense. We'd signed up as human sacrifices to the nation after all and our oaths were not flippant. If Irish national soldiers could fight with such resilience and courage in Katanga under Commandant Quinlan when they had nothing personal at stake how yet more resilient and courageous they'd have fought when defending the ancient walls of Derry.

The situation would have changed radically if the nationalist people of Derry, Belfast, Newry, Armagh, Crossmaglen, Dungannon, Coalisaland and Dungiven were armed and supported by the Irish government and friends overseas. It would have been significantly harder for a B Special or RUC man to smash a nationalist over the head with a pick-axe handle or truncheon if an Irish army FN 7.62mm assault rifle was pointing in their direction at the time. The causal factors weighted against an intervention from the Irish army and this influenced the morale and reputation of our national army for decades after. The men serving at the time were morally obliged to intervene and cross the border, but fear, British agents at the heart of the Dublin administration, woeful leadership, ambiguity towards the North and the underfunding and demoralisation of the army by successive governments over decades weighted in favour of not intervening. Apart from little more than bluff and bluster we did exactly what Jack Lynch said we wouldn't do, stand by.

If units from the Irish army crossed the border to take the city of Derry by force and arm nationalists where and whenever possible the protracted hell of decades of violence propelled by the Provisional IRA and other paramilitaries need not have happened. After initial engagements the mechanisms of international diplomacy would have swung into action. Irish army units could have agreed to a withdrawal south of the border on condition that the gerrymandering, legal discrimination and state brutality be addressed in a bill of rights somewhat like the ambitions of the Good Friday Agreement. The Irish army as the military element of the will of the Irish people could have won in a matter of weeks or months what it took the Provisional IRA and its' supporters decades to achieve.

Northern Ireland's prime minister at the time James Chichester-Clark understandably tried to dismiss the pogroms as a nationalist insurrection. To everyone else outside the bubble of prejudice Chichester-Clark and his friends moved in it was another sectarian pogrom against those damned by history to live in Catholic enclaves in the North. The IRA in Belfast at the time was too insignificant to even consider insurrection. At the height of the violence on the 14th August 1969 the IRA's commander in Belfast Billy McMillen called out all his members for defensive duties. In total thirty IRA volunteers answered McMillen's call to arms, along with twelve women, forty boys from the Fianna and a dozen or so girls. They had one Thompson submachine gun, a Sten gun, a Lee-Enfield rifle and six old revolvers, along with whatever petrol bombs they could make. They were hardly the forces of insurrection mentioned by Chichester-Clark.

Even the most conservative voices on the island of Ireland spoke out after the fires were put out and those injured were taken to hospital. Cardinal Conway and his bishops said-

The fact is that on Thursday and Friday of last week the Catholic districts of Falls and Ardoyne were invaded by mobs equipped with machine-guns and other firearms. A community which was virtually defenceless was swept by gunfire and streets of Catholic homes were systematically set on fire. We entirely reject the hypothesis that the origin of last week's tragedy was an armed insurrection.

It's not for a humble ex-private from the Irish army to try and rewrite history. No matter how many words we chose to dedicate to events in Ireland in 1969 the facts remain the facts. The official military arm of our state, the Irish Defence Forces or Oglaigh na hireann, or the Irish army as known by its common name, did not rush to the defence of the Irish nationals burnt out of their homes, injured or in some cases murdered by enemies of the Irish state and its nationalist aspirations. In 1981 as we were forming up for Lebanon our history as an insignificant player in the events of 1969 weighed on our shoulders.

Our failure to cross the border in 1969 and our failure to protect civilians against both civil and state terror deflated our morale and reduced us to even more subservience to An Gardai Siochana. The one moment in the history of the state when we had legitimate reasons to act resolutely, we didn't act at all. Looking back now the roles of self-serving and fearful politicians are more in focus. Without orders from the very top the Irish army of 1969 was going nowhere.

After August 1969 it was far more understandable for anyone interested to regard the Irish Defence Forces as true inheritors of the Free Statism so hated by republicans. It was the Free Statism which accepted partition in 1922/23. It was the Free Statism which supported the twenty six county administrations of a subdued and semi-theocratic state dependent in so many ways on our former rulers in London. It was the Free Statism which looked the other way when the North's institutional bigotry and paranoia made a mockery of whatever concepts of equality and human rights were around at the time.

If we thought about it for longer than two minutes, we'd hang our heads in frustration and humiliation. Standing by had become our modus operandi. It was far more convenient to distract ourselves with whatever was happening in Lebanon than to think about the questions brought into the open by events in the North.

The student of history can only point to the disgraceful state of the army in August 1969 as the primary reason for its inability to do anything useful in relation to what was happening in the North. It had been allowed to become a depot soldier's army of pot-wallopers and unfit men who went home for their tea. The chief of staff at the time handed in a defeatist and dismal report to the government as to the effectiveness of the army. As if affected by the overall ennui of his organisation General McEoin's estimation was negative in the extreme, emphasising how his entire army was only capable of holding the town of Newry for twenty four hours.

Maybe British agents had worked in the background for to ensure the army of the

South was so demoralised and poorly led that any idea of an intervention up North was out of the question. General McEoin's gloomy estimation of his own men's abilities has the observer of history wondering just why as chief of staff he remained in his post. If he'd have offered his resignation in the years leading up to the crisis of 1969 in protest at army underfunding and stagnation it would have at least focused attention on the army's dire state.

The realist might point out that the army's stagnation was an extension of an overall stagnation in the country. From the archives a Radharc television documentary from the nineteen sixties is an unsettling glimpse of poverty and despair. The photographer Alan McWeeney's award-winning photographs of Travellers camped at Cherry Orchard in 1965 is also a poignant record of poverty, discrimination and hopelessness. Anyone unfamiliar with the hated status of Irish Travellers and the depths of their poverty in the nineteen sixties would be forgiven for assuming McWeeney's monochrome images were of starved refugees running from war, pestilence and genocide. The destitution and emaciation of the unfortunates photographed at the Cherry Orchard halting-site in 1965 is a damning snapshot of a society ill at ease with itself. Such conditions are not readily associated with European standards of civilisation. As a nation we had quite a road yet to travel.

McWeeney's photographs were the basis for a John T. Davis documentary simply titled Traveller. It is probably the most insightful and moving documentary made not just about Travellers, but to ever come out of Ireland. The documentary's stress on human vulnerability touches the hardest heart. Its greatest compliment was when RTE bought the rights of the film as the establishment in Ireland would have blanched at the thought of a broader audience viewing such degrading poverty in the Dublin of 1965. Since RTE bought the rights of Traveller it's not been aired on the national airwaves, or has it been offered for viewing on an international stage. It's as if the documentary has disappeared, buried deep in the archives at Donnybrook in the hope that it's implied shaming of the Ireland of our fathers will be forgotten.

In such a time of inequality, high emigration and squalor is it even reasonable to ask why the army of 1969 was so dismally unprepared for an intervention in the North? Nobody had bothered to liberate the hated caste known as Travellers from their poverty, or to ask why such a liberation had not happened in a state pledged to the equality of all its citizens. Nobody had bothered to prepare the desperate emigrant heading for the cattle boat for the travails of urban England and the NO BLACKS, NO DOGS, NO IRISH signs on the doors and windows of a number of English boarding houses. Nobody had bothered liberating the Irish poor from their soul-destroying poverty and Irish women from their roles of subservience, so why should a national consciousness be primed and ready to liberate nationalists in the North from their Croppies Lie Down status under Stormont? We'd drifted too far from the republican ideals of 1916 for a national consciousness to override the selfishness of individuals and the exploitation at the beating heart of how human communities generally organise themselves. Could we even save ourselves, let alone our fellow Catholics north of the border?

If there is such a thing as national shame we probably endured it through much of the Troubles of 1969-98. As Taoiseach at the time Jack Lynch went from a glorious, televised moment of declaring the nation would not stand by to bringing criminal action against members of his own cabinet for signing off what was agreed in government, or at least implied. The implications of direct involvement in the North must have given Lynch nightmares during his waking hours, a dawning horror of a war with the Northern state and its British ally that nobody south of the border was remotely prepared for.

Lynch ate the words he delivered over the national airwaves in 1969 by sacrificing his more energetic cabinet colleagues in a show-trial and retreating into the kind of cooperation with the British state that would wake the republican dead at Arbour Hill and Glasnevin and have them shaking their ethereal fists in the direction of Dail Eireann. Lynch's volte-face was completed inside a year. He'd gone from a national address on television where he'd implied direct military action in the North, to offering weapons, money and respirators to Northern civilians under siege - finally arriving at a total denial of intending to do anything outside normal governmental and diplomatic channels. The woeful state of the Irish army at the time and Chief of Staff McEoin's morbid defeatism would not have given Lynch any confidence in an action even a hairs' breath outside normal diplomatic channels.

After Lynch's arms trial in 1970 the Irish state's role in the North's violence was set in stone. It would be a role of cooperation with Westminster and Stormont, along with consistent and occasionally imaginative diplomatic and legal challenges to the violence of the Northern state. It was a massive climb-down and yet another national humiliation to add to all the other humiliations handed down by our old colonial masters.

All this history might seem totally incidental to the Irish army soldier bound for Lebanon in 1981. After all what's this UNIFIL business got to do with us? But don't the events of the past largely define our present circumstances and reality? Because hundreds of us didn't die in a re-run of the old Pettigo-Belleek battles a few of us will die in Lebanon. Because we lost so much respect by not intervening in 1969 we're trying to salvage respect by intruding on a conflict on the other side of the world which has nothing to do with us.

Propaganda with a visceral hatred of all concepts of Irish consciousness independent of London condemned the Provisional IRA with all the venom of the English language. But the Provisional IRA and their supporters were taking up the fight the Irish army could not take up for a variety of political, diplomatic, economic and practical reasons. A number of them, as opposed to us, were the real national soldiers who deserved medals pinned on their chests.

If it were not for the pressure they applied on the political status quo would the exploitative classes of Stormont Toryism, Lowland Scottish planter and what remained of the Anglo-Irish ascendency have gone to the table to meet their Catholic neighbours in what would lead to the Good Friday Agreement? Any progress in the North would have had to have happened on Stormont's terms, endorsed by the always only a breath away arrogance of High Toryism or the Centrist, legalistic pragmatism of Labour.

Westminster politicians for some unfathomable reason still think they know the right course for the Irish people, even though their record in Ireland is best forgotten for the sake of the generations to come. The IRA's war filled a gap left vacant by the inability of the Irish army in 1969 to intervene in the North when it had the moral right to do so. As the legitimate soldiers of the Irish people, we were pushed to the margins of the most critical national crisis in living memory. Irish soldiers from a more unconventional constitution were needed to redeem national pride in the absence of a national intervention from somewhere else. Instead of a re-run of Pettigo-Belleek we had a revision of the old tactics of Tom Barry and Dan Breen, complemented by the devastating tactic of urban car-bombings.

None of this is intended as history or as another analysis of the complexity of the troubles in the North, but merely a study of sorts of the causal factors relevant to our day before Lebanon in 1981. It was impossible for us to ignore accusations that we'd turned our backs on the North, running away from the most serious political and civil conflict of our time. In effect we were accused of institutional cowardice, of not fulfilling the primary role of our arms.

I have never personally supported Sinn Fein or any republican grouping or movement, never that interested in nationalism per se. It's just that it was obvious to us then and even more obvious now that something had to be done in the North, and we were not doing it. The circumstances in 1969 were ripe for intervention, but we didn't intervene. Some force or other from nationalist Ireland had to intervene to compel the planter mentality to look more closely at its Croppy Lie Down ethos, it's up to the knees in Fenian blood mentality. As it wasn't going to be us, it had to be somebody else.

We carry these doubts with us to Collins Barracks and onto Dublin airport and on further to Lebanon. In Lebanon we'll meet Norwegians, Fijians, Ghanaians and others who don't have contentious borders drawn across their national territories. We'll struggle to answer questions about Bobby Sands and his fellow hunger strikers. At times we'll struggle to adequately explain who exactly we are and why we have no active role in the conflict in the North of Ireland. History swings as a deadweight from around our necks and the might of England and her commonwealth is still fixed against Irish national consciousness and Irish arms.

The student of history looks back on the available facts and can only wonder how the Irish national soldier evolved from men like Tom Barry and Dan Breen to the depot soldiers of 1969. There's an RTE interview with Dan Breen in the archives when Breen was in his twilight years. He's tenacious to the camera and although an older man his eyes are on fire with revolutionary righteousness. He explains he is not one bit sorry for killing Crown forces.

If any man comes into my house, my country, and tries to take over by force I will kill him … and I apologise to no man and no god.

Breen's affirmation of his revolutionary role is chilling. It's easy to imagine him emptying the magazine of a Mauser C96 or Howth rifle with its foot-long muzzle-flame into the body of a Royal Irish Constabulary policeman or a British soldier. In the same interview Breen talks about how the Irish peasant of his boyhood was little more than a serf, a slave to impersonal economic forces directed by faceless and ruthless men from the English ruling classes. From a wider reading of exploitation on these islands Breen was a reincarnation of Wat Tyler, the leader of the Peasant's Revolt of 1381. He was as much in the tradition of the Chartist as the Fenian, the socialist as the republican.

Breen suffered much hardship as a child as his family circumstances were tough and his outrage at the conditions he was born into was deeply personal. Some men prefer to die with a gun in their hands rather than live in poverty and what they see as hopeless oppression. For Breen, Michael Collins was a god he'd have gladly died for. For some men economic exploitation and class inequality are simply intolerable. The exploitation and subjugation of Ireland by land-owning elites who classed themselves as English or Anglo-Irish was so objectionable to a few that the violent death of a revolutionary was preferable. The Ireland of 1916 had a number of such men and in 1919 too such men emerged when Dan Breen and his comrades gunned down the RIC at Soloheadbeg in rural Tipperary. Such men again stood up to their full height and answered the call when guns at Pettigo-Bellek were heard in 1922.

How the ruling caste in London must have fumed at the thought of peasants rising up to fight against the economic and social forces perfected over centuries that condemned so many millions of men and women to wage-slavery and penury. How quick they were to send in the Black and Tans and to reinforce Pettigo-Belleek with the Crown's best regiments. How anxious they must have felt at the thought of the spirit of Michael Collins, Dan Breen and Tom Barry spreading to the slums of

England's cities and to the collieries and dark Satanic mills of their own hinterlands. How frantically Fleet Street's propagandists worked to damn Irish rebels and by association the Irish people to the seventh pit of hell.

The revolutionary zeal which led to the birth of the modern Irish state faded quickly, largely because economic forces and resources were not allied with the spirit of revolution. The same old systems of exploitation continued much as before, with Irish-born factory-owners, landlords and bankers replacing their English predecessors. After only a few years of the counter-revolutionary Irish government of Cosgrave people began to realize that there had been no revolution as such, merely a change of administration whereby the sons, and occasionally the daughters, of ambitious Catholic families were given the good jobs hitherto reserved for people sent from England and Scotland. Poor people began to somewhat bitterly observe that the only difference they noticed in their lives was that their eviction notices and court fines were stamped with a harp and the word Eire, rather than the crown of England.

Dan Breen and his revolutionary comrades were exalted as national heroes and given government jobs and pensions. But the economic conditions remained much as before with the same old practised regime of exploitation and class disparity. The tricolour flew over public buildings and a president rather than a governor general was now in the Phoenix Park. But the slums remained and the exodus to the cities of England and further afield carried on much as before, with hundreds of thousands of Irish citizens joining the exploited classes of England in her factories, workshops and construction sites.

The Irish army of 1969 under General Sean McEoin were regarded by the state as inheritors of the spirit of the men of 1916, but others saw them as the living embodiment of a counter-revolution organised around the Irish Free State's first government. Perhaps it is kinder to see them as the inheritors of both traditions, with more of an emphasis on a Free State, twenty six county identity. None of the soldiers of 1969 had known revolution or experienced much by way of a revolutionary spirit. The enlisted man would have had no imperative to fight on the border. They were volunteers not conscripts and any or indeed all of them could have simply walked away if ordered North.

But they were proud Irishmen under arms and would have followed orders to the letter. As General McEoin's report to Jack Lynch's government pointed out the two thousand or so men available for combat would have needed to have trained under combat conditions at section, platoon and company level. They were not trained for real combat because McEoin reported there was not enough men available to guard installations, go on U.N tours of duty and be available for training.

General McEoin would have to take some responsibility for the underfunding and complacency of the army in 1969. Army headquarters under McEoin had applied for extra funding more than once in the years before the crisis of 1969 but the government of the day had ignored their requests. Given the combustible nature of the North McEoin could have resigned in protest and his resignation would have brought attention to the lamentable state of the army. McEoin had commanded twenty thousand peacekeepers during the U.N's volatile mission in Congo. He was the nephew of Sean McEoin, the Blacksmith of Ballinalee, one of the IRA commanders with notable successes against the Crown during the struggle for independence. History expected more of McEoin than what he gave.

In 1969 General McEoin was almost sixty years old. When his uncle and namesake Sean McEoin was appointed chief of staff of the Irish army in 1929 he was 36 years old. Sleepy decades of a twenty six county state succoured by a conservative Catholicism had progressed the Irish mind not very much. In an old man's country it made sense that our chief of staff was an older man with a limited capacity for offensive military thinking.

The reports from General McEoin's planning staff were unbelievably defeatist and negative. The rational mind is puzzled how a country like Ireland could produce men like Michael Collins and Dan Breen in the same century it produced the army officers on McEoin's staff who authored *Document 8. Planning Board on NI Operations. Interim Report* on 27th September 1969. In this best forgotten document the authors conclude-

The Defence Forces have no capability of embarking on unilateral military operations, of any kind (either conventional or unconventional) from a firm base at home.

Further on they add:

... in light of modern surveillance techniques available to the security forces in the North guerrilla operations in Northern Ireland would be difficult to conduct over a protracted period.

The staff officers conveniently forgot the two thousand men fit for service and who had mortar, armoured car, artillery and medical support available. They could have crossed the border from Donegal and turned Derry into a fortress city. If the British forces in the North did counter-attack Irish army defenders and civilian volunteers could have resisted until diplomatic intervention focused the eyes of the world on the North. For planning staff to advise General McEoin that there was absolutely nothing the Irish army could do in August and September of 1969 was both misleading and sinister.

Likewise, their summation of guerrilla operations on the border is simply laughable when the Provisional IRA's Fermanagh-East Tyrone and South Armagh Brigade's operations in the nineteen seventies and eighties are considered. Just what exact modern surveillance techniques were the army H.Q planners worried about in 1969? They sound like men who were looking forward to going home every evening to the more affluent Dublin suburbs to enjoy their family lives. They come across as firmly in the tradition of the Free State partitionists who accepted a twenty six county state as far removed as possible from the eccentric and barbed Protestantism of Lowland Scottish descendants in the North.

In the longer view British agents probably did not have to infiltrate the higher echelons of the Irish army of 1969. These colonels and commandants had clearly no stomach for intervention in the North. The revolutionary spirit of 1916 was tagged to the legitimacy of the state and celebrated in official ceremonies but did not extent beyond the Boundary Commission's final demands.

The state of the Irish army in 1969 and the attitude of its self-serving H.Q staff shadowed all of us who pulled on the army's green uniform in the following years and decades. An intervention could have saved thousands of lives in the subsequent conflict and redeemed the honour of the Irish state in the eyes of our Northern compatriots and the wider world. Diplomacy and intervention from the US government would have limited the British response to the annexation of Derry. The defenders could have returned across the border to Donegal and the cross-government talking could have then begun in earnest. There was a moral and historical obligation to act, but we didn't act. Not surprisingly one of the three staff officers who authored the Planning Board on N.I Operations report later became one the army's senior men. Whether he slept well at night as the Northern conflict raged on is not recorded in what archives and diaries we have access to.

Events moved quickly. The Irish army in 1969 was used as leverage in talks with the British government, the reserves were called up. Jack Lynch's dramatic televised address to the nation implied a military intervention. Residents on the Falls Road in Belfast did in fact stand in the street waiting for the Irish army to arrive. Once the lamentable state of the army of the time and the defeatist attitude of its general staff was fully digested by the government the emphasis switched to training, arming and funding nationalists in the North.

Jack Lynch appeared to very quickly change his mind on any direct support for nationalists in the North and in 1970 brought criminal proceedings against his own ministers which would become known as The Arms Trial and would distance his government from their earlier plans of intervention. A few politicians and an Irish army intelligence officer, Captain James Kelly, were duly scape-goated, wrongly blamed for acting independently of Lynch when all the facts to hand indicates they were following government policy. The narrative quickly changed to cooperating with the British forces in the North and beefing up security on the border.

By the time we were forming up at Collins Barracks for Lebanon in 1981 all thoughts of intervention in the North were as abstract as the stirring words of the 1916 Proclamation. It was now all about a threat from rogue Orangemen, an incursion into our twenty-six-county territory by columns of Unionist paramilitaries and activists. All thoughts of the North hinged on the concept of the Irish soldier standing guard on the border, watching and waiting for an Orange incursion. And we'd been drafted by the British into the struggle to contain the Provisional IRA and the INLA. We guarded installations and magazines and escorted IRA/INLA prisoners when they were moved from A to B. We also escorted movements of cash and explosives and stood on the roof of E Block at Portlaoise Prison guarding captured terrorists, or nationalist freedom-fighters if you prefer.

We'd helped create the Provos by not intervening in 1969 and now they were a force to be reckoned with. Lebanon was a merciful distraction from a legacy of ineptitude and complacency towards the North. Thanks to the U.N there were other places in the world where an Irish soldier might distinguish himself without walking headlong into the killing rage of descendants of Scottish planters in the North and their English defenders.

At Jack Lynch's funeral one of his loyal Fianna Fail comrades excused the debacle of 1969 with the following words-

Thirty years ago as a nation ... we were confronted with a stark choice ... we could have caved into sinister elements and put our country at risk.

Reading between the lines it is now more obvious that General McEoin and his men were stymied before they had even begun to

think about the North. The Southern
political class from the decidedly Free State
mindset would have literally stolen the
bullets from their weapons rather than see
them cross the border. If there were sinister
elements influencing the Irish army of 1969
then even more sinister elements were
subverting the government's importation of
arms at Dublin airport, arms intended for
the defence of Catholics in the North. The
senior civil servant who was instrumental in
intimidating the uncertain Jack Lynch into
abandoning all thoughts of intervention in
the North was the same civil servant who
signed the death warrants of the IRA men
executed by DeValera's government. This
civil servant also had a dark hand in the
obstruction of Robert Briscoe's attempt to
rescue Jews from Hitler's death-camps by
offering them sanctuary in Ireland.

It is now night-time at Collins Barracks.
How totally different the mood is in these old
stone buildings. Darkness eases the mind
away from the hard logic of barrack-squares
and the decisions in history Irish leaders had
to make. Who else is present here? What
measure of psychometry have these austere
walls and squares honoured? It's unsaid, as
so much in the world is unsaid.

In 1916 the 10th Battalion of the Royal Dublin Fusiliers were called from these very billets and squares to help quell the rebellion in the centre of Dublin. Irishmen killed Irishmen in the nation's capital city. An English infantry captain went mad and murdered the pacifist Sheedy-Skeffington. Tenement-dwellers with not much by way of food in their bellies were bayoneted to death by English soldiers. Children died in crossfire. Much of the very centre of Dublin was ruined by fire and shell in what became the most conspicuous moment of blood-sacrifice in the regeneration of Irish nationhood. Bullet-holes in the neo-classical pillars of the GPO are the wounds yet visible in the soul of modern Ireland.

The Irishmen from the 10th Dublins who died on Easter Sunday 1916 were forgotten in DeValera's Ireland, damned by a quirk of history to die at the wrong time, wearing the wrong uniform. Soldiers were they, good ones too by all accounts. They lived at the same time as Yeats, O'Casey, Casement, Joyce, Collins and Shaw. And the young gaunt Dev too, spared the executioners' bullet by a whim of fate.

Surely nothing before or nothing since comes close to such a moment of total history for the Irish people. The Irish soldiers who hurried from the Royal Barracks on Easter Sunday 1916 couldn't have been aware they were marching on the wrong side of history. Their comrades are yet grinning from the archives in old grainy photographs - Pals' battalions bound for Gallipoli. They were photographed at this very barracks during the war to end all wars.

Irrespective of Irish national consciousness the British regiments at Loos and on the Somme and elsewhere are a part of our story too. We were part of the United Kingdom at the time so legally Ireland was also at war with Germany. Irishmen fought in every branch of the British military and were among the shell-shocked soldiers led by the arm or carried from the trenches as husks of the men they once were.

Francis Ledwidge, Tom Kettle, Willie Redmond and Yeats' suicidal flyer merge the soul of Ireland with the blooded obscenity and travesty of the First World War. Men from the Dublins would have staggered too in recuperation with shell-shocked, broken minds, their mental health confounding the psychiatric professionals of the day. They diagnosed the broken men from the trenches in the spirit of their own bewilderment at what they were faced with. *Shell-shocked man battling against the wind,* because one patient looked exactly like a man walking into a strong wind. *Shell-shocked man on slippery ice.*

Empires, autocracies and the political states which colluded in the war to end all wars richly deserved to wither and die, their authority forever tarnished by their collective crimes against humanity. Many Irishmen from the 10th Dublins would have had their minds broken by the savagery of the 1914-1918 war. It was as if a cabal of mass-murderers had hijacked entire nations and peoples and herded them into a slaughterhouse of hell. A number of the orchestrators of slaughter were related by blood, like the cousins King George of England, the Kaiser Wilhelm and the Russian Tsar.

The only sane response of progressive citizens after the war was to distance themselves as much as possible from the power blocs responsible for it. Who could blame the leading lights of the emerging Irish state from distancing themselves from the inhumanity of the trenches? What sane person would wish to have any part in a war of such horror and obscenity? The absurdity of dada was logical in the context of what it was responding to.

Demobbed soldiers from the Dublins were not embraced by the emerging Irish state. The British Legion was concerned about how Irishmen who'd served the king were treated in Ireland under administrations with a growing national consciousness. The County Kildare writer John McKenna mentions a soldier who survived the trenches in his book The Lost Village, an account of life in Castledermot in 1925. The soldier and his brother were brawling with a third man at the end of a drunken Sunday. The former soldier was sent down for a month's hard labour. From the dock the former soldier says-

I was in the war and when I get a few drinks I lose my head.

The sentence was judged heavy by the locals, with no thought given to the man's war service or to the probability that he was suffering from a neurological condition related to the trenches. The individual is at the mercy of so many great forces, indifferent sweeps of tumultuous change.

How easy it is for any of us to find ourselves on the wrong side of history.

Somewhere in the bowels of this Collins Barracks are the timeworn remains of prosthetic masks used by maimed soldiers after World War One. Missing jawbones and pulped noses were hidden behind such masks by men who coughed up particles of lungs ruined by gas years after war's end. The spirits of the men taken in the war are yet asking why they had to die in such a way. As this day before Lebanon turns into a night before Lebanon the deeper mind of the Irish soldier is more exposed to the restless spirits of Irish soldiers who went before us.

So many souls passed here. In the 1880s the Royal Barracks was condemned by the Commissioners of the War Office as unfit for human occupation. Men from the 8th King's Royal Irish Hussars died here from enteric fever. Death stalks this day before Lebanon. The deaths of the two soldiers at Deir Ntar are conjoined in a longer narrative of death. Collins Barracks is a mausoleum for history's mostly forgotten men. It's among such impressions from the past we slumber as we form up for Lebanon.

Post 7th October attack on Israel. London.

When facing a death-cult as an enemy who use human shields and tunnels, the Israeli military are faced with the impossible task of freeing hostages and defeating its enemies whilst at the same time avoiding a humanitarian catastrophe in a heavily populated area. All the while the world is watching, waiting for the first sign of bad news to come. Israel is now the Western world's favourite pariah, its every failing pounced on by a media that can never get enough negative content about the world's only Jewish state. In everyday walkways of life it's increasingly difficult to voice any kind of sympathy for either the state of Israel or the people of Israel. It really isn't appreciated.

A Soho shopkeeper argues with me when I placidly suggest that there's usually two sides to every conflict. She brought up the question of Gaza, not me. I was only buying flowers for my wife, minding my own business. The woman is furious, her eyes flaring into a self-righteous rage. What's going on? What is it about this particular conflict that brings on such reactions? Is it because it's on the T.V news nearly all the time? Is it because it's to do with Jews? I'm not Jewish, nor am I Muslim. I don't have a stake in this. Except that there's something called truth and that the truth is worth struggling to pin down. One of the examples of antisemitism the International Holocaust Remembrance Alliance give is-

Denying the Jewish people their right to self-determination, e.g., by claiming that the existence of a State of Israel is a racist endeavour.

The Soho shopkeeper as much as said that in her angry monologue, that Israel shouldn't even exist. She's heard enough of Ireland in my voice to take it as a signal for a quick put-down of a country and its agonies a long way from here. After all I'm from the most antisemitic country in Europe and that it seems is a come-on to all who feel like getting a little Jew hatred off their chests. That's how it is now. And the truth lies bleeding in some dark alley, hidden from so many who want nothing to do with it.

Dublin. April 1981.

The torpor of hanging around all day in the billets of Collins Barracks vanishes as the clock ticks towards the hour for us to leave. A self-satisfied captain from Army H.Q at McKee barracks enters the billet to give us a short talk on what to expect in Lebanon. He runs through the ground-rules of engagement, what is expected from us and what is not expected from us. We know when staff officers show up to give talks something is happening. We'll soon be out of here and on our way to Dublin airport.

The commissioned officers of the Irish Defence Forces in the early nineteen eighties were a mixed bag, much like any comparable collection of men. Most of them came from Catholic Ireland's middle-classes, the sons of successful farmers, merchants, solicitors, auctioneers, civil servants and publicans. Some came from families with both money and connections with the Catholic hierarchy, or with the old revolutionaries of what's referred to as the Irish Troubles by the British and the War of Independence by the Irish. Only a few were commissioned from the ranks.

The class divide was strong and based on the old British army model. Quite a few of our officers mimicked the class-conscious idiosyncrasies of the British colonial officer. There was no sense of the army's organisation conforming to the revolutionary role of our supposed predecessors in the Old IRA. It was often more like an armed body of men led by Catholic conservatives who'd held onto the old class prejudices of Imperial Ireland. The derogatory tag of Free Stater was hard to shake off.

We had officers of great compassion and integrity, the truest sons of Ireland. The pedantically administered class divide between officers and enlisted men was a continual gripe for the ordinary soldier. Accommodation, pay, uniforms, kit, food, status and general conditions were demarcated in strict accordance with the class division between enlisted soldier and commissioned officer. The depot officer of the time was a pampered creature waited on hand and foot.

The army was an extension of the class divide in Irish society. Many private soldiers came from the poorest families in the land, or from Industrial Schools and orphanages.

It was often a choice between taking the boat to the uncertainties and second-class status of an English city or showing up on the Curragh in the hope that they were looking for recruits. Obsequiousness to snotty officers meant nothing in a time of high unemployment. The relative of a famous person served with us as an infantry captain. He came across as likeable, sharp and gifted, too gifted for the dull routines of depot life. He had flaws which to be fair would not be tolerated in any army and he resigned his commission early. He was in the wrong place at the wrong time, like so many more of us.

We had a few brilliant officers who were rightly promoted to senior rank and helped guide the army through many challenges and changes. We had brutes, bullies and thugs, gentlemen of quality and mediocre men too. We were very much a mixed bag as members of small, garrison armies of neutral countries tend to be.

Its 1981 so there's no lip-service paid to anything to do with diversity or equality. There are no women in our ranks and we're all pretty much from the same homogenous group. There are a few Church of Ireland men with us and even a convert or two from

Catholicism to Pentecostalism. They are excused from mass parade whereas it's compulsory for the rest of us to attend mass. There are atheists and agnostics among us but they are nominally Catholic so must attend mass parade too. In a spectrum of colours of only black and white all shades of grey are ignored or distrusted or looked down on as suspiciously foreign.

We're marched to the Catholic garrison church in the Curragh during Mission week, a week of mass-going, confessions and religious activities organised for our spiritual wellbeing. The fact that it's an unpopular event even among many religiously inclined soldiers is beside the point. Officers, chaplains and missionary priests have gone out of their way to organise masses and talks for our benefit, so the least we can do is not to complain about having to march to church and sit through extraordinarily long masses whilst not nodding off.

The Catholic vibe is not as pronounced as in earlier years. It was already diminishing before scandals in the nineteen eighties and nineties forced the nation into secularism. Some soldiers are very religious and devout and most of us understand the Marian codes and reductive Jansenism of our native church at a visceral level. We are Catholics in our blood and our instincts but don't like the trouble of mass, vigils, confessions and all the rest of it, at least not herded together like a docile flock of unthinking serfs.

The controversial Dublin priest Michael Clery showed up on the Curragh in the early eighties during Mission Week. The garrison church was packed with a thousand soldiers, most of us embarrassed or not entirely happy with being marched to mass in the middle of the week. Clery was an unusual choice for Mission Week on the Curragh as a long-haired, bearded, chain-smoking media-priest. But there he was anyhow, up on the altar in front of a thousand uncomfortable national soldiers.

As in keeping with the traditions handed down by our old colonial masters the congregation was divided on strict class lines. The senior officers including the commanding officer of the Curragh Command were in the first front pews. Behind them were their fellow commissioned officers and then behind them were the enlisted men. Revolutionary zeal died at the battles of Pettigo-Belleek and at the death of Michael Collins. We kneel as a body of men in thrall to Catholic conservatism and the brute forces that drive ordinary people out of their homes to find and keep a steady wage.

Clery's words as he took to the pulpit were startling and pitched to catch our attention.

Ninety five percent of us here masturbate ... and the other five percent are liars.

It was extraordinary by the standards of the church at the time. Calling the senior ranking officers on the Curragh a bunch of wankers and liars to their faces took some nerve. From where I was sitting I could just about see the bull-like head and neck of a kneeling colonel up ahead. The skin on the colonel's ample neck reddened in embarrassment or anger.

Clery went on to father the two children of his housekeeper Phyllis Hamilton, a former psychiatric patient at St. Loman's hospital. The authorities in Ireland used their power and influence to cover up Clery's failings as a supposedly celibate priest. With the usual contempt for ordinary people after the media-priest's death in 1993 Phyllis Hamilton's claim of having two children fathered by Clery were denied by the Catholic hierarchy. When Hamilton's former psychiatrist from St. Loman's came out in support for her he was censured by the Irish Medical Council. In telling the truth about a hypocritical priest's illegitimate children the respected psychiatrist was denounced by the Irish Medical Council for going beyond what was *ethnically permissible.*

It was yet another of the grubby little controversies whereby Catholic conservatives in Ireland tried to hold onto their control of the Irish state and the Irish mind. More grubbiness was to follow before the Irish mentality finally drifted free of the Episcopal letter, the Papal Bull and Sunday morning pulpit denunciations by disapproving priests. On hearing about the mess left behind by Clery the colonels who blushed at the priest's masturbation joke during Mission Week on the Curragh must have laughed, in private at least.

We were a Catholic militia for a Catholic people, on an island cursed by damp weather, a high fertility rate and bitter history. We claimed a revolutionary legacy but were damned by our own complacency and by high-stool idealists and fanatical Republicans as Free Stage stooges of a cynical British and Anglo-Irish hierarchy.

Yet our roots were in the peasant revolt of 1798 for as men we were as close to the peasants of Vinegar Hill as any men. We were the poor Irish who had their skulls smashed in by the Suffolk Fencibles and the Ancient Britons at Ballitore as recorded in the diaries of the Quaker Mary Leadbeater. We were descendants of the Croppies who lay in the ditch with an sagart bocht, pikes at the ready.

Our people before us dug about in the dirt to scratch a living as tenant farmers and the labourers of tenant farmers and went hungry when destiny ordained they went hungry. Our histories were recorded by Cecil Woodham-Smith and James Plunkett and our rights reasserted by James Connolly, Jim Larkin and Dr. Noel Browne. We kneel dutifully in garrison churches when ordered to do so, glad for a reprieve from the dole queue, the brutality of consistent and heavy manual labour or the boat to England. Debates and references to our Free State predecessors were abstract because righteous arguments can never be offered as payment for rent or carved up on a plate to be served for dinner. We were more saighdiuiri an chearnog barraic than soldiers of destiny, more the working-class pragmatist than the tool of Free State oppression.

But as we had the spirit of Collins on our side, were we so diametrically opposed to the principles of 1916 as we were made out to be? Dan Keating, the last surviving Old IRA volunteer who died in 2007 at the age of 105, was remarkably sharp up to his dying day. In his gentle Munster tones he denounced Free Statism and the Free State army in particular as the devil incarnate. For Dan, the Free State army of 1922/23 destroyed everything the martyrs of 1916 sacrificed their lives for. Dan stuck with an undiluted Republicanism after truce and treaty and was interned by DeValera's government at the Curragh in 1940. It's worth noting for the student of history that it was DeValera and not Cosgrave who imprisoned Dan and who executed his fellow idealists in the nineteen forties.

Republican idealists insisted they were betrayed by McNeill and the Irish Volunteers, so they organised the Rising of 1916 secretly. They complained they were betrayed by Redmond's Nationalist Party when Redmond pledged to fight for England in WW1 for the promise of a revised Home Rule Bill. They denounced Michael Collins as a traitor and put their faith in DeValera instead. Later they denounced DeValera.

The IRA's idealists reinvented themselves as Marxists in the nineteen sixties and were denounced a few years later by a new breed of IRA who relegated Stickies, Free Staters, the SDLP and other constitutional parties North and South to degraded roles of collaborators, gombeen-men, traitors, informers, spies, British sympathisers, West Brits and other derogatory categories and lesser forms of life. It goes on and on, predictably, a needle stuck in the groove of a cracked record.

More than one student of history has questioned whether Collins would have accepted a torpid Catholic state economically dependent on Great Britain. Would he instead have rallied the resources of the new state and built up its military as earlier he'd built up the revolutionary capacity and fighting spirit of the IRA? If anything can be judged by Collins' life and character the modern history of the island of Ireland might have panned out very differently if he had lived.

There would almost certainly have been a military show-down with the forces of the

North. Collins by his very nature could not have accepted economic dependency and stagnation, Orangeism and partition. The chances are that under Collins many more Irishmen would have lost their lives in re-runs of the Pettigo-Belleek battles.

Without someone of the stature and energy of Collins the newly created Free State followed the script held out before it by the authorities in London, defaulting to a political oddity as part of the British Commonwealth. It became an introspective state of mass migration and Catholic political interventionism, a de facto theocracy. Without an intention to march on the North it needed little by way of a standing military force. Only a handful of men were needed to watch the skies for signs of omens and RAF aircraft gone astray.

This is the vacuum into which we marched as soldiers of the Irish Republic, or Free State stooges of the British, depending on how you see it. The North orbited our lives like a vulture orbiting a dying beast. Psychologically there was no escape from it. There was especially no escape from it from 1969 onwards when there was only one moral and practical reason for an Irish army claiming linkage to Richard Talbot's

Jacobites, the United Irishmen, the Fenians and the volunteers of 1916. The only possible reason for an army was to intervene in the North. History ordained we could not intervene, so we didn't.

It was always there, always the elephant in the room. There was a contained civil war in the Northern six counties of the country and for a complexity of reasons we had no role in it worth mentioning. In Lebanon the South Lebanese Army leader Major Saad Haddad liked to shout to the Irish UN positions situated closest to his positions.

Why are you here? Go back to Ireland and fight for your own country. Don't come here to interfere in a war which has nothing to do with you!

Officially one Irish soldier died during the Troubles - Private Pat Kelly from Athlone's Custume Barracks. Pat Kelly was part of a joint Garda-Army operation searching for the kidnapped businessman Don Tidey in the woods of Leitrim. A young Garda recruit in training at Templemore, Gary Sheehan, died alongside Private Kelly. The Northern Ireland Troubles scorched nightmarish marks into the psyche of the Irish soldier. Many soldiers dealt with it like many Irish citizens dealt with it, by distancing ourselves from it. Most of us had never seen an RUC or UDR man in the flesh or experienced firsthand the fierce tribalism of an Orange march. We had never set foot in Northern Ireland and couldn't understand why anyone would want to do such a thing. It was strange, alien territory populated by strange, alien people.

The former Provisional IRA man Eamon Collins lived in Dublin and in Scotland after he'd fallen out with his revolutionary comrades. He wrote about his experiences, pointing out how he felt more affinity with the Scots because of the strong links between Scotland and Northern Ireland. He felt more accepted in Scotland and easier in his skin than he felt in Dublin. Certain Scottish and Northern Irish accents are indistinguishable from each other, as if the Plantation of Ulster happened only a few years ago rather than hundreds of years ago. Although we are the same people, Catholic people from the island of Ireland, there are regional and other differences. In somewhere like Ireland where people from a neighbouring county or townland can be seen as suspicious the Northern accent with its Scottish inflections can come across as discordant and unusual.

If we were to intervene in the Northern six counties how exactly would it pan out? And in what circumstances would such orders be given? In 1981 the North was constitutionally part of the national territory of Ireland, so if any of us stepped over the border into Down, Armagh, Fermanagh, Tyrone or Derry we would not be usurpers or trespassers according to our constitution. But in legality and referencing Collins' treaty the Northern six counties of Ireland were a part of the United Kingdom. We would in effect be stepping onto the ground of a neighbouring country.

We would be regarded by London much how the soldiers and marines of Argentina were regarded when they invaded the Falkland Islands in 1982. There would be a re-run of the Pettigo-Belleek battles of 1922, with the expected retreat of Irish national soldiers. The consequences both economically and militarily were unthinkable, the potential for a civil war involving the entire island were very real. Little wonder the nation viewed the North with such distrust and horror. If the Irish army of 1981 tried anything on the border with Northern Ireland it would have had to be decisive, rapid and ambitious. Given the tensions between Nationalists and Unionists in the North's hinterlands even a miscalculated gesture by the Irish army on the border could result in pogroms and mayhem to dwarf the murderous anarchy of 1969 and 1972.

In 1981 we live on tender-hooks, hoping somehow the violence in the North will miraculously fizzle out. The more conservative Southern voices, the voices of property, wealth, political office and tenure, blame the Provos and their supporters. Without the Provos' contribution to the conflict, the argument goes, the overall situation could be normalised. Globally much of the world's population are cowed by the fear of nuclear war between the USA and the USSR and the proxies of both powers. Similarly, the collective psyche of the Irish people is troubled by the prospect of an eruption of the Northern conflict into civil war involving the entire island.

Against this sullen backdrop the humble Irish soldier stands on the walls of Portlaoise Prison and rides in the back of land-rovers through the boreens and unapproved backroads of the border with Northern Ireland. The Provos' Green Book instructs their volunteers to stay clear of the security forces of the South, so generally we don't have to worry about the IRA taking pot-shots at us or setting off mines underneath our trucks.

It's a strange existence of perpetual watchfulness and paranoia, punctuated by an occasional incident, not unlike our duties with UNIFIL. The thousands of jobs provided by the army and the army's civilian contractors save many from the dole-queue and the boat to England. What can we do but drink when drinking is possible and watch re-runs of Debbie Goes To Dallas in our guardrooms with smoke from Rothmans and Major cigarettes choking us in a toxic fog. The politics of the day and the history of our island box us into an often tedious life on the sidelines of a merciless conflict in the Northern counties of the island.

Politically the Irish army are not a threat. There are more chances of the British Royal Family becoming signed-up members of the British Communist Party than the Irish Defence Forces making any kind of political gesture, much less threatening an army coup or refusing orders. A docile, barrack-square mood defines our days and nights. The idea of an Irish army colonel with pistol drawn entering Dail Eireann like a Spanish colonel had entered the Spanish parliament is ludicrous.

And what about a Greek-like revolt of the colonels? Simply impossible. Our rank and file were mostly uneducated and fearful sons of peasants and factory labourers, with venial, carnal minds. Any word or gesture beyond the brute necessity for bread and circuses was unheard of. Political education other than what was written in the Dublin newspapers or discussed on RTE did not exist. And what self-respecting private soldier or NCO would take a blind bit of notice of whether Fianna Fail were doing better in the polls than Fine Gael or vice versa?

The boat to England and the humiliation of the dole-queue are spectres haunting the collective lives and the most personal thoughts of the ordinary Irish soldier. Politics and existential questions falling anywhere outside the norms of talking about sex and sport, smoking fags and watching endless re-runs of Debbie Goes To Dallas simply don't exist. Any soldier naive enough to mention politics is brutally shouted down and might even catch a slap or a kick. In the valley of the blind even limited vision is an impediment.

The officer class is conservative and
Catholic, the ruddy, big-boned nephews of
parish priests and the sons of pious men who
volunteer for organisational roles in
Catholic charities and fraternities. They are
men with property to develop and land to
inherit, men with a stake in both the past
and the future of Catholic Ireland. They have
real interests in the sacred history of the
state, with grandfathers and granduncles
who marched with Pearse and Collins. They
have more than a rudimentary grasp of the
Irish language, understand the unspoken
codes of Irish Catholicism and are often
devout in their religious duties and mass-
attendance. It would be impossible to ignite
a revolutionary thought in any of us, enlisted
men or officers.

Legally and constitutionally, we cannot
approach a citizen without an on-duty
police officer present to speak on our behalf.
On border duties we cannot communicate
with the RUC or British Army on the other
side of the border. We are dumb mutes
ordered here and there by our police force,
An Gardai Siochana. This emasculating
subservience dates to the foundation of the
state. A significant percentage of the
population had sympathies for the anti-
Treaty lobby and regarded the deaths of

anti-Treaty activists at the hands of the National Army as unlawful judicial killing at best, or at worse as bestial murder of a sinister intent.

To encourage reconciliation and constitutional respectability the army had to take a backseat, for their very mention in certain quarters of the country and in families touched by Civil War atrocity was an affront. Army strength was radically reduced and soldiers retreated to their barracks, surfacing only now and then in the life of the state. They showed up momentarily in British Pathe News film-clips in the nineteen thirties wearing ridiculous German Army-type helmets, in pageants and in moments of propaganda or ceremonial state occasion.

The conflicts between pro-Treaty and anti-Treaty forces in the cradling years of the state are not easily forgotten. Even today, a long time on from the Four Courts bombardment and the deaths of Collins and Brugha the most bitter criticisms of the Irish Defence Forces are couched in subsumed hatred of the Free State Army of the early nineteen twenties. Old wounds never fully heal, or they leave scars to remind generations to come of battles yet to be fought and arguments to be won.

The true proclaimed saviours of the state were An Gardai Siochana, an unarmed police force with a Catholic, nationalist ethos. They, not the army, inherited the nationalist hopes of a people. As an organisation they had played no role in the truce or treaty and had no organisational links to their predecessors in the RIC and Dublin Metropolitan Police. State power and the moral authority of the Catholic Irish people were duly invested in the Gardai and not the National Army with its Free State and British Army connotations.

Whatever people think about An Gardai, they not us are the inheritors of Free Statism and the enforcers of the Irish Catholic mentality which defaulted as the moral credentials of the Irish State in its first seven or eight decades of existence. Once the National Army were reduced in numbers and marched back to their crumbing old barracks and forts in 1923 they were of no further threat to the constitutional authority of the Irish state. There was sabre-rattling at Army H.Q in 1925 and on a few other occasions but in effect the army was disbanded as a combat-ready military force.

Irish soldiers lifted their heads again in 1960 when they were needed by the U.N for a spot of soldiering in Congo. From the perspective of national pride and respect among the nations we needed the U.N more than it needed us, whether it was the Congo in 1960 or Lebanon in 1981. Hanging around old British army-era barracks and holding the shirttails of An Gardai Siochana is not everyone's idea of soldiering.

Post October 7th attacks on Israel. Berlin.

Just off Kurfurstendamm on Joachimstaler is a small bookshop. In the window they have copies of the Torah in both Hebrew and German. I'd love to have a look inside but it's never open. This morning, I seen a man walk out from there, lock the door behind him, get on a bicycle and cycle away. He's an older man with a white bushy beard, dressed in the broad-brimmed hat and dark clothes of Orthodox Judaism. Just by the bookshop there's always a police officer standing by. Sometimes there are two or three officers, and a police car parked nearby. I'm sure they're guarding the bookshop. What else could they be guarding? It makes you wonder what's going on when the police are guarding a small bookshop in Berlin. There are only nine thousand Jews in Berlin, a city of seven million. It's a tiny minority. Yet they are on their guard again, especially since the Hamas terror attack on October 7th.

Synagogues, kindergartens and schools are attacked, private homes too. Molotov cocktails were thrown. People wearing masks came in the night and painted crude Stars of David on doors and buildings. Have the BBC, RTE and ITV reported that? I guess they haven't. Maybe they haven't got the time. Maybe it doesn't fit in with their editorial guidance. Who knows what's going on in the depths of their minds? There is fear again on the streets of Berlin.

There's a suburb called Neukolln. In Neukolln there's a street called Sonnenallee. Many of those living there are migrants who fled Syria in 2015. They have big signs up that say DEFENDERS OF PALESTINE. On Kurfurstendamm there's a weird feeling, a bad vibe in the air. Ghosts are stirring. I can feel them everywhere. There's a plaque in memory to the medical researcher and doctor Rachel Hirch. She only just about escaped to England before the Nazis got their hands on her. She took a big psychological hit, hallucinating about her persecutors. She was admitted to Friern Barnett asylum on the northern outskirts of London and died there in 1953. The plaque to Rachel Hirch never seems so obscure, so unseen in this modern Berlin.

I visit a museum they've named Topography of Terror. They've put it on the site where the Gestapo had their headquarters on Prinz Albrecht Strasse, now renamed Niederkirchnerstrasse. It's the part of Berlin where all the tourists go. Checkpoint Charlie. Brandenberg Gate. Reichstag

Building. The Memorial to the Murdered Jews of Europe. One of the museum's perimeter walls is formed by what remains of the old Berlin Wall. They had lots of visitors, the usual high school groups and tourists from God knows where. These cities have become places for tourists to orbit around endlessly. So much of Europe has become an open-air park for tourists, the nice bits that is. I didn't stay long. It's the same horror. How beastly people are to each other. They put the museums up to remind us of the past so as we don't do it all over again. But of course the people around today who'd love to do it all again wouldn't be seen dead in a museum.

Dublin. 1981.

In Collins Barracks something is happening. Someone is bawling out on the square in a loud Dublin voice. It's probably how the Dublins would have sounded as they got ready for Sion Kop and the Somme. The NCO out on the darkening square is shouting so loudly I'm sure the spirits of yet-lingering old-sweats from the days of enteric fever and galloping clap are stirring in response. For a moment or two it's possible to imagine them groping around for pith-helmets and Lee-Mitford rifles before realising their days of soldiering have passed.

Whether the NCO out on the square has got anything at all to do with us is not really the question. He might be shouting out a detail to do with the ordinary routines of the 5th Battalion. The urgency in his voice is in synch with a new urgency in the barrack-room where we are waiting. Nobody's interested in lying about the bunks any longer. Something is happening.

Fu Manchu tells me to get ready as we'll be on the trucks and heading for the airport any minute now. What a smashing big brother he must be, naturally suited as he is to actually caring about others. Everyone's on their feet by now, waiting for the word to file through the door leading to the square and into the sweet air of night. The number of hours hanging around billets and guardrooms cannot be underestimated. It's a core skill, coping with the brain-numbing necessity of hanging around.

The engineer privates are really getting into the swing of it, laughing and horse-playing in the corridors separating the billet-rooms. They clearly had a good skinful and are loving the novelty of Collins Barracks and the absence of officers and other spoilsports. They roar into the billets, repeating the usual old guff and gossip so familiar to ordinary garrison soldiers. By now the Transport company sergeant has joined the short, red-faced engineer corporal in completely ignoring the engineer privates. The vibe is less tense. If anything, the joking moods of the engineer privates are a blessing, a distraction from the tedium of spending so long cooped up in the billets.

An officer from the 5th Battalion gives us a final pep-talk before we leave the barrack-rooms. There's a sanctimonious ring to his words. The two dead soldiers in Lebanon are referenced with the same respect as the martyrs of 1916. People around here have to be killed to get any respect. If the two dead privates were here with us now the officer would treat them bluntly or with class-conscious contempt, much like he treats the rest of us.

It's probably more a human problem than a problem specifically to do with the Irish army, how we can cope better with the dead than we can cope with the living. It's the dead Elvis syndrome. Death transforms the dissolute, drugged-up singer and the eccentric modernist painter into a god-like legend. It's easier to praise the dead and drive up the price of their records and paintings than to deal with the living person with all the foibles and ego of a living person. And even peacetime armies of small neutral countries need a number of soldiers killed in action for credibility reasons.

The guys who take all this barrack-room malarkey seriously drool over the men killed in Lebanon as it legitimises their soldiering fantasies. It helps them to spice up yarns about their time with UNIFIL. When they repeat the yarns often enough, they themselves begin to believe they were part of a soldiering adventure on a par with the US Marines on Iwo Jima or grunts shooting it out with the Viet Cong. The male ego is famously fragile after all. We are men with testosterone in our tanks. We need people to know we did something out here other than get drunk and sun-bathe.

A sickening outcome of soldiers dying in action in Lebanon is how others who might have known the dead soldier look for sympathy with self-pitying monologues. They falsely claim they've been heroic or totally selfless toward a dead soldier weeks or days before the man's death. Even if they were from a different company or battalion and had never actually met the dead soldier in question, they weave fantasies where they not only knew the dead man but saved him from disaster a few days before he died. The kindest thing is to blame it on the vulnerabilities of the male ego and the glut of soppy Hollywood war films. It's quite a combination, an endless diet of war-glorifying Hollywood trash and the underemployed energies of a peacetime depot soldier.

The officer from the 5th Battalion is one of the more benign of his species. From what brief experience I've had of them officers from the Dublin barracks are a little more civil than the officers from the Curragh. On the Curragh we had rare brutes from the nation's middle-classes, rugby-playing louts with a Neanderthal glaze in their eyes. These officers got drunk on whisky rather than pints of Harp lager or Guinness like the lower ranks. They'd been to the best Catholic schools in the land and many of them regarded the elitist sport of rugby as their personal religion. They were civilised thugs kept in line by the privileges of a class system lovingly retained from the days of British rule and by a legality which relegates the army to a poor second behind An Gardai Siochana.

Yet where better to send a middle-class thug than to the army? If by a complete freak of history there was a re-run of Pettigo-Belleek these same rugby-loving sons of the nation's prosperous farmers and merchants would be exactly what are needed. There was an innate brutality to many of them, a brutality honed into shape by a stubborn Catholic orthodoxy. They had older brothers and uncles who were bishops and senior priests teaching in the Irish College in Rome or in seminaries in Boston or Melbourne. They had a major stake in the often-sanctimonious union between the state and the Catholic Church in Ireland.

We fall in on the darkening square at Collins Barracks one final time. The trucks which will take us to Dublin airport are revving up nearby. The torpor of a long day hanging around the billets is finally over and is now only seen in yawns and the stretching of stiff muscles. Out in the crisp air of early night the engineer privates appear to be already sobering up. They stand in the ranks indistinguishable from the rest of us. A passing officer would not notice anything different about them and would not assume they'd drank anything stronger than garrison-strength tea.

A favourite line of conversation with the soldiers is the influx of females into the army, expected a little later in the year. They will be the first enlisted females to serve with the Irish army and not unexpectedly they are already causing quite a lot of interest and conversation among the serving men. Some guys are hoping to get their hands on an army female, while others are worried that females in the guardrooms and barracks will change the mood and temper of army life forever. Jokes about fanny-farts and re-runs of Debbie Goes to Dallas will never be the same again.

Another recurring conversation is about the slum housing provided by the army to many of its married soldiers. A soldier from Cathal Brugha barracks mentions the Today Tonight programme broadcast on RTE on the squalid living conditions of the wives and children of enlisted soldiers. He's living in Griffith Square with his teenage wife and infant twins, the slums the RTE programme focused on.

The buildings where he and his family live were built by the British army and inherited by the Free State army. In 1981 nearly all the notable buildings of Dublin are a legacy of the second city of the Empire. O'Connell Street is pretty much unchanged from the days when we had a Governor General living in the Phoenix Park rather than a president. The concept of independence is fluid.

The toilets at Griffith Square married quarters are shared by three families and there's only one cold water tap per house. The families report damp and dry-rot, rats and broken drainage pipes. The cameras of the RTE documentary-makers record the evidence and broadcast it nationally. Irish slums are peculiarly unpleasant because of the nature of our weather. A miasma of freezing fog and rain is an unhappy backdrop to rotting and neglected old buildings. Hardy winters and an abundance of rain deepens the pit of misery for the Irish poor.

In James Plunkett's Strumpet City and Frank McCourt's Angela's Ashes the Irish slums are introduced as the glum destroyer of hope, the wrecker of families and the final stamp of humiliation on the urban poor. The misery of the Irish slum is magnified not only by lousy weather but by classism, snobbery and the frustration of listening to lip-service about a revolution which never really happened.

Although having been brought up in a similar slum to the Cathal Brugha slum featured on the Today Tonight programme I can't say it was a problem. We had an outside toilet and one cold-water tap for an overcrowded household. On winter nights the winds howled in from the Curragh plains. The cold rooms and overcrowding were the more immediate reminders of relative poverty. But we didn't regard ourselves as poor as we had a strong community spirit. We belonged as much to the neighbourhood as to our families.

Yet the most unsanitary deficit was not delineated by class but by culture. In the British Isles there was no culture of using water at toilet. For us in married quarters on the Curragh it was only the dry rub of coarse army-issue toilet-paper, or sometimes paper torn from sheets of old newspapers. A drop of water in the toilet would have greatly improved the hygiene of many families and would have cost nothing. Such an innovation would have been regarded as foreign and the preserve of Africans, Muslims and the French. And the connation of cleaning with water was too suspiciously close to the ritual ablutions of Islam to be accepted in our Christian islands. It wasn't unusual to smell stale shit from other boys from the neighbouring married quarters.

In 1981 the slums at Cathal Brugha barracks were logical extensions of the divisions in capitalism societies. Hunter-gatherer or feudal days are at best historical distractions in academia. An age of stratified capitalism with its illusions of meritocracy is ascendant. The families of Griffith Square are working class, regardless of the army uniforms hanging in their bedrooms. Slums, exploitation, income disparity and stigma are as much their true legacy as hopes for a better day.

There's a final rollcall before we board the trucks. Fu Manchu and the other corporal from the Curragh are in a different truck, so I can gaze out at the passing sights of Dublin without having to talk to anyone or to occasionally reassure Fu Manchu that I'm all right. Home means something around here. The Curragh and its environs are sacred codes to the soldier travelling away from the Curragh. The yellow acorn emblem on a red flash denotes not just the Curragh Command but a tribal affiliation encompassing family, community and territory. Inevitably when we're drunk in Lebanon someone will have a bash at singing The Curragh of Kildare.

Our morale is high as we travel through the night-streets of Dublin. After a long day cooped up in a barrack-room with the spirits of the Royal Dublins as company the night-air is an elixir. Civilians occasionally wave at us in passing without any apparent cynicism or ill-will. We're subdued by conservative, legal and historical forces after all, so civilians have nothing to fear from us. Our Free State roots are vague and rarely referenced by any of us. We're merely wage-slaves, escaping to the new sights and sounds of the Middle East for six months, our oaths on the flag mostly abstract in a world brutalised by economic necessity. Our married men are thinking mostly about money and double-glazed windows, confirmation clothes for children and paying off loan-sharks. The words Free State are an insult we hardly respond to anymore, just a curious historical thing.

In the wider scheme of Irish life, we are powerless, confined mostly to barracks and guardrooms and excluded from controversy or confrontation. The power and authority of the state are very much invested in An Gardai Siochana, our mostly unarmed police force. They are the true Free Staters, the ground troops of O'Higgins, Cosgrave and O'Duffy. Civilians or An Gardai or the body politic have nothing to fear from us. We have enough cigarettes, garrison-strength tea and re-runs of Debbie Goes to Dallas to get us through the long hours of yet another guard-duty.

Personally, Lebanon is a coming of age, a rare chance to leave the dull routines of County Kildare and face the world in a different context. There might be trouble, a moment or two of drama where survival might depend on an FN rifle and the standard Irish army issue of forty rounds of ball ammunition per man. Someone might die. There might be an incident. The country might hear about the 49th Infantry Battalion in the newspapers.

These things are possible. Part of me is hoping to shoot someone. Are such impulses absorbed from the spirit of revolutionaries or rebels lingering at Collins Barracks? I'm longing to feel the kick of an FN rifle against my shoulder in a moment of crisis. Any change to the ordinary reality of our days and nights would be welcome, another angle from which to view the world. For depot soldiers in perpetual peacetime mode this Aer Lingus flight to the Middle East is a bolt of lightning from whatever heaven is yet out there.

Post October 7th attacks on Israel. London.

Voices are again raised against UNIFIL. A former IDF intelligence officer, Lt. Col Zehavi, believes UNIFIL is not only ineffective but harmful.

The problem is not the mandate, the lieutenant colonel claims. *It's the lack of willingness to act.*

It's a complex and large entity that's been around for decades on Israel's northern border. To say it's ineffective is not entirely true. However, to say its ineffective in containing Hezbollah is largely a true statement. From an Israeli defensive perspective UNIFIL is an imposition from a host of friendly, neutral (or with a bias towards the Arabs in the region) and indifferent nations. Maybe we could say it's the world's conscience. From a humanitarian perspective it's been generally quite helpful to the Lebanese population it serves. Roads and infrastructure have improved. US dollars have benefitted almost every household in the UNIFIL area of operations as the various contingents buy everything from gaudy knickknacks and egg and chips to gold chains and crates of Sprite from the locals.

Thousands of mines set by Arab militias including Hezbollah and Bouncing Bettys dropped from IDF cluster-bombs have been made safe by UNIFIL ordnance teams. Military doctors, dentists, nurses and health workers have improved the health of locals and saved lives. There's been a lot done over the decades to ease the burden of war and its miserable outcomes from the lives of those surviving in the hilly towns and villages of the parts of South Lebanon that face Israel. U.N patrols have done much to face down local militias and to stand between those on either side of ancient squabbles. In efforts to keep the peace UNIFIL soldiers have been hit with rocks, shot, injured by shrapnel and have given their lives.

But for Israeli defence analysts like Lt. Col. Zehavi this is not nearly enough. Hezbollah have operated freely in the UNIFIL area of operations more or less since their inception in the nineteen eighties. To tackle them would mean an all-out war, and a dirty war at that. It'd mean losing the hearts and minds of most Arabs in the hills of South Lebanon. The ensuing casualty rates among U.N peacekeepers would be unacceptable to their respective nations. In tactical terms any effective assault on Hezbollah would be doomed before it began. And the U.N resolution needed for such an assault wouldn't even make it as far as the secretary general's desk at U.N headquarters in New York.

In the mindset of Israel's defenders the Palestinians that fled to Lebanon should have long-since assimilated with their Arab kith and kin and built new lives, just as many millions throughout the world after the tumult of WWII assimilated in strange lands and built new lives. Lebanon's Palestinians are perceived to have institutionalised their sense of victimhood and perpetuated their refugee status with the help of agencies of UNRWA, claiming to be refugees generations after the displacements of '48. From a sense of rage that's never dimmed they radicalised Lebanon's Arabs and attacked the Christian population, leading to a civil war that bottomed out in outrageous depths of barbarity. Lebanon became a fragmented and wounded land where the PLO and later Hezbollah were allowed to set up bases from where they bombarded the north of Israel with Russian-made Katyusha rockets.

From a reductive view south of the Lebanese-Israel border UNIFIL's humanitarianism is but an addendum to the real problem, the threat of more terror attacks from militants with an undying hatred of Israel and the Jewish diaspora. Reports of a UNIFIL patrol engaging insurgents and then capturing or even killing them would bring a grim nod of approval from IDF intelligence officers monitoring UNIFIL's area of operations. All the rest of it is either sugar-coated interfering from the U.N and its more dubious agencies, or collusion of one kind or the other with Israel's most bitter enemies.

When it comes to it national soldiers defending their families and the sacred ground of their ancestors are most likely to step forward for to fight men with fanatical hearts that wish them only the very worst fate. The IDF's border conflict with Hezbollah flared into open warfare at times with UNIFIL standing by as the deaths and injuries on both sides were added to the grievances that weigh heavily on the collective psyche of a people. What could they realistically be expected to do but stand by?

From an Irish perspective it's too much to hope that Lieutenant Colonel Zehavi remembers Lieutenant Aongus Murphy, killed by a command wire activated by

Amal, an ally of Hezbollah. In an inquiry into his death Murphy was praised for the *valour and persistence with which he sought out and incapacitated improvised explosive devices.* In an incident linked to Aongus Murphy's death three Irish UNIFIL soldiers were targeted by the same Hezbollah-affiliated terrorists and were killed by an IED on the outskirts of the village of Bra'shit in the Irish area of operations.

On 22nd December 2022 Private Sean Rooney from UNIFIL's Irish contingent was killed in the village of Al-Aqbiya. Those involved were identified as members of Hezbollah but Hezbollah as an organisation denied any involvement. Maybe it doesn't mean much in the scheme of things, at least not when viewed through the lens of the IDF's defence of Israel's northern border. But those Irish soldiers died a long way from home. The only real battles Irish soldiers killed in Lebanon were morally obliged to take part in was a re-run of the old Belleek-Pettigo battles. There was no moral obligation for them to give their lives in a bitter and drawn-out war in a land where they had no meaningful connection. No matter how its framed it's not an Irish war but Irish soldiers have died out there anyhow. Soldiers from other U.N contingents paid with their lives too.

If the ghosts of Irish soldiers from past wars stirred at the exact moment when Irish U.N soldiers were killed in Lebanon they might have been perplexed at why Irish soldiers had to die in somewhere like South Lebanon. UNIFIL can't stop militants like Hezbollah and their fellow travellers in terror. But hundreds of UNIFIL soldiers gave their lives for the U.N Security Council resolutions that pledged to confirm the withdrawal of Israeli forces from Southern Lebanon, restore international peace and security, and assist the government of Lebanon in ensuring the return of its effective authority in the area.

Morally and spiritually the South of Lebanon is a long way from Pettigo-Belleek and Irish soldiers are under no obligation to give their lives out there in the battles that traumatised, killed and maimed so many. But they did so anyway. In such a broken world that's worth remembering now and then.

Dublin Airport. 1981.

Night-time. The night hours are a surreal intrusion in the life of the depot soldier. As a teenager I'm ignored, as generally teenagers are ignored at that time. I'm deemed to have nothing to add to any conversation or interaction and am only required to shut up and follow orders. The older and married soldiers are at least given credit for having a basic humanity and for existing as sentient beings. As someone not seen to have a personality, I keep my mouth shut. I haven't much to say anyhow.

This is not an unreasonable position as I am so repressed in my spirit and in my mental development it's as if I don't exist. I am alive only in my ability to function at the lowest levels of human survival. I can look, act and sound just like a young soldier from the Irish Defence Forces is meant to look, act and sound. Otherwise, I am quite deadened, numb in both spirit and in personality. It can happen. In truth it's more common than we think. Much like the argument where a foetus in the womb is not regarded as fully human because it lacks human characteristics, teenage soldiers with underdeveloped personalities can be regarded as not fully human.

The weight of expectation from others and the confines of depot life in a stunted army impedes the development of the personality. We are kept in place by brutalised mythologies and tired old ideas of what is expected of humble soldiers. Our betters seem perplexed by our very existence, unsure of what to do with us. They have no war to send us to. Instead, we are marched up and down barrack squares built by the British army in the Ireland of our great-grandfather's day. We are posted on duty to guard the state's assets, as subservient as backward children to the true inheritors of Free State authority, An Garda Siochana. A war of terrifying inference is happening on what is constitutionally our national territory. This war we ignore or try to ignore.

We're caught up in not just one mind-trap of Orwellian doublethink, but several. The people of the Black North are distrusted for their heretical Protestantism and irreverence towards the Vatican and its ordained princes and servants. But at the same time, they are cherished as all the children of the nation are ostensibly cherished in deference to the nation's most idealised document, the 1916 Proclamation.

British military interference in the political life of the country is excoriated and damned by folk songs bawled out in closing-time pubs throughout the land. But we cooperate with the British military on the ground along the border and right up to the highest levels. Our history in schools and our national legends glorifies military resistance to English and Scottish colonialism, but our military is conflicted and uncommitted on the question of what to do about the conflict in the North.

As we are forming up for Lebanon prison officers in Northern Ireland's Maze prison are torturing Irish Republican prisoners on a daily basis, smashing their naked bodies with boot and baton in filthy cells, wiping disgusting bodily effluence into the prisoners' food. These British officers inflict physical and psychological violence on defenceless Irishmen, naked in cells, who have dared to take on the British presence in Ireland in the absence of any other body of men to step up and do so. When these prisoners go on hunger strike the world will sit up and notice. Those in authority in London at the time will get away with the torture and human rights' outrages of the H-Blocks even though it will drag their names through the gutters of international opinion.

There's nothing we can do about the treatment of Irish nationalists in the North but even the mildest among us registers the brutality deep in our hearts. After all, if the circumstances were a little different it could be us. We're from the same socioeconomic, cultural and religious background of those getting kicked in the genitals and ribs by British prison officers. The only thing that separates us is a quirk or two of history and a hundred miles or two of terrain.

We are riddled with a multitude of schisms, saluting our uniformed manhood as they march off to vague U.N duties in distant countries while at the same time torn apart by the death of Bobby Sands and the other hunger strikers. As the old come-all-ye goes the greatest war of all is at home and not just at home but in the psyches of individual Irishmen and women. It's so much easier to talk about the failings of nations a very long way from here, to feel outraged at the grievances of others.

In the barrack-rooms and billets of the depot soldier the agonies of Northern Ireland are mostly ignored or waved off as someone else's problem. A serious analysis of the North's sufferings has too many sharp edges for the self-respecting Irish soldier to swallow. Occasionally an old sweat from '69 when the army was sent to the border is heard. He'll talk about damp nights under canvas in the fields of Monaghan, waiting for orders to cross the border which never came.

We had over two thousand fit soldiers at the time. The rest were mostly alcohol-dependent depot men hardly fit to climb without help into the back of a truck, or men too old or troubled by medical conditions to do any actual fighting. But we could have done something, a Quixotic gesture if nothing else. Two thousand men could have managed a decent re-run of the old Pettigo-Belleek battle, a brief incursion to let the world know we exist. But nothing happened. For the sake of the nationalists inside the Northern Ireland state at the time this was the best outcome. During the Pettigo-Belleek battles of 1922 Catholic civilians were burnt from their homes in Belfast and lucky to escape with their lives. Others were beaten and murdered by Orange mobs.

In March 1921 Dail Eireann declared war on Britain, the only war it has ever declared to this day. Tom Barry's flying column of a hundred or so volunteers took on British infantry units of over twelve hundred men at what became known as the Crossbarry Ambush. Barry's men avoided encirclement and killed up to thirty British infantrymen. The previous year at Kilmicheal Barry's column ambushed and killed 18 Auxiliaries, a specially recruited militia sent to Ireland to fight the IRA. In an overall conceptualisation of Irish nationhood, the actions in 1920 and 1921 must rate as the noblest order in a nation's struggle in arms.

Revolts in the nineteenth century by the Fenians and a century earlier by the Croppies were heroic but the rebels were quickly defeated and their political movements brutally suppressed. The men of Kilmicheal, Crossbarry and hundreds of smaller scenes of death were very much different, insofar as they were successful. The resolve and ruthlessness of these men was such that even the toughest British army officer, many of them dehumanised in the great war against Germany, must have sat up and asked themselves just who exactly they were fighting. At certain times they were fighting against their own former comrades, for prominent IRA fighters like Tom Barry and Emmett Dalton were former frontline British army soldiers. Matters between Ireland and England are often an incestuous business.

There was heavy fighting in the Pettigo-Belleek battles which might have kick-started a second revolutionary war in Ireland. Good communications between Collins and Lloyd George helped calm things down on the border. Pogroms against Catholics in Belfast consolidated Graig's vision of Ulster as a Protestant state for a Protestant people.

Lloyd George warned Churchill and his fellow hawks that-

Our case in Ulster is not a good one. In two years 400 Catholics have been killed and 1,200 have been wounded without a single person being brought to justice.

By the time London sent two brigades of infantry and a battery of artillery to Pettigo-Belleek the fighting had ended with both sides withdrawing to their respective territories. The end of the conflict on the border did not prevent this large force from crossing over to County Donegal and attacking the Free State army post at Pettigo. Taken by surprise and overwhelmed by numbers and artillery the post fell, and seven Free State soldiers were killed. The pogroms in Belfast were seemingly acceptable to the London government, as was the crossing of an international border to attack an independent territory and then kill seven of its soldiers. Such aggression and contempt for national boundaries are revealing when juxtaposed with the fearful reticence of the Irish state to do anything remotely assertive in August 1969.

In Munster where much of the revolutionary IRA's battles took place the reprisals were at times dubious. Historians have questioned whether the IRA executed informers or simply people they regarded as the enemy. Apparently, Protestants, tramps passing through on the high roads and ex-soldiers were especially at risk of an IRA bullet. Tough luck for the ex-soldier who happened to be a Church of Ireland man, lapsed or otherwise, and who decided to tramp the roads of West Cork and Kerry for the summer months, only to bump into the local IRA.

A number of Protestant families and former Royal Irish Constabulary policemen left Ireland forever, caught up in a polarisation not too difficult for anyone connected to Ireland to understand. When the Sinn Fein Lord Mayor of Cork, Terrence McSweeney, was shot dead in front of his family there was almost certainly collusion between the killers and the local RIC. The RIC district inspector believed to have had a hand in McSweeney's death fled the area but was tracked down by the IRA to a quiet part of Northern Ireland and shot dead.

The killing of tramps and ex-soldiers traumatised in the trenches of WWI was another dehumanising outcome of war to add to all the other dehumanising outcomes. Before truce or treaty, the IRA had burned down over four hundred empty RIC barracks to ensure they were not re-occupied, along with a hundred tax offices. Court services were suspended, martial law enforced in much of the country. The IRA roamed the land at will. The country was ungovernable.

More worrying for the London government was the IRA's next stage of the struggle, bringing the war home to England. Plans were in place for a war of attrition against English cities, with hundreds of IRA agents, bombers and gunmen getting ready to demoralise the English public by attacking installations, military bases and the major cities of England. Collins and his confidantes whispered of carnage on an apocalyptic scale in Liverpool, Manchester and London. Mercifully before the England stage of the IRA's campaign began a truce was called. Apart from limited actions, most notably the killing of General Sir Henry Wilson in London, the war in Ireland was confined to Ireland.

In Dublin airport none of this is really relevant or is only relevant in an abstract sense. What do we have to do with revolutionary killers from our grandfather's and great-grandfather's age? When War of Independence veterans die, they have the option of an Irish army funeral party, a volley of shots fired over the grave and the last post played on a bugle. Not all families are interested in such honours for all wounds have not yet healed.

There are plenty of barrack-room yarns about funeral parties lost in the countryside or showing up at the wrong funeral, or once when the entire firing party disappeared because the grave they were standing on collapsed. We like to think we are linked to the War of Independence IRA men. Many of them who took no part in the Civil War of 1922/23 or who were sympathetic to the Pro-Treaty side were pleased at the thought of an Irish army firing party blasting a volley of shots over their graves or playing the last post at their graveside. Others would have spat on the ground we walked on.

Interestingly the North was not the pressing question for the refuseniks of 1922. Few would have envisaged the Boundary Commission's work in creating a state within a state and consigning hundreds of thousands of Catholics to what defaulted to second-class citizenship in their own land. The pressing question was the actual deal struck by Lloyd George and Collins, a Free State within the Commonwealth with an oath sworn to the English king for all holders of public office. It was not the republic the men and women of 1916 had pledged their lives to. More than one student of history has questioned if Lloyd George could have cut more slack for nationalist Ireland.

The question of membership of the secret society the Irish Republican Brotherhood was also important, for history counts the influential supporters of the treaty as members of the IRB and the important voices raised against the treaty as from outside the IRB. Personalities, frail human ego and jockeying for power must have played their parts as they predictably play their parts when there is anything much to gain.

Brugha and DeValera, the two most vociferous voices raised against the treaty, were very critical of Collins' natural leadership qualities. Brugha's verbal attack on Collins in a critical session of the Dail was said to be unforgivably low-minded and unfair. Several representatives present who had decided to vote against Collins and the treaty changed their minds and voted for the treaty after hearing Brugha's unfair words against Collins. There's bitterness in people after all, an ugliness quick to show itself when there's anything at all to gain.

More idealistic minds interpret nationalist Ireland's acceptance of Collins' treaty as a coup d'état, a counter-revolution in response to Easter 1916. And even worse, a British-sponsored coup d'état. Such minds are not easily satisfied by the ordinary grubbiness of politics. They reject compromises as sell-outs and point teary-eyed to the Starry Plough and the tricolour, quick too with the poet's words of self-sacrifice.

We don't live in such a world. Idealism and purity of word and deed are but a small part of our world, only factors rather than defining factors in humankind's affairs. Earthly and beastly compromise are more recognisable, the shady handshake of middlemen. More than most the lowly depot soldier only a few wage packets away from destitution understands the limitations of the idealist argument.

At Dublin airport we're ushered into a nondescript waiting-space with plastic seating. There's a lot more happening here than at Collins Barracks, with people coming and going and taking more of an interest in our departure. The married men and older privates with fiancés are using the airport's payphones to call loved ones. A priest in a heavy dark overcoat is wringing his hands as he talks to two commandants from army H.Q at McKee Barracks. I sit in an obscure part of the waiting-room so as I don't have to talk to Fu Manchu and the other corporal from the Curragh.

There's not much idealism here, not much by way of reference to national legends. It's a matter-of-fact business. There's a contained civil war in the northern part of our national territory and we're waiting for a flight to take us to Lebanon. It's a practical business. A stint in Lebanon with the U.N is a good deal for men without very much by way of capital or assets. Ordinary soldiers have second-hand family cars to buy and children to rear. UNIFIL money is one of twentieth century's equivalents to money posted back to Ireland from emigrant sons and daughters in Boston, London and Melbourne. Its money is not to be sniffed at. In the financial reality in the lives of men without assets and property it's serious business. How else can an ordinary soldier get his hands on a couple of grand?

In the airport there's not much talk about the unpleasant facts of the day, the Hunger Strike in the North or the deaths of the two soldiers in Deir Ntar. It's more about the private lives of the soldiers, a parting call from an airport pay-phone to a wife or mother. Another priest has joined the priest in the heavy overcoat and the two army HQ commandants. The class identification of the priests with the HQ commandants couldn't be more obvious. They are from the same families and have a serious stake in the wealth and reputation of the state. They are not the Irish who take the boat to England with their earthly belongings in a battered and borrowed suitcase for whatever work is going, the back-straining work nobody else is rushing to do. When they leave Ireland, they leave as tourists or pilgrims, and not as semi-paupers in search of labouring work. Lucky them.

The two army HQ commandants and the two priests are animated in conversation, clearly enjoying the pleasing company of each other. They might have studied in the same classrooms, Rockwell or Blackrock or Clongowes Wood. They might play golf on the same courses or know each other from a Catholic fraternity or from the private bar of a GAA or rugby club. It's all jolly good fun when men of good standing and good family are endorsed by a solid conservative Catholic society. None of the four men are heading for the Lebanon but it's nice for them to call out and see us before we go.

Class distinction and class prejudice in the Ireland of 1981 is just another fact of daily life. There's no way past it, not here in this country or in any country signed up to what we understand as international capitalism. People do well, build up wealth and property over the years. And then they pass this wealth onto their children. The families of privilege have a generous head-start in life.

Privilege is beefed up by education and propaganda. Equality and meritocracy are impossible in such a system, but an illusion of equality and meritocracy is cobbled together by educationalists, media-types and politicians in thrall to money. Talented, gifted people can achieve much but sooner or later someone will ask what school they went to or what exact street they were raised in or what their father did for a living. It's just another fact of life. The sanest of citizens just shrug and accept it, understanding class inequality and income disparity is as inescapable as taxes and death.

A little later both priests drift away from the company of the army HQ commandants and begin circulating among the rank and file waiting to board the flight to Tel Aviv. It's difficult for them of course, to pretend to find even a few minutes social contact with poorly educated common soldiers interesting or easy. It goes with the job, to pretend we're all part of a shared venture and the disparities between us in class and income are incidental and not worth mentioning.

The common soldiers are faking it too, pretending the circumstances of our financial status are not the only reason we are here. We are submissive to the priests, knowing they are the commissars for the wider system we are all subject to. There's a fair share of sham, self-deceit and hypocrisy here, as there is in practically every human interaction. Civilisation it seems is to blame.

Yeats' brown lieutenant is missing from our ranks. Is anyone really afraid of us? Has any military even been so subservient to a civilian population and its national unarmed police? The priests circulate with their heads held a little to one side in a gesture of empathy and ask the married soldiers about their families. There's talk of confirmation suits and communion dresses. The priests come across as decent men with good skills in listening. It's hardly their fault the world and its human societies are organised as they are.

For the Japanese philosopher Hajime Tanabe the first step in philosophy is to confess. At Dublin airport there's no signs of anyone wishing to either philosophize or confess. The priests don't look like they have any time for such things anyhow. I guess they are really here to let us know we have their support. They are living symbols of the higher aspirations of the Irish Catholic.

Tanabe's concept of confessing doesn't easily coalesce with the Catholic version of confession. Tanabe's confession is more about admitting we know nothing or know hardly anything at all. It's much like when Socrates asked the Oracle at Delphi was there anyone in Athens wiser than Socrates.

The Oracle confirmed that there was indeed nobody in Athens wiser than Socrates. But as Socrates was convinced of his own ignorance he set out to prove the Oracle wrong. After a series of conversations with various people in Athens Socrates had to admit the Oracle was right as he couldn't find anyone who would admit they knew nothing or hardly anything at all.

It's from this point of admitting we know practically nothing that Tanabe's philosophy begins. His concept of confessing translates as accepting that we know hardly anything. For Tanabe philosophy is not about logic, ethics or debate but rather about relating to our own deeper selves. Only through confessing can we hope to continually rediscover who we really are and in doing so overcome a limited view of self to arrive at an awareness of enlightenment. It's a mental version of death and resurrection, the forsaking of ourselves for the grace of another power. In essence it's a borrowing of ideas from the Pure Land School of Buddhism and certain concepts from the writings of Martin Heidegger. Such thoughts are a universe away from this simple reality at Dublin airport. We are soldiers after all and not philosophers, although our anti-soldering role on the ground as U.N peacekeepers can be in essence as complex and counter intuitive as the reasoning of an Enlightenment thinker.

I avoid the priests at the airport as I'm an awkward eighteen-year-old with nothing to say. My thoughts are elsewhere. In my steel locker in the billets of my home unit on the Curragh is a stack of magazines, mostly the New Musical Express. I read Hot Press too, the pop and rock publication printed in Dublin. My thoughts are on music, on the emerging post-Punk bands and personalities that front such bands. Music to define a generation is happening in cities like London and Manchester. In Paris an early line-up of The Cure opened a televised set with different lyrics to A Forest. The housing estates of greater Manchester are giving anguished birth to bands like Joy Division, The Buzzcocks and The Fall. This very idea is depressing, because I'm nowhere near this music, nor am I likely to be get anywhere near it any time soon.

Fate has somehow shepherded me here to this airport where I'm waiting with one hundred and twenty or so others for a flight to the Middle East. Whatever else happens I know it won't have anything to do with the seminal music of an emerging generation.

This is Sartrean Bad Faith in technicolour, a vivid, eyes-wide-open reality and there's no easy way out of it. There are Punkish girls out there somewhere in garish make-up, eighteen-hole doc marten boots worn down at the heels and ripped fishnet stockings. And I'm here with a bunch of married men who are already spending their UNIFIL money in their minds on double-glazed windows and second-hand cars. I'm sure there are many worse examples of Bad Faith, but just now I can't think of any.

A braver soul would simply walk out of here. Walk and keep walking and never look back. A braver soul would dump the uniform in some forgotten place and beg, borrow or steal the price of a one-way ticket to an English or European city. But I'm tied to all this by a thousand invisible steel cables, crippled by fear and inadequacy and maybe even a sense of honour and national pride too. It is pointless railing against it. I'm destined for this Lebanon business.

There's not much discussion about the overall political context we'll soon be entering. There are only rumours, the predictable dumb rumours of garrison army life. Irish soldiers have died in Lebanon because there isn't anywhere else for us to die. The Provisional IRA has for the moment omitted us from their list of enemies, the vanguard of Republican violence barely interested in our existence.

As far as the Provos are concerned we don't exist, or are seen as a mutely subservient addendum to An Gardai Siochana. Now and then, when they are in a tight spot they turn their armalites on us. Bizarrely we come across the Provos at PLO checkpoints in Lebanon and when we are both on our separate training jaunts in the Wicklow and Donegal hills. We give a wave, a short shout of greeting and then we're on our way.

When Fine Gael are in power, we're re-packaged as a pro-British, pro-Free State, Pro-Unionist security force determined to keep the country safe from Republican bandits and general troublemakers. This is a ruse of course. We are ham-strung by a legal framework assigning us as the dummies of An Gardai Siochana. The Gardai don't trust us. We are their social inferiors. They often regard us as semi-literates and assorted failures who escaped the boat to England and the dole-queue by catching a bus to the Curragh's General Training Depot on a lucky day when they were taking recruits.

In fact, because of our socio-economic backgrounds, we're perfect candidates for the radical policies of Sinn Fein and other Leftist parties. Maybe this is why the Gardai have no liking for us. Our officers are from the same educational and social background as the Gardai. They've all passed the Irish Language component of the Leaving Certificate of Education. The Gardai would only object on social grounds to sit in one of our guardrooms in clouds of cigarette-smoke, watching yet another re-run of Debbie Goes To Dallas.

The class divide in the Ireland of the eighties is so demarcated that it's hard not to wonder just what Ireland the Hunger Strikers are willing to die for. In their own shit and filth, they are on their way to martyrdom. Have they really thought it through? Have they even had a chance to meet very many of the Irish people they will effectively die for? When Bobby Sands and his comrades are feeling their first hunger pains, stomachs growling for food, we'll be on our way to Lebanon. The H.Q Coy soldiers are well-fed, with no shortage of overhanging bellies and fatty jowls. From the beastly practical view of the common Irish soldier the sacrifices of the men on hunger strike are incomprehensible. The idea of willingly depriving oneself of food and nourishment on idealistic grounds is as unfathomable to the depot soldier as refusing to watch Debbie Goes To Dallas on aesthetic grounds.

Down South politics usually means choosing one complacent and corrupt rightist party over another, one cute hoor in preference to another cute hoor. The dreary rituals and soon-to-be-doomed social dogma of the Irish Catholic church are draped over almost every political decision in the state. The defining symbol of Ireland in the nineteen eighties is a party of national soldiers carrying a coffin-like container with fragments of a revered Catholic saint inside. All thoughts of revolution here are abstract.

Often the common Irish soldier of the nineteen eighties is an unemployed or precariously employed labourer, bar-tender or low-skilled worker looking for a steadier wage and an easier life. There's little more to it than this. It becomes more apparent when we look a little closer at the Irish soldiery ordered to the border by Jack Lynch in 1969. Lynch electrified the nation when his 'we will not stand by' speech was broadcast on national television. An alarming percentage of the men were unfit, alcohol-dependent and too old for active duties or they were categorised as grade c, the categorisation grading the serving soldier as fit only for light duties in the barracks.

In 1969 the lessons of the past decided against military action on the border, tending more towards training Catholics in the North and giving them arms and the training to use such arms. Reserve soldiers were recalled. Calling up the reserves was a stunt, for if Jack Lynch was serious about beefing up his forces on the border, he'd have recalled U.N units serving overseas at the time. Calling up the reserves was more useful as a pawn for Foreign Minister Patrick Hillary to use in his verbal chess match with Britain's Lord Chalfont.

In an Irish army memorandum of the time the numbers of personnel available for frontline action in the North in 1969 are set out on paper. From an overall figure of 8,860 serving personnel 1,700 were over the age of 40 and unfit for active duty. A further 560 were categorised as Grade C and as such fit for only light barrack duties. When Naval personnel, ancillary units, Observer Corps, band-boys and recruits in training were considered it left only 2,500 men fit for combat duty.

The analysis of the available soldiers' combat readiness was just as grim. The memorandum from 1969 goes on to state-

Because of the low strengths of units of the Permanent Defence Forces, their dispersal over a large number of permanent posts and border posts and their high incidence of duty, it has not been possible to relieve personnel for essential sub-unit and unit training to fit them for combat conditions. Thus while their individual skills may be described as reasonably satisfactory, they have not received adequate training as part of the team at section, platoon, company and battalion levels. Therefore their standard of combat effectiveness in present conditions is low. The standard of FCA (reserves) training is much lower.

The memorandum goes on to summarise the absence of modern weapons and equipment as dire.

Deficiencies exist in almost every type of armament, ammunition and military equipment.

There would be no re-run of the old Pettigo-Belleek battles, not with such a depleted, combat-unready military so fond of the extra ration of bacon and sausage, cigarettes and subsidised beer. The narrative would quickly shift to gun-running and the extra-judicial involvement of Irish politicians and Irish army intelligence officers in funding and arming what would become the Provisional IRA. The Provisionals would be naturally favoured over the Marxist-orientated Official IRA. The political and actual violence against Northern Catholics would be answered not by the Irish army but by the Provisional IRA.

History it seems prevented Irish soldiers from defending their fellow Catholics from pogroms, a second-class status as citizens, gerrymandering and state injustice. Instead, we were sent to Cyprus and Lebanon wearing the U.N's blue beret to help keep the peace on internationally demarcated peace-lines. The inability of the state in 1969 to use its military at least as some kind of bargaining chip in the Northern crisis was largely due to underfunding, under-training and undervaluing the Defence Forces over decades, along with the expected contempt for the ordinary soldier. In her Belfast Magazine series Military Aspects of Ireland's Arms' Crisis Angela Clifford is succinct in her analysis of the dire situation of the army in 1969.

Following the 'Mutiny of the Generals (1924)' a military structure was devised that would discourage military flair and political ambition in the army. The policy was continued by successive Irish governments. Apart from the 'Emergency' years, the army was kept short of funds, below strength, and physically divided in separate commands to prevent a coup d'état. No single officer exercised ultimate command. Authority was shared between the troika of Chief of Staff, Adjutant General and Quartermaster General. Each reported directly to the Minister of Defence, who was able to exercise direct military authority.

Later in the same publication Clifford links the Irish governments' indecisiveness and lack of resolve in 1969 with the acceleration of the subsequent conflict which took the lives of thousands and ruined the lives of thousands more, casting sinister shadows across these islands. It's why armies exist after all, to fight and die, if need be, for national interests. The lyrics of the old come-ye-all The Shores of Gallipolli could be sang with Irish army service with the U.N in mind.

You fought for the wrong country, you died for the wrong cause ... when the greatest war of all was at home.

All these aspects of our history as a national military registered with us, either consciously or unconsciously. When we heard Maj Saad Haadad from the South Lebanese Army was shouting to our comrades at At Tiri, telling them they were in the wrong country, at the wrong crisis, it angered us. Maybe we just didn't like hearing such things from someone like Maj. Haadad as he was perceived as an enemy of Irish contingents in UNIFIL. Or maybe the truth hurts more than we think it does.

Thousands of casualties and decades of civic trauma could have been avoided if the Irish state was ready in 1969, prepared both politically and militarily. It wasn't. Hundreds of Irish soldiers might have been wounded or killed in an incursion north. We'd sworn our lives on the tricolour and on the bible. It's what we were intended for as the military arm of the Irish people. The Catholics of the north were no longer willing to remain as a cowed minority in an Orange state hostile to their aspirations. Jack Lynch's government did not expect such spirit and defiance from a generation whose cries of freedom were fired like missiles from the lips of Bernadette Devlin, Nell McCafferty and Eamon McCann. We were not ready for war, unconvinced as a nation that the northern Catholics were worth fighting and dying for.

Irish military chiefs had managed to ignore Northern Ireland for almost fifty years, but in 1969 were asked by their government to draw up plans for an incursion. There'd have been a sleepless night or two in the Dublin suburbs where generals and such luminaries tend to live. Ultimately, the Irish army took hardly any role worth mentioning in the Northern Ireland Troubles of 1969-1999. This fact weights on the consciousness of anyone who ever pulled on an Irish army uniform. How could it not?

Yet the young men who went to the border in '69 were good men, game lads who'd have given a superb account of themselves in a re-run of the Pettigo-Belleek battles of 1922. For the equivalent of a labourer's wage, they'd have slept out in the wet fields of Monaghan and Fermanagh and matched their marksmanship and guts with the enemies of nationalist Ireland. Armies and tyrants the world over can always rely on the economic illiteracy of peasant soldiers who trade their lives for a rate of pay they could often find in nearby farms and factories.

The only battles relevant to the Irish national consciousness are the next re-runs of Pettigo-Belleek. And if anyone really believes Churchill had any intention of helping to re-unite Ireland if DeValera declared war on Hitler's Germany they are a stranger to Irish history. He'd have gone back on his word with the same indifference that he'd have flicked cigar-ash on the floor of the war office. Irish citizens were free to travel to Britain to join the fight against Hitler. Tens of thousands did.

Switzerland, Portugal, Spain and Sweden were neutral during Hitler's war and other European countries would have stayed out of it if they could have done. Soviet Communism and its Comintern had uncorked a most malevolent genie from its bottle and nationalist forces across Europe responded forcefully. The more individualised voices ask why should a farm labourer or factory worker pull on a uniform for to suffer the stress and dangers of war when no army is threatening his island state? We left the European Jews to their fate, the brand of Christianity dearest to our hearts viewing them as heretics long overdue a mass conversion to the true messiah.

In the context of history all this Bad Faith makes more sense, waiting at Dublin airport for a flight to the Middle East. We know why we're going there. We're volunteers anyhow so any one of us, even at this late stage, can walk out of here. There's a young soldier with us who loves Elvis so much this is his personal homage to Elvis in his G.I years. Married soldiers are here for the money. For others it's a matter of prestige, a blue and white UN ribbon pinned to a dress uniform.

It's not a re-run of Pettigo-Belleek so spiritually it should mean little to us. Deep in my soul I'm just about interested enough to show up. There's a possibility something might happen out there. We're not going in any other direction by the look of it. If nothing else, it's an escape from the rainy dark nights of County Kildare.

The battalion chaplain has showed up. He'll spend time with us at A Coy so we'll get to know him a little. He's a gentle soul, a man touched by grace. It's hard not to like him. Locals from the Arab villages of South Lebanon will soon fear him. He's smitten by the old weakness, the Irish virus. He'll stagger drunk through the villages most days with the locals literally running away from him. A man of God who is nearly always drunk on whisky doesn't compute in villages pretty much unchanged since medieval times. The belief in Jinns in the villages of South Lebanon is real, the possession of the individual by malevolent spirits. They'll soon believe our chaplain is possessed, unable to find in their cultural wisdom any other contextualisation for a man of God to appear so drunk so often in public. The kids from the villages of the Irish area of operation in South Lebanon often mimic the dance of a drunkard when they see an Irish jeep or truck passing on the road. It's often how we're seen by others from further afield. We drink too much and our behaviour in drink is more often sad and excessive.

The gentle chaplain is circling the spaces of the airport waiting room, talking to soldiers. He's a compassionate man with a gift for putting people at ease. He chats with Fu Manchu, both men obviously pleased by each other's words. One of the great medical conundrums of the age is how the Irish liver holds out for so long against the onslaught of alcohol. It jars with the Muslim Arab population of South Lebanon particularly, our drunken ways. Through the consistency of a sturdy percentage of our kin we've managed to build up a global reputation as jolly drunkards who can booze the night away and still get up for work the next morning. Conservative Shiite Muslims from agricultural villages struggle with this aspect of Irishness. It lands more than one Irish soldier in trouble. The kindest way of regarding it is to regard it as a means of coping with the challenges of the human psyche in a changing world.

Post October 7th attack on Israel. Berlin.

On Kurfurstendamm the column of men and women have rushed past in a blur of purpose and excitement, leaving an impression in their wake of people with important things to do. Even though we're in Germany they are shouting in English.

From the river to the sea, Palestine will be free.

There's something disquieting about the whole thing. This is Berlin after all. One of Germany's more strident organisers of anti-Israel protests is Marlene Engelhorn, a young woman who inherited millions from her family. Her great-grandfather Friedrich Engelhorn made a fortune from producing Zyklon B, the gas used by the Nazis to murder Jews during the Holocaust. That's quite a loop in time to get one's head around. It brings to mind Faulkner's quote from Requiem for a Nun.

The past is never dead. It's not even past.

Dublin. 1981.

Looking at the world in its wider configuration is it any wonder so many people drink too much alcohol? It can be a rational reaction to pitiless irrationality. In the early nineteen eighties we're waiting for the nuclear holocaust to come. Nuclear weapons are routinely carried on strategic bombers. This is how people are living, watching the skies and horizons for the first signs of a mushroom cloud. On 26th September 1983 Stanislav Petrov was the duty officer at a Soviet nuclear early-warning site. His computer screen began to blare out warning after warning, with readouts confirming that NATO had launched nuclear missiles against the USSR. Sirens blasted out as Petrov's equipment alerted his post to more incoming nuclear strikes. Petrov's standing orders were for him to pick up a designated phone and report the nuclear attack to his commanders. Thankfully for the sake of humanity Petrov did not do this. Instead, he waited, hoping the information conveyed so urgently from the large red screen with the message *launch* on it was false.

Years later Petrov described the terrifying moments to German documentary-maker Karl Schumacher.

I had all the data (to suggest there was a continuous nuclear missile attack). If I had sent my report up the chain of command, nobody would have said a word against it. All I had to do was to reach for the phone; to raise the direct line to our top commanders – but I couldn't move.

Instead of reporting a missile attack to his commander Petrov rang the duty officer at army district headquarters and reported a system malfunction. After another pause in time Petrov realised he was correct in his estimation - no missiles had been launched against the USSR. In later investigations the Soviet military concluded that the potentially apocalyptic glitch was caused by satellites mistakenly identifying sunlight reflecting on clouds as the engines of in-coming Intercontinental Ballistic Missiles.

The Nobel Peace Prize in 1981 was awarded to the office of the United Nations High Commissioner For Refugees. In 1995 the prize was awarded to Joseph Rotblat and the Pugwash Conferences on Science and World Affairs for their-

... efforts to diminish the part played by nuclear arms in international politics and, in the longer run, to eliminate such arms.

In 2017 the Nobel Peace Prize was awarded to the International Campaign to Abolish Nuclear Weapons for its work to-

... draw attention to the catastrophic humanitarian consequences of any use of nuclear weapons and for its ground-breaking efforts to achieve a treaty-based prohibition of such weapons.

Stanislav Petrov got nothing, no award or medal for his clarity of thought in a stressful moment of crisis where a man of lesser nerves would have followed orders to the letter. Petrov himself put his lateral thinking down to a lack of rather than a glut of military thinking. He didn't follow orders as soldiers are generally conditioned to follow orders. He explained that his colleagues at the missile early-warning centre were all professional soldiers, drilled from boyhood to obey orders. He himself had an ordinary state education rather than a military education and could think more independently than the others at his station. If Stanislav Petrov was not on duty at the precise moment of the early-warning malfunction chances are there'd have been a very different outcome.

In the nineteenth eighties people were haunted by such things, whether we were meant to be or not. No Peace Prize for Petrov. Although he probably saved the world from a nuclear holocaust, he probably didn't know any influential people or wasn't favoured by a well-funded university for to be mentioned in the same breath as any of those on a Nobel Prize short-list. And anyhow, he was on the wrong side of Churchill's Iron Curtain.

The situation in Lebanon at that time can be looked at in various ways, depending on a multitude of fluid factors. Literalist interpretation of monotheistic scripture weakens any serious attempt at conciliation. A narrow strip of land is where the three mighty monotheistic religions of Judaism, Christianity and Judaism converge. It's a tense place. Not that I'm any kind of expert on the region but in my brief experience people out there are on a short fuse. Killing a stranger for an abstract reason isn't as big a deal as it should be. The Israeli Defence Forces and their Lebanese Christian militias face north into Lebanon, backed by the USA and their allies. Various Arab Muslim factions and the PLO, backed by the USSR and its allies, face south towards the Lebanon-Israel border.

It's a proxy war as much as it's anything else, another Cold War face-off in yet another part of the world caught up in what shouldn't really be their business. It's another episode in a saga of war which just stops short of an actual war between the Americans and the Russians. Berlin Airlift, Bay of Pigs, Cuban Missiles, the killings of Patrice Lumumba and Dag Hammarskjold, Ethiopia's Red Terror. Now and then just like in the Congo or in Lebanon the U.N are parked in the middle of the proxy forces.

The PLO and Arab Muslim militias take out their frustrations on UNIFIL from time to time - the opposing side do so too. The U.N Secretary General in 1981 is Kurt Waldheim, an Austrian with his reputation as a diplomat dogged by war-time service in Hitler's Wehrmacht. There's evidence that Waldheim had a role, albeit administrative, in Nazi atrocities against Serbs, Jews and British Commandoes. The Chinese see Waldheim as a dupe of the Americans and want him out. Later in the year he'll step down as Secretary General. Stuff happens. Life goes on.

Post October 7th terror attacks on Israel. London.

The man looks healthy and well-cared for. He's holding up a sign in support of an organisation that's been banned by the British government on account of its links to terrorist acts in various parts of Britain. He's in the centre of London on a Saturday afternoon, protesting with thousands of others, many of whom are holding similar signs. The camera zooms in on him and we see kindness and something that's wounded in his eyes. He's almost in tears as he speaks. Maybe if the cameras zoomed in a little closer we might actually see tears. He says he had to show up at the protest, that he felt he had no choice. He says he's terrified, literally shaking as he's afraid of getting arrested. He's never protested before and has managed to reach his retirement years without any contact with the police or the courts.

Why is he there? What compelled him to travel from his home in the suburbs to protest in the centre of London? It's a warm and sunny summer's day and he looks fit so surely there's more to do than to travel into the centre of London and break the law by supporting a proscribed organisation. He's not an Arab or a Jew and has no stake in the Middle East yet there he is. What information is he tuning into that's animated him thus?

When Orwell wrote his famous novel back in the nineteen forties he wasn't to know that we'd shrink the telescreens used by the party to control the people and carry them around with us in our pockets. The applications of power channelled through the telescreens are now more subtle. In fact, they're often so subtle we're not even aware of them. We're often so distracted that we hardly notice we need a credit card to buy a coffee or an app to register a complaint. We're even getting used to the endless rebuttals that instruct us to submit our applications and queries online. Orwell's instincts were prescient - it's just the details that don't tally.

The retired and gentle protestor probably hasn't read Orwell recently, if at all. For it seems a version of the telescreen has invaded his psyche, compelling him to leave the life he knows and take to the streets of London where he's at risk of labelling himself a domestic terrorist. Content from the BBC, ITV, Sky and other Western outlets have saturated the man's psyche with pitiful images from a faraway conflict pieced together with a morality tale that casts the IDF as ogres and emaciated women and traumatised children as their victims. There's an added narrative for the more thoughtful whereby the modern state of Israel has internalised the horrors of the Holocaust and in conforming with the Western refined classes' take on a classic psychotherapy model is acting out such horrors on their innocent neighbours.

The close-to-tears man with his unlawful sign is responding to how a conflict is represented by suave individuals who have in their control a version of Orwell's telescreen, rather than responding to the ancient, complex conflicts involving Israel. The map after all is not the territory. What others present to us as truth may not be the truth. And what we believe to be the absolute truth carried within the throne of our hearts may be just a fickle thing that we use to prop up the unseen and wounded parts of us.

April 1981. Dublin.

The lowkey arrangements at Dublin airport are almost concluded. The commandants from army H.Q at McKee Barracks have gone on home, the two civilian priests too. An Aer Lingus jet is taxiing on a nearby runway. It's time to go. We'll play a small role in Lebanon's tragedy, a humanitarian watch on the hills of an ancient land. It's not Pettigo-Belleek and from an ancestral or national or tribal perspective we have no business out there. But whatever world order the U.N represents we're signed up to it. We're here because we're here ... because we're here, as the old drinking song goes. And besides, there are confirmation and communion clothes to buy and second-hand family cars too. Double-glazing windows are not cheap. The real excitement about U.N service is the US dollars it puts in the pockets of Irish soldiers.

The setting up of a Jewish state in the Holy Land in 1948 is largely what all the trouble is about. The Israelis and the religious aspects of their state are widely blamed for much of the trouble in the region. Their critics are vociferous and global. Conspiracy theories are plentiful. People see Mossad agents everywhere, working hand in glove with the secret police of other lands. The Palestinians are included in a generic struggle for global equality along with Mandela's ANC and our own Sinn Fein. The campus activist of the time wears a Palestinian keffiyeh with ANC badges on a Che Guevara tee-shirt.

As Irish soldiers we're conservatives to the bone. Any talk of class-consciousness or solidarity with oppressed peoples is unheard of. Our lack of general education and political education is fully appreciated by our patriarchal superiors, nodded at with indulgence at every twist and turn. Stupidity, drunkenness and violence within reason are tolerated. When it goes too far soldiers are punished by lock-up on Spike Island and in the Glasshouse on the Curragh. Political sympathy with marginal groups is rare, largely because any political sympathies or thoughts of politics are rare. Our servitude is a fixed thing. We have not pulled on a green uniform to think politically, or in fact to think very much at all. Our thinking is done for us. For many people that's one of life's great blessings.

Post October 7th attacks on Israel. London.

When children are victims of war it rightly enrages those with any level of growth in their personalities. Images of children suffering in war burns into the world's soul. There are those watching who'll plan revenge. There are even those who see every Israeli military action as an act of revenge against the world. Recently when paging through an online record of those who died in Auschwitz I came across a picture of Annie Nakache, a young girl holding a football and staring into the world's conscience with eyes that saw the very worse of human nature in her young life. She died alongside her mother at Auschwitz but her father, separated from his wife and child, survived and went on to compete as an Olympic swimmer. Perhaps on a certain level the very establishment of Israel is a memorial to young Annie and so many like her.

In August 1976 twelve year old Majella O'Hare was killed in Whitecross, County Armagh, shot in the back by a British paratrooper as she went to church. The paratrooper who killed her was acquitted by Judge Maurice Gibson who heard the case alone as part of the Diplock system in place at that time. Ten years later Judge Gibson and his wife were killed by a car-bomb activated by the IRA.

In the deeper reaches of mind this was in part at least vengeance for the killing of an innocent girl, for such an act of violence begs vengeance of the world. There's a sense of vengeance too for little Annie Nakache and millions more like her when Israel strikes back against its enemies. Vengeance is as much a part of human history as compassion and empathy. It puts fire in the human heart and compels people to cross mountains and bide their time over generations if need be, before hitting back. Although the world may find moments of peace and creativity when the scars of vengeance are unseen, history and the world as it stands tells us that vengeance and all that goes with it will remain with us for the foreseeable future.

Lebanon. 1981.

Fallacies can be fatal. When an ordinary man from Catholic West Belfast allows his thoughts to be warped by conspiracies against Jews how could he not get everything wrong? What has another faith and a faraway nation got to do with ordinary people in Ireland? It'd be at least intelligible if someone like Michael McAleavey was worried about the pay and conditions of family and friends or was worried if any of us were ready for another re-run of Pettigo-Belleek. Worrying about things with no noticeable impact on our lives is a disassociation leading down a thousand blind alleys. It's a prize fallacy totally detached from the reality of our day to day lives.

In the Belfast of McAleavey's experience inequalities and distrust were embedded in the civil administration, policing and governance of everyday life. Not until the Good Friday Agreement were these institutional inequalities addressed in an acceptable way. McAleavey was born and raised under legal, social and political injustice in a city of fear and machismo. The curious history of the island of Ireland and the commonplace inequalities of life reduced him to a kind of second-class citizenship. And yet somehow the workings of his mind interpreted all this as somehow related to Jewish matters.

Without having to go into it in any great depth we can see there was something wrong. Sending a young man so influenced by such a disassociating fallacy to somewhere like Lebanon wasn't the most enlightened decision. Private Micheal McAleavey travelled south to Dublin and joined the Irish army, later sent to Lebanon on U.N duty. On the night McAleavey shot dead three colleagues at Tibnine Bridge there'd been an incident involving an Israeli army officer. McAleavey's fallacy, deeply personalised over several years, flared up into rage. He saw before him the living embodiment of his most skewed misconceptions - a Jewish man. And not only a Jewish man but an Israeli officer, a pawn in the great international Jewish conspiracy to humiliate Christianity and enslave all Gentiles.

Not long after the Israeli officer was waved on his way McAleavey shot his three comrades dead. It's too coincidental for someone with such a hardwired fallacy to come face to face with an Israeli military officer shortly before exploding in a killing rage. I'm reminded of our commandant meeting his first Israeli at Ben Gurion airport, the confusion and annoyance in his expressions and gestures. It was as if the spirit of Charles Bewley had awakened from the ranks of the Nazi dead and taken possession of our skittery commandant, polluting his thoughts with every antisemitic trope imaginable.

When we internalise conspiracies and international news' events which oversimplify extremely complex geo-political conflicts we risk obscuring all sense of personal identity. Taken to extremes we sacrifice our individuality for an argument we have no real part in. Did events in the Middle East or the affairs of the Jewish people really have any impact on the life of a private soldier in a Dublin battalion of the Irish army? In accord with what Maj. Saad Haadad used to shout at the Irish positions at At Tiri we had no fight in South Lebanon. In a moral and psychic sense there was only one battle we were obliged to avoid, another re-run of Pettigo-Belleek. Yet people get caught up in distractions and obsessions which have no actual meaning to them personally. It's probably more common than we think.

It wasn't that Private Michael McAleavey kept his dangerous misconceptions about Jews and Jewish conspiracies to himself. Officers and NCOs would have known about his views as he hadn't tried to hide them. In hindsight it's the easiest thing in the world to condemn the army's decision to send a guy like Michael McAleavey to South Lebanon. If McAleavey could kill three of his own comrades, he could kill the two Israeli soldiers who'd driven past the Tibnine Bridge checkpoint earlier on that horrible night. How disastrous for the Irish state if this had happened, an openly antisemitic Irish soldier sent to the Lebanon and who then kills the first Jews he encounters.

Sending a battalion-sized contingent to UNIFIL stretched the manpower of the Irish army. McAleavey was sent out there as a replacement, in the absence of a more suitable soldier. There are traits in the human personality so problematic that they can take a lifetime to correct, or decades of confinement or the self-annihilation of the personality in conflict.

Later, McAleavey spoke of the chaos of his unit. Men were sleep-deprived and driven hard. Rations and water were chaotic and scarce. Men went to checkpoints without weapons and the men they were relieving had to hand their weapons over to the new arrivals. There'd been rumours about this from soldiers on the ground. With what I'd seen out there I've no problem imagining such chaos. By the early nineteen eighties we hadn't yet evolved into an organisation capable of sending a battalion-sized unit to a U.N-declared warzone in a planned way.

How much the chaos and poor leadership were causal factors in McAleavey's crimes is yet to be decided. The delusions he held dear and his encounter with a living embodiment of such delusions, an Israeli officer, were surely factors too. Belfast machismo and what he experienced growing up in that city in those years must have been a factor also. For the Irish army and for UNIFIL it was an appalling crime. McAleavey was released after serving twenty-seven years in both military detention and civilian jails. So much for fallacies and conspiracies.

Bad Faith is signing up for another man's war. Of course, this is what we are doing as we queue at Dublin airport. For the entire stint in Lebanon little about UNIFIL struck me as authentic. The Israelis and their allies looked like they knew what they were doing. Everyone else seemed lost, or phoney. So much of life seems to be about playing roles handed to us by those in power at given times and in circumstances chosen to suit others, not us.

Only Private Mick Ryan from County Tipperary struck a brief and genuine note by walking on a Lebanese road one afternoon, naked and draped in a blanket in memory of Bobby Sands. Everyone viewed it as a joke. But humour often masks deeper truths. In the light of Mick Ryan's gesture everything else stank of hypocrisy, torpor and stupidity. I didn't witness it personally but Major Saad Haadad shouting to the Irish positions at At Tiri must also rate as a moment of authenticity. *Go on back to Ireland,* Haadad shouted. *You have no business here.*

He was right. We had no business out there. But soldiers need money to buy second-hand cars, double-glazed windows and to help them to save up to get married. So, we're here ... because we're here. We're mostly dishonest because so much of the affairs of humankind are mostly dishonest. The U.N Secretary General Karl Waldheim lied about his war-time service in the Wehrmacht. His initials appear on documents consigning Greek Jews to death-camps, British Commandoes to unlawful execution and

Serbian civilians to a dubious faith at the hands of a hated German occupation. We are all living a lie to one extent or other. Maybe now and then there's a peak experience but mostly it's all charade and ego or an act of pure survival.

Maybe as the pragmatist says there is nothing deep inside us except what we ourselves put there, or how we interpret what's there. The pragmatist searches but cannot find eternal truths about ethics, measuring the depths of a human soul with the verve of human imagination. Truth for the pragmatist is what our contemporaries let us get away with saying. Truth for the enlisted men of a peacetime, neutral army is very much constructed on what is allowed to be said or not said. Legends, rumours and mythology are substituted for actual thinking and creative conversation.

We stand on the walls of Portlaoise Prison or at U.N checkpoints in South Lebanon quite literally brain-washed by other people's ideas, as so often entire populations are brain-washed. Thus, we are controlled and will do what is expected of us. As reward we'll avoid the dole-queue or the boat to England. There is nothing deep down inside us except what was put there for us, and mostly it's not very much. There are no transcendent truths, unless we ourselves have a superpower to think independently and to then plant vivid ideas deep in our psyche.

In Lebanon the Israeli Defence Forces will tolerate UNIFIL until they are ready to invade again, just like they did in 1978 when they pushed as far as the Litani River. In 1982 Israeli armoured columns will move north into Lebanon, ignoring the UNIFIL checkpoints and bases. They'll fight conventional tank and air battles with the Syrians and face ambushes and skirmishes with the PLO and other militias. On their way to war they will pass UNIFIL posts so quickly that UNIFIL soldiers will yet be sun-bathing in their swimming trunks or underpants.

It could in a way contextualise the relationship between the European soldiers of UNIFIL and the Israelis. European soldiers in their underpants and swimming trunks shouted out excited hurrahs to the passing Israelis on their way to war. No matter how it's presented it's not the UNIFIL soldier's war. The African contingents understand this fact more than the Europeans. The Ghanaians and Nigerians kept their heads down, stayed in their bunkers and did only a percentage of the patrolling of Irishbatt. Why should they die in the Lebanon by trodding on a mine or driving a truck off the side of a precarious mountain road? Human lives are far more valuable than that.

Post October 7th 2023 terror attacks on Israel. London.

Already a great many celebrities, internet influencers and both left of centre and right of centre political commentators have boosted their profiles, increased their subscriptions and added to their followers as they repackage themselves to the world as almost saintlike in their concern for the victims in Gaza of the Israeli-Hamas conflict. A saviour complex that's generally strong within them breaks forth from their psyches and the popular world pauses to listen. Their names come up again and again, linked in the common mind with the agonies of Gaza. At times it can seem as if their very names are synonymous with Gaza. In a broken world the wrong names are remembered.

In the documentary 'The Children of October 7th' the youngest survivor Ella Shan led the documentary-maker to the attic where her father Yitzhak was murdered. Blood stains could still be seen on the floor. Ella was one of the thirty seven children killed on that day, while hundreds more survive the terror but were left with lasting injuries. That's one of the names that should be remembered, Ella Shan. Her father

Yitzhak was murdered by the Iranian-sponsored terror group Hamas for the perceived crime of being Jewish.

The fact that the names of the Palestinian and Israeli children are not as known to us as the commentators covering the war and the celebrities sympathetic to Hamas tells us more about the sinister histories in the West than it does about the actual war in Gaza.

Lebanon 1981.

Walking around Tibnine for the first time was a profound experience. It was almost other-worldly, an adventure of psychic exploration. The village and the surrounding area were pretty much unchanged since medieval times. A knight from the Crusades could have stepped out of history and instantly recognised Tibnine. At the marketplace they slaughtered goats in the ritualised ways of their fathers and their father's fathers, slitting the throat while the animal was hoisted up by the back legs.

As I wandered Tibnine alone the locals looked at me with the expected suspicion of a people on the cusp of war. I wore a pistol in a holster borrowed from an armoured car driver. Carrying a rifle around the village while alone wouldn't have looked right. We were tourists in essence, under the mighty patronage of the U.N who in turn were under the patronage of the mighty USA. We took photos of Tibnine Castle and visited the holiday resorts of Israel and the holy city of Jerusalem. All things said the UNIFIL experience was mostly an experience of privilege. Under American patronage we lived on the edge of a warzone, witnesses to a precarious peace.

Over the years there were many incidents and misunderstandings between UNIFIL soldiers and the Israelis and their Christian militia allies, a number of them fatal. Others were farcical like the Norwegian armoured cars trying to stop Israeli bulldozers from building a roadway on the boundary of UNIFIL operations known as the Blue Line. For the Israelis the UNIFIL contingents were an inadequate and for the most part unwanted line of defence against AMAL or PLO raiding parties which yet somehow managed to sneak through the wadis under U.N control to fire an RPG 7 rocket or empty a magazine or two from an AK47 at an Israeli border post. For the locals UNIFIL could be seen as an extension of USA/Israeli influence in South Lebanon. At certain peaks of increased tension, it wasn't unusual for UNIFIL to be disliked from both sides of the peace line.

Tibnine Castle looks down from the eight hundred and seventy metre high Tibnine Hill and was built in 1104 during the Crusades by Hughes de Saint Omer. Saladin and his brother King Adel occupied Tibnine Castle after the battle at Hattin in 1187. It was once a fortress of twelve rectangular towers, with one of the towers used as a dungeon. The castle was razed in 1266 by the Mamluks and re-built five hundred years later in the mid-eighteen century by a Shiite sheikh during his battles against the Ottomans.

In 1981 the castle had nine towers, and the main entrance and temple vaults were well preserved. Its Western flank offered impressive views of the surroundings wadis and hamlets. The sense of history at Tibnine Castle is a strange manifestation as real as the air or the sky but somehow at the same time a little unreal. Crusaders, Shiite kings, Ottomans and French Colonialists are somehow present here. It is a place of power, a sacred link with the past.

Experiencing perceptions of Ireland and the Irish outside of our own native perceptions was an eye-opener. In the Middle East people knew little if anything about our island nation. We had a connotation with drunkenness and high spirits, seen as one-dimensional ginger-haired, pink-skinned party-animals prone to lachrymose moods and quick to burst into sentimental songs about Mother Macree and The Old Bog Road. Many people assumed we were Irish soldiers in a formation or other of the British army. When we explained we were not in any way part of the British army, although diehard republicans might have believed we were, our explanations were sometimes met with surprise. Nobody had heard about Pettigo-Belleek or Commandant Quinn's men in Katanga or showjumpers who competed internationally in Irish army uniforms.

Everyone had heard about Bobby Sands. The popularity of the H-Block hunger strikers was phenomenal. It touched the very deepest reaches of the post-colonial mind. People of all ages and backgrounds understood the symbolism of Sands' death. It was an emotive time. Apart from Private Tipp Ryan's blanket protest in a South Lebanon village there wasn't much said or done by us Irish soldiers. It was better to block out what was happening back home. What could we ever hope to do about it anyhow?

Getting enough money together for double-glazed windows and second-hand cars or wanting to wear a U.N service ribbon on a dress uniform was all very different to what was happening in the Northern six counties of Ireland. The only way to cope with it was to pretend it wasn't happening, to look the other way. The Troubles brought out subsumed Free State instincts. It was harder not to see ourselves as successors to the peacetime soldiery of Saorstat Eire and its later nominal re-birth as the Republic of Ireland, rather than as successors to the national soldiers at Pettigo-Belleek.

In Cyprus while on leave from UNIFIL Bobby Sands was big news. I took a taxi from one end of Nicosia to the other and when the taxi-driver heard I was from Ireland he shook my hand. He only wanted to talk about the very recent news of the death of Bobby Sands. At one point he was tearful. When he dropped me off, he refused take my money for the fare. He was adamant. There was no way he was going to charge an Irishman a taxi fare when Bobby Sands had just died for the conscience of the post-colonial world. I hadn't time to outline the nuances of Irish politics and why as an Irish soldier from the South my feelings about Bobby Sands were not straightforward. It was an emotional time. I could sense emotion on the streets of Nicosia and Larnaca. I tried not to imagine what the pitch of fever was like back in Ireland.

The Ghanaian soldiers we played football against and happily cheered in passing went home to a tumultuous country. Flight Lieutenant Jerry Rawlings had taken power, and the Ghanaian military were on the streets of the former colony's towns and cities. There were reports of extra-judicial killings, and ordinary Ghanaians fled to neighbouring countries. Our own tensions between the state and the military were resolved in the nineteen twenties. We were going home to an invisible existence as armed ghosts, mostly unneeded by the state and the people.

Our police force, An Garda Siochana, handled all the dirty laundry and answered all the awkward questions. The Ghanaian soldiers were returning as conquerors of their land, part of a military force that anyone with sense and a liking for personal survival would not defy. We were returning home as a neutered force subservient to the police and to any other state agency interested enough to bother with us. We were often ridiculed or cursed by citizens and journalists who questioned our very existence. Little wonder we drank.

Post October 7th 2023 attack on Israel. London.

A Jewish comedy duo was cancelled at the Edinburgh Fringe Festival. Why would anyone be offended by comedy sketches such as 'Shall I Compare Thee in a Funny Way, 'Jew-O-Rama' and 'Ultimate Jewish Mother'? We can imagine the insensitivity of cancelling Irish-themed events in Britain during the IRA's bombing campaign in the nineteen eighties and nineties. Something very odd is going on. This level of antipathy involving a foreign conflict thousands of miles away is usually reserved for hatred and targeted minorities in a time of war or in the days leading up to war.

It's as if a host of parasites have infested the collective unconscious of entire populations and are continually bringing into existence the ugliest Jew-hating tropes dredged from history. If it's a psychic problem then the cure must begin with the psyche.

Dublin. 1981.

At Dublin airport here's no sign of anyone with a doctorate in Sartrean Bad Faith to remind us that we are condemned to be free and condemned to use our freedom to create meaningfulness. An Aer Lingus jet is what it is and can't be shaped into something else. There isn't time to look into our souls for to try and avoid unconscious rituals of behaviour. The doors to the Aer Lingus jet are already opening. Nothing can be solved anyhow by wriggling out of this army business. To borrow an idea from the highly regarded philosopher of science Karl Popper, every solution to a problem creates new unsolved problems. Once we shy away from any one given direction there is a new direction to choose. It's easier to go on walking this way.

Fu Manchu is having one quick final smoke before we board the aircraft. He seems reconciled to the whole deal by now, ready for whatever the hills of South Lebanon have to throw at him. As it happens, he's a grafter, a man who'd do two men's work on a factory floor. He'll quickly take on driving and signalling duties in the battalion area of operations as a highly responsible and goal-orientated man. It's easy to imagine him making decent money in a civilian job. But it's the early nineteen eighties and as our politicians keep telling us jobs don't grow on trees.

Aristotle regarded every action as due to seven causes: chance, nature, compulsion, habit, reasoning, anger and appetite. The great philosopher might have added double-glazed windows as Fu Manchu has mentioned them often enough for to believe they are his sole motivation for showing up here today. As it happened, he was the perfect U.N soldier, always correct and sensitive around civilians. He wasn't remotely interested in politics of any kind and had a particular hatred of Middle Eastern politics. None of it concerned him, the plight of the Palestinians, the poverty of so many of the Shiite families in the South Lebanese hills or what the Israelis and their Christian Arab allies were getting up to or not getting up to. He did his job to the letter and was professional and practical in everything he did. He was the pragmatist who interprets the world around him through his own existential reality.

As the corporal responsible for communications in A Company he'd plenty to keep him busy. He never seemed to stand still for a minute, volunteering for duties outside his own remit, helping other soldiers out. He smoked cigarette after cigarette and drank tins of Amstel beer when off duty like everyone else, but never to excess.

The Lebanon existed long before Fu Manchu was born in a humble County Kildare town and would exist long after he's gone from here. He would have had very little influence on its destiny or well-being. Whether he had sympathy for the Palestinians or the Israelis or for both sides at the same time was not the question. He did exactly what the U.N and the commanders on the ground asked of him. He was impartial, detached, busy and preoccupied with what he was doing at any given moment.

He kept his emotions for his own private life, obsessing at times about his wife and family back home in Ireland. All his free time was dedicated to those back home. He made phone-calls and wrote letters and postcards. He posted mementoes and small gifts back to his young children. Lebanon was but a bump in the road for him, a distraction and a chance to get enough money together for double-glazed windows. The Lebanese had their own wives and families as Fu Manchu had his wife and family. Why did he need to concern himself with their worries when he had his own worries?

For the American philosopher Richard Rorty everyone has a final vocabulary, a summation of their views and feelings on any given topic. Rorty tried to find a way out of the moral language which can be so ineffective in influencing or making sense of human affairs. For Rorty the person who can review their final vocabulary has a better chance of making humankind less cruel. Fu Manchu's final vocabulary on nearly every topic of conversation was always two simple words - *fucking bastards.*

Fu Manchu nearly always summed up his feelings on every matter with those two words, whether we were talking about the local Arab militias or the Israelis or the South Lebanese Army or Irish battalion headquarters or whoever. It was his final vocabulary on nearly every subject. He hadn't the time or the mental energy to analyse the complex situations caused by the ambitious personalities that tend to rise to the top of hierarchies and shrugged off so much of the world as horrible and cruel. Why should he have to dissect the motivations of the Assad government in

Damascus or the leading lights in Israel's Knesset or the Christian Milita's Maj Saad Haadad when he had another letter to write home to one of his kids? What did the economy of the entire Middle East mean when Fu Manchu hadn't yet got the money together for double-glazed windows?

Fu Manchu carried his personal weapon around the area of operations like a handyman carrying a ratchet. The weapon had to be carried everywhere, so he carried it everywhere. But the idea of aiming or firing his Carl Gustav 9mm machine-pistol at anyone or anything was would have been alien to Fu Manchu. He was in Lebanon to do the job the U.N asked him to do. He was there for the peacekeeping experience and to make money for him and his family. Pointing an automatic weapon at someone didn't enter the equation. This absence of a military mentality was just what UNIFIL liked about its Irish contingents. There was enough machismo and inflated male egos in South Lebanon as matters stood. The volatile regions of the Middle East needed as many Fu Manchus as they could get.

At the end of his six-month stint in South Lebanon Fu Manchu had earned his UNIFIL ribbon more than most. He'd clocked up thousands of miles on lousy mountain roads in land-rovers and old ex-US army trucks to deliver water and supplies to outposts and to dump the swill-bins from the company cookhouse. He'd laid field-telephone lines across wadis with unexploded cluster bombs underfoot and maintained generators, radios and checkpoint spotlights. He'd done security duties and radio operator duties and hardly lost his cool more than once. He was the ideal U.N soldier insofar as he'd no bone to pick with anyone and was not prejudiced against any of the sides involved directly or indirectly in the Lebanon conflict. His two-word final vocabulary summed them all up.

Lebanon and the travails of the Lebanese people would drag on long after Fu Manchu slung his kitbag over one shoulder and headed back home to County Kildare. He did what he was asked to do and was paid for his work. He did well in UNIFIL's frontline as an excellent servant of peace. He harboured no fantasies or fallacies about Jews or Muslims and was as level-headed an Irishman as the men who rebuilt Britain's infrastructure after the war or who made their name in America. His final vocabulary saved him from unnecessary chatter as to who was right or who was wrong in a volatile land of endless propaganda and conflict.

Maybe if certain politicians in Dublin at the time had shown the same impartiality as Fu Manchu there'd have been less Irish casualties in South Lebanon. Did it really concern us after all? Were the national interests of Ireland in any way implicated in the contested boundaries of countries thousands of miles away? Were the struggles of Middle Eastern people more important than the national struggles on our own island of Ireland? When Irish politicians were meddling in Middle Eastern affairs by promoting the Bahrain Declaration the conflict in the North of Ireland was reaching another pitch of violent intensity. H-Block prisoners were putting their names forward for hunger strike. A young political prisoner and patriot by the name of Bobby Sands was preparing for martyrdom.

Arguably we'd slunk away from our obligations as the military of the Irish people by not taking on the Orange state in 1969. For a multitude of reasons, we were not ready for such a serious conflict anyhow. The role of the Irish military defaulted to a very small percentage of Northern Catholics and nationalists, supported by men and women of conscience south of the border. Another possible re-run of Pettigo-Belleek metamorphosed into a torturous decades' long agony of tit-for-tat killings, punishment shootings, collusion from the British forces in the North with Loyalist death squads and bombings that shook the Irish soul. Morally it was far easier to make statements about conflicts in distant lands which in real terms had little to do with us.

Fu Manchu was the ideal UNIFIL soldier and the ideal national soldier too. He had no wish to kill anyone or anything. The army was a job, a means to an end. Young families had to be provided for after all, double-glazed windows bought and paid for. The obligations of a father and husband had to be somehow honoured. Fu Manchu's final vocabulary applied to all parties in Ireland as it did to Lebanon. *Fucking bastards.* Everyone had their agenda after all and their own narrow interests. Why would Fu Manchu or any of us think otherwise?

In the middle of our stint in Lebanon I was in the back of a land-rover as it laboured up a steep and winding mountain road. The driver struggled to navigate the battered land-rover past dips and rocks on the road.

He could only drive at a walking pace. Fu Manchu was sitting in the front seat beside the driver. Out of nowhere one of the Lebanese warzone's feral, mangy dogs appeared.

The large black brute ran to the back of the land-rover and tried to jump in. I can see its slobbering yellow fangs even now. Rabies or some such disease had turned the dog crazy. I poked it in the snout with the barrel of my FN rifle to keep it from jumping into the back of the land-rover. I called to the driver to speed up as there was a wild rabid dog trying to jump on me. The driver couldn't get much more speed from the land-rover, such was the poor state of the mountain road and the steep incline of the route. I poked the mad dog in the face again to keep him away and it snarled and tried to bite the rifle-barrel.

I had a vision of the land-rover coming to a complete halt on the road and the rabid dog jumping on top of me in a rage. I had to do something. I cocked the rifle, flicked off the safety catch and pointed the barrel directly at the dog's snout. I called to Fu Manchu, telling him there was a rapid dog trying to jump into the land-rover and I was just about to shoot it. Fu Manchu reacted as if a firecracker had gone off in his back-pocket. He pulled rank and said there was no way I could shoot the dog. He yelled out a direct order for me not to shoot even though the crazy bastard of a dog was jumping up and snapping at my rifle-barrel. I put the safety-catch back on and poked the dog again in the face. This time I caught him with some force right in the snout so as he yelped with pain. Yet he still tried to jump up on the tailboard.

The land-rover picked up speed and at last we began to put distance between us and the wild dog. Fu Manchu was angry I'd even wanted to shoot a rabid dog as it tried to sink its diseased fangs into me. He just wasn't into killing, full stop. He'd have put me on a charge and had me up in front of the company commander if I'd have shot that horrible dog in self-defence. In so many ways he was the perfect peace-keeping soldier for the Irish army at the time and for UNIFIL too.

London. Post 9th October attack on Israel.

Leading politicians in the governing Labour party here in Britain are making yet more statements and passing yet more motions in the House of Commons to do with a conflict a very long way from home. Probably every aspect of life for ordinary people in Britain has become a crisis, from pot-holed roads, the lamentable state of the NHS and social care, to the exploitation of much of the population by a vicious form of international capitalism that's long-since out of control. Yet our government appears more worried about a two-state solution in the Middle East.

And yet again we'll buy it, desperate for a distraction from the real problems facing us. One can only imagine the suffering we'd go through if there wasn't a Jew about the place to blame.

Dublin. 1981.

At Dublin airport it is not the scene from Hair where Treat Williams as Berger miraculously manages to substitute himself for a real soldier bound for Vietnam. In the Hippy-era film Berger along with hundreds of GIs march into military transport planes to the soundtrack of Sunshine. It's a powerful anti-war sentiment with a thousand-strong cast of singing Hippies. In the longer narrative of war and soldiering the often creative anti-war protests of the Hippy movement are but a blip, a curiosity at best in the great glorification of war. Quakers, Jehovah Witnesses, Greenham Common women, CND marchers, Conscientious Objectors and Hippies can only ever be an oddity, for war and the business of war are too important to be disturbed for longer than it takes for the next generation to be psyched up to fight.

Inside the plane the Aer Lingus stewardesses are only slightly condescending. We are their social inferiors after all, the social inferiors of almost everyone in the country as it happens. Social divisions colour all our days and nights as we stumble on after the American dream of how to organise societies. After a while we'll catch up with the rest of the free world and greed and naked self-interest will overtake the political goals of social cohesion, cultural identity and ecological integrity. Hardly anyone will admit to believing in the Faeries or honouring the Nine Fridays or that blasphemy against the Holy Spirit is unforgivable. It'll be harder to pretend to believe in the old ideas of a shared national identify.

Our unawareness and servility are the outcome of a finely tuned mechanism of oppression calculated to ensure there's always a rump of human labour and willing consumers to keep everything ticking over. Very little actual time and proactive thinking are devoted to trying to design and introduce anything different for the coming man. We are required to accept unfairness, inheritance rights favouring tiny elites, radical income disparity and exploitation as much as we accept the natural conditions of the planet we live on.

Soviet-style Communism and the atrocities against the human spirit it brings in its wake proved to be an even greater insult to the human condition than the exploitation and class disparity of the kind of capitalism we have. If there are alternatives humankind has not honed them into working social and political entities. Maybe we are doing all we can do.

Irish schools, what media we had and common discourse hammered home a mind-numbing status quo, a hopeless acceptance of rich and poor. Social mobility under such a model might be possible when certain very favourable conditions are in place. For those who consistently find fault in the culture of cute hoorism there is always a one-way ferry and train ticket to England or a long-haul flight to somewhere farther afield. The expected answer when a farmer or businessman or rich spinster inherits another tract of land or another property down the end of a lane is to say good luck to them, almost as if it is the accepted response to a common prayer. We are more conditioned into swallowing the party line on property and the rights of property as any citizen of the old Soviet Union was conditioned into swallowing the Communist Party line.

Our ignorance and servitude are a jealously guarded shibboleth of national life, for without an ignorant, economically dependent rump of citizenry the art of exploitation is a redundant art. Who can imagine the chaos if the one hundred and twenty or so men on this journey to Lebanon begin expanding on their own ideas and personal values, delving deeper into their humanity and asking questions it was always taboo to ask? If the repressed homosexuals or bisexuals in our ranks began exploring their sexual impulses, where would that lead us? If men began to think for themselves and to really question the socio-economic conditions of their lives, what conclusions would they arrive at?

Such refinement of thought is impossible as army life reinforces every societal instrument and method of keeping people in their boxes. If a soldier is seen reading a book there's a strong likelihood he'll be laughed at. A Sven Hassel or Len Deighton novel might be accepted. If a soldier was to somehow get his hands on a book of dialectics or political philosophy, then someone further up the food-chain would have something to say about it. It wouldn't happen anyhow.

Lebanon is a long way from Pettigo-Belleek and as such has nothing to do with us. There are no tribal or national or religious interests for us in a land of Maronite/Eastern rite Christians, Jews, Druze and Muslims.

Money from UNIFIL is prized and without it there'd be little interest from ordinary soldiers, especially married soldiers with little ones to feed and clothe and double-glazed windows to buy. For others to travel to somewhere like the Middle East with the promise of cheap Amstel and Heineken beer and with hours of precious sunshine is not an uninteresting option. Many Irish soldiers fly wives and girlfriends to Israel or Cyprus and meet them there on planned leave from UNIFIL.

The slums of Griffith Square and the humble, dreary living of the ordinary Irish soldier at the time uplifts Lebanon to a wondrous moment of freedom. For the briefest span of time the socio-economic conditions of reductive codes of living are lifted from the shoulders of men starved of stimulation and opportunity. For this alone Lebanon is a triumph, a cause for excitement and celebration. Good luck to the Irish who went there and to the Lebanese who endured.

Post October 7ᵗʰ attack on Israel. London.

The Chief Rabbi Sir Ephraim Mirvis addressed a rally at Trafalgar Square attended by thousands of protestors who'd marched through the centre of London to Downing Street where they demanded the release of the remaining hostages held by Hamas terrorists in Gaza. The Chief Rabbi was critical of the UK government, saying that when Hamas, a terrorist organisation proscribed by the UK government, is congratulating Downing Street on its Middle Eastern policies then something is seriously wrong.

Rabbis had the power to shun or ban members of the congregation for certain ritual lapses and for minor transgressions. Niddui could be imposed for a week and longer if necessary. A one day version of niddui known as nezifah was also used. An indefinite ban known as cherem was famously handed down to the Dutch philosopher Baruch Spinoza. The Chief Rabbi's words were more than just words. They summoned up ancient powers and carried with them a subliminal message to the world, apocalyptic in its implications.

Lebanon 1981.

On a hot, sunny Middle Eastern day a Ghanaian soldier walks through a checkpoint of the Irish area of operations. He's wearing a woollen Ghanaian army overcoat and green gumboots, smiling and waving to any Irish soldiers he passes.

On the ball Irish!

It's the friendly shout which rings out when Irish and Ghanaian soldiers pass each other's checkpoints. *On the ball Irish! On the ball Ghana!* The contingents from Ghana and Ireland were ideal for UNIFIL, both small non-aligned nations part of the Anglophone world. Generals from both nations, Erskine and O'Callaghan, went on to lead the UNIFIL mission.

The Ghanaian soldier with the gumboots and overcoat is unarmed, or you could say only armed with disarming natural smiles. Tribal marks from the Ashanti nation are sliced into both his cheeks. He exudes much by way of good nature and positivity. Like Fu Manchu and so many of the others the Ghanaian soldier's thoughts will never stray too far from the reason he's here in the troubled hills of South Lebanon. A U.N payment in US dollars goes a long way in the developing economy of a West African state.

An anti-soldiering posture helps rather than hinders national contingents of UNIFIL. Infantry training involving enfilades, dead-eye shots and the accurate lobbing of grenades and mortars are not needed out here. Much of the standing around at checkpoints and patrolling wadis in present-day Lebanon could be done unarmed but ordinary soldiers have their dignity and can't be separated for long from their small arms. There's an experimental vibe to U.N missions as much as there are diplomatic, political and pragmatic vibes. If the modern soldier can bring humanitarianism, diplomacy and as much restraint as possible into daily operations it must register as real headway in the overall organisation of nations.

Reconciling the fragility of the ego with the passivity of the U.N's expectations of its soldiers on the ground is very much a work in progress. The sun-bathing Dutch, Irish and Norwegian UNIFIL soldiers waving in their swimming togs and shorts to the passing Israeli armoured columns was a representation of an army leaving for war as they passed cheering civilians. The disgust in the European consciousness at the bestial killing excesses in the opening five decades of the twentieth century has matured into a moral, political, legal and humanitarian framework unusual in the history of human affairs. Trial under international law at The Hague is now mentioned as the highest moral test of a culture at odds with whatever gods or God it once held sacred.

The Western European mentality has tempered to a point where it insists on analysing the impulses and soundings of war, demanding diplomacy and peace talks even when one side is not interested in peace. This fascinating development, most notable in the relationship between France and Germany, is widely seen to have saved Western Europe at least from World War III and from lesser wars.

Subsuming the instincts and impulses of war is as much an achievement of this European project as reassuring populations that the wars of the past are worth not repeating. The puerile mind craves war with all the petulance of the junkie craving the needle. U.N boots on the ground are living testimony to a new age of humanitarianism, international law and pervasive diplomacy. By this reasoning the ideal U.N soldier is an anti-soldier, unable to respond in kind to aggression or insults in the time-honoured ways of the soldier.

Increasingly the U.N soldier on the ground is female, as the female soldier is less of a risk to a civilian population often stripped of peacetime civil protections. Sexual crimes and abuses against civilians by U.N personnel are sadly more common than we think. In Lebanon the impositions of sex were dissipated by regular weekend passes and longer periods of leave in Israel and Cyprus. Yarns from the bordellos of Tel Aviv and Haifa were the most popular yarns among depot soldiers at the time.

Sexual activity between teenage boys and young Arab men in the villages of South Lebanon was common. One of our corporals was surprised by the rocking motion of an M3 Panhard APC parked at a checkpoint. When he went to investigate and pulled open the backdoors of the vehicle he saw two Lebanese soldiers inside making the beast with two backs. It wasn't unusual for an amorous Lebanese soldier or young male civilian to proposition an Irish soldier they liked the look of. As far as I'm aware the offers were not widely accepted. I once seen a young effeminate boy guiltily leaving the room of one of our corporals. The boy carried the rewards of whatever took place in the room, a large pack of Duracell batteries and a few cans of sprite.

Women were off-limits, so even the most harmless chit-chat between U.N soldiers and young Lebanese women was harem, forbidden under pain of very real retribution. Now and then a soldier got drunk and made an arse of himself in front of the local women. But as far as I heard the soldiers of the 49th Battalion at least steered clear of any major trouble with the local Arab women, saving it all up for the bordellos of Haifa and Tel Aviv.

One night in particular is burnt into memory. We were on sandbags on what must have been the starriest night in history, with the Israeli border only a few miles to the south. Israeli border guards panned immensely powerful searchlights into the night. Green luminous flares fizzed into life from several directions. We were the observers of a majestic and fragile peace.

London. Post October 7th attack on Israel.

The mass murder, ethnic cleansing, rape, persecution and forced conversions of minorities by Jihadis is the greatest outrage against humanity in the Middle East. Yazidis, Kurds, Christians and Druze are targeted by a medieval mindset steeped in the murderous motivations of religious fanaticism. The Jews have been targeted too by this savagery and would have been exterminated in that part of the world if the state of Israel hadn't come into existence for to protect Jews and preserve the sacred legacy of Judaism. The Jews of that region would get the same treatment from the Jihadis if they did what Western liberals have been pressuring them to do for decades, that is to compromise or even dismantle their security apparatus and allow their sworn enemies to take advantage.

All this is recorded by NGOs and journalists and cannot in any way be regarded as a secret. Recent Jihadi atrocities against Druze communities in Western Syria have been well documented and there is plenty of video evidence of firsthand accounts of the crimes in question. If such atrocities do not meet the criteria of genocide they do at least fall into the category of ethnic cleansing.

The real threat to human rights, the dignity of women and minorities and political stability in that region is clearly Jihadism and the despotism of Arab regimes, alongside the tyranny of the Iranian mullahs. Yet on an hourly basis only aspects of Israeli defence actions are broadcasted by Western media organisations such as the BBC and Sky. Such a continuum of biased reportage over time is sure to seep into the deeper reaches of the public mind and in doing do cast the Israelis as an evil force among a plethora of innocents.

Why do they do this? Why do they insist that Oceania is at war with Eurasia and has always been at war with Eurasia? It's as if they've internalised the very worse of the methodology of misinformation from Orwell's dystopian novel. There are those who put forward plausible arguments that there has been an infiltration of Jihadism in British institutions, and certainly British media outlets has been slanted by this infiltration. But most people in Britain are not Jihadis so why is there such an emphasis on ignoring the pernicious workings of Jihadism in the Middle East and instead demonising a country like Israel which is first and foremost defending itself against Jihadism? There are a number of answers to this question, with self-preservation up there as a causal factor in all of them.

By overlooking or downplaying Jihadism and focusing on Israel the more influential Western media organisations and commentators are sidestepping the risk of a David Amess or Charlie Hebdo-like attack, steering wide of any repercussions for their views. As Israelis are democrats they allow free comment and criticism and although they must by now be quite demoralised by the endless misinformation aimed at them by Western liberals they are not going to show up outside a broadcaster's office wearing a suicide belt or carrying a lethal knife like a Jihadi might.

So we continue to live under lies and misinformation, our conscious and subconscious thoughts on the Middle East conflict modelled by fearful broadcasters who do not tell us what the truth is, or explain that despotism, Jihadism and a pathological hatred of Jews in the Arab countries is as much the reason for violence in the Middle East as anything to do with the Israeli instinct for survival.

Lebanon 1981

I went on leave to first Israel, then Cyprus. I stayed at the American Colony Hotel in Jerusalem and walked the way of suffering to Golgotha. I took photos by the Garden Tomb and Damascus Gate with my childhood Christianity fanned into fervour. I entered the Old City through the Jaffa Gate, trying to imagine what Second Temple Jerusalem looked like to the Messiah. I travelled alone as I knew it would have been difficult if not impossible to find someone from the battalion keen to hang around the sites of Jerusalem's Old City for very long.

On the crossing from Haifa to Cyprus I spent most of the time standing on deck, absorbed by a tumultuous Mediterranean Sea. The ferry dipped as waves crashed into its sides, spray cascading over hundreds of sea-travellers with third-class tickets obliging them to travel above deck. Handsome, sun-kissed people laughed and sang to the rhythm of a solitary guitar. A dozen or so Greek Orthodox monks sat quietly together on-deck, seemingly not caring about the rough crossing, maybe on their way home to Mount Athos or some such haven of peace.

Any traveller with a spark of romance in their heart left the comfort of the lounges to travel on the exposed deck with the handclapping, singing free spirits. If only such nights never ended. If only the solitary traveller could travel with such fellow travellers eternally. I met two German sisters on-deck, the younger sister my exact age. They were travelling onto Greece, and from there travelling by land and sea back to Germany. We spoke together quietly, looking out on the disquieting tempers of the sea. The idea was as influenced by the beautiful unreality of the moment as much as by a teenage urge for sex and intimacy.

For hours I planned in my mind to continue on travelling with the blonde German sisters, to travel on past Cyprus to Greece and on further. What did the Lebanon and the U.N mean to me anyhow? It was all a very long way from another re-run of Pettigo-Belleek. As Major Saad Haddad from the South Lebanese Army liked to shout to the Irish UN positions, the troubles of Lebanon had nothing to do with Irishmen. We were there mostly in an abstract sense, as anti-soldiers trying to make better a conflict with nuclear apocalyptic potential. When we did slip from an anti-soldiering to a soldiering role it was straightaway punished or criticised. Sure, second-hand cars were bought and double-glazed windows were fitted from UNIFIL money. But it wasn't really our fight.

The fantasy stayed with me until the ferry docked at Larnaca early the next morning. I'd travel with this beautiful young German, the younger of the two free-spirited sisters, and find a job somewhere in Europe. There was no need to return to the banal and perpetually frustrating routines of the Irish army. I'd heard enough and seen enough. If I stayed a day longer in the billets of dehumanised men with spirits brutalised by forces calculated to keep them ignorant I'd literally rot in spirit. Our thought-life can sink to places in the spirit from where it's very hard return to normality again.

It was a combination of the beauty of the young German woman and the spiritual intoxication of the night-journey by sea. Of course the plan evaporated in the reality of dawn. A soldier disappearing from U.N service in Lebanon would make the newspaper headlines. Given the uncertainties of the region they'd speculate on all the worst possible outcomes. Interpol and every other police force and every border post west of Jerusalem would be alerted. The romantic spirit in full flow is stupid, but not that stupid. I wouldn't desert and tag onto the young German sisters' itinerary. Of course I wouldn't.

Every year thousands of people go missing for similar reasons to the reasons I tried to rationalise on the night-crossing from Israel to Cyprus. People are rarely gifted such freedom. We are generally tied by complicated bonds to families, jobs, institutions, brute economic necessity, permanent addresses and daily responsibilities. Often the missing are only classified as missing by others who have not twigged on why certain bonds can be the difference between life and physical death, or the spiritual death so familiar to the modernist.

I'd return to Lebanon and from there return to Ireland. I'd be required to jump through a thousand experiential and psychic hoops before finding anything that looked like personal freedom. There are yet a number of barrack-squares to cross, yet more mass-parades to get through and security duties to endure, before light illuminates the horizon.

Post October 7th attack on Israel.

Gay rights and an accompanying LGBT agenda has been among the most vigorously promoted campaigns in recent decades by Western liberal agencies, but not unexpectantly there's a blind spot when it comes to Israel. The countries that are the most antagonistic to Israel and the Jewish diaspora have appalling records in Gay rights and rights for minorities. In truth the Jihadis and their fundamentalist paradigm is diametrically opposed to the rights-based, democratic systems in the West where equality under law is about as sacred a tradition as we have. The hatred so vivid in the hearts of so many Arabs for Jews, Gay people and other minorities is kept secret by the media organisations that dominate the airwaves.

It's not only an inconvenient truth but a taboo. Even the conservative Orthodox Chabad emissaries from the Jewish faith are supportive of Gay people's dignity and aspirations. The director of their annual Kinus Hashluchim get-together, Rabbi Yehuda Pink, had this to say.

We have people from the LGBT community who attend our events. We accept and welcome any individual unreservedly. When you respect others, it gets mirrored back.

In returning to Orwell we are again reminded of truisms in his day that are just as relevant today.

Intellectual honesty is a crime in any totalitarian country; but even in England it is not exactly profitable to speak and write the truth.

Lebanon 1981

Another enduring memory is of the humility of the Shiite villagers in hills overlooking Israel. They suffered much through the years and lived in Biblical simplicity. The block walls of many of their houses were without plaster, much less paint. Pictures of Mecca and portraits of Muhammad al-Mahdi or other imams were pinned to the bare walls. They were simple small-holding people who sweated over crops of tobacco for their daily bread. Their elders' knowledge of religion was impressive.

They celebrated Fatimah's birthday on the 20th of Jumada al-Thani as the day of women and mothers. The elders spoke reverently of the Imam Husayn Shrine and the Imam Ali Mosque in Najaf. They remembered the destruction of the Tombs of the Imams in the Al-Baqu cemetery in 1925. The elders encouraged the villagers to think about creation, for Allah granted intelligence to humanity for this very reason. Following Allah by imitation rather as a consequence of reasoning and reflection on creation was not encouraged. The call to prayer was played on a record-player from the mosque's minaret, with the record sometimes scratchy or catching on a groove so as one word was played over and over until put right by the hand of the Mukhtar. Even to someone from the Christian lands it was a chilling sound, an ethereal link to another world.

On evenings we eat eggs and chips in a simple house of unpainted breezeblocks close to A Coy headquarters in the village of As Sultaniyah. The family invited me to watch television with them in their only other room. It's a tiny black and white set but the signal's good. It's a television station from Damascus, the only service in Arabic they can pick up in the Southern hills of Lebanon. Rows of both male and female dancers in full Arabic dress dance to loud traditional music. They dance and dance in mesmeric coordination, line after line of dancers covered from head to foot in flowing robes.

I sit on the bare concrete floor with the mother, father and three young children, absorbed by the dancing from Damascus. The mind is seduced away from conscious thoughts, lulled into a wondrous and symbolic zone. The repetitive dancing and singing goes on for hours, uninterrupted by advertisements. Every hour or so there's a news bulletin from the Assad government and then the music and dancing return. It's a television experience several worlds away from the interruptions, inane babbling and annoying advertisements of Western television.

How the mostly moronic television channels of Western countries are somehow regarded as superior to Syrian state television is another questionable sleight of hand. The dancing and singing which goes on for hours is calming and reassuring at a level beyond the conscious mind. It sedates and pleases the psyche. It is an experience of transcendence and unsophisticated pleasure. After absorbing the dancing and singing in the sweet company of the poor Shiite family the mind is lifted high, the soul is anchored in something ancient. The lines of Dabke dancers and the music of the Levant are lasting sedatives.

When a culture is undivided and strengthened by mosque, church or temple it impacts powerfully on the human spirit. Among such people the Westerner realises our losses are incalculable. Remembering lines from The Wasteland doesn't help. At such times we are the hollow men. In parts of the world where they've somehow managed to hold onto a coherent cultural narrative and recognisable identity the Westerner's relativism is exposed as something lax, weak and shot through with indecisiveness. The Shiite villages of Lebanon of 1981 were animated by mighty and at times ferocious cultural, familial and religious forces. To tap into these codes of daily reassurances with their references to the very apex of creation comforts the very soul of man.

Our crates of Heineken and Amstel beer, our bags of chintz from the mingy shops, our US dollars and dreams of meeting Elvis or Marilyn Monroe in a life to come are exposed as hopelessly phoney when juxtaposed to a real culture. Home is more about relationships than physicality and the Lebanese peoples' relations with each other was refined and mediated by communal and transcendent significance. Spending a little time with them made sense of just why Western interventions and Western societal models are so often damned as Satanic in the Middle East.

Our own native Irish culture was in decline by then, as people looked more to England, the USA or to the wider Anglophone world for inspiration, pleased when an Irish singer made it into the UK charts or when they found out the drummer from a famous US rock band was born in Westmeath. DeValera and John Charles McQuaid's shared vision of a glorified Irish peasantry was doomed from the beginning, for American and British culture had colonised the Irish mind far too seductively by then. A small percentage of people who liked woollen jumpers, Sean-nos singing and who own holiday cottages in Donegal or Connemara might have half-heartedly believed in an Irish culture independent of the wider Anglophone world, but it was far from a universal vibe.

Catholicism as defined by a Gaelic-inspired and an introverted Irish consciousness was nowhere near strong enough to stand toe to toe with Elvis, Kojak, Star Wars and the Beatles. The more it tried to discourage people from swallowing up every scrap of popular culture from the Anglophone world the more greedily such scraps were swallowed. Irish Catholicism with its stern Jansenist undertones only succeeded in tormenting, stifling and regressing the Irish mind, introducing harsher layers of unneeded guilt and shame. Deep down we didn't buy it anyhow.

DeValera hadn't manage to re-introduce the Irish language to the nation, as the Hebrew language was re-introduced to the Israelis. He'd failed to re-unite the country, going so far as to execute Republican militants hoping for a re-run of the old Pettigo-Belleek battles. Instead, he settled for a pseudo-theocratic introspection doomed to failure because Irish people in Ireland and elsewhere are part of the Anglophone world and could hardly be expected to deconstruct their conscious and unconscious conditioning for the sake of a blind old patriot's vision of Kathleen ni Houlihan looking down benevolently on cold nights of endless repeats of the rosary and dreams of a life to come. Irish conservatism as personified by DeValera, the papal Count Oliver J. Flanagan, Archbishop John Charles McQuaid and a legion of often good-hearted and self-deprecating Catholics only managed to hold back the development of the Irish national consciousness. In a country where the most valued export is its people it was critical to at least make an effort to prepare the young for the cattle-boat to England, or for the longer routes to Canada, New Zealand, Australia and the USA.

These deficits were painfully obvious in places like the South of Lebanon. Civilians laughed at us when they saw us drunk out on the roads in front of whatever mess or canteen we'd been boozing in. Soldiers from other contingents looked at our arms and equipment with curiosity, like men looking at objects in a museum. We hadn't moved with the times. Yet for all our imperfections we were the perfect peacekeepers for the U.N to offer to the killing passions of the Middle East. Our easy-going sense of humanity and innocence along with our underperformance as killing soldiers were just what were needed in a macho world horribly maimed by death and war.

Natural aggression and the tenacity of the Irish National soldier at Pettigo-Belleek are not needed in the political impasse of a post-Hiroshima/Nagasaki world. The more reasoned, even-tempered, pseudo-police role of the U.N peacekeeping soldier insists on an anti-soldiering rather than a soldiering mentality. Standing eternally at checkpoints and having a gentle disposition towards civilians are the key strengths.

For the foreign soldier Lebanon is different. The southern hilly villages of Lebanon are yet more different. Maronite Christians and smaller Christian denominations, displaced Palestinians, Shiite, Druze and radical Islamists alike share an age-old reverence for sexual propriety, public decency and restraint in matters of human sexuality. The idea of a foreign soldier welcomed to their lands and who then seduces a single young woman or girl, impregnating her and then abandoning both the expectant mother and the child to come, is an immense insult. There are also literalist interpretations of sacred text to consider too.

The infant born from a careless, loveless fuck and then rejected by its father is cursed for life. Orphans are pitied in the Middle East, for the people understand personal identity is deeply enriched by knowledge of and emotional connection with both a father and a mother. Impregnating vulnerable young women and girls and then disappearing is seen an act of grave social vandalism, for it destabilises the fragile bonds between male and female, between one generation and the generation to come. It can create an often-unbearable sense of rejection in the unfortunate children born in such loveless circumstances.

Whatever their faults the people of South Lebanon understand the implications of the careless, loveless fuck and the psychological and spiritual burden dumped on the illegitimate child born into poverty with little or no knowledge of their father. Popular culture may at times romanticise such human tragedy but in the Middle East the culture condemns the absent father with a chilling cry of *harem*. It puts into place its familial, societal and cultural norms as a bulwark against the kind of short-sighted, contemptuous, woman-hating carelessness typified by a number of U.N soldiers who served in Haiti.

Is it any wonder our current fads and neglect in the most serious matters known to the human family are hated in parts of the world where they've managed to hold onto a social order judgemental of the loveless congress and its abandoned, rejected off-spring? In Lebanon the feckless U.N soldier could not have just acted out sexually and then ran away like his counterparts in Haiti because the communities of Lebanon would not stand for it. They understand a child at least needs a father and a mother in its early years and needs to know both its father and its mother, whether they are poor or not or disadvantaged or disabled or whatever.

They understand these basic facts at the deepest level of the human experience and they order their societies and kinship bonds accordingly. Pitted against so much valueless propaganda they know this is to their credit. With the global spread of a far more selfish mentality in mind the existence of cultural norms which protect against the kind of abuses and careless fathering of children by U.N soldiers during their mission in Haiti, Congo and other places of war may not last in perpetuity.

Humanity has never travelled on this road before. The concept of the United Nations is alien to the human narrative. In history empires and armies expanded by their military prowess and strength of numbers. Imperial or colonial forces patrolled the towns and valleys of conquered lands. The idea of a neutral force inserted into a war zone or place of natural disaster is a curious modification not yet fully absorbed by human consciousness. The U.N is one of the world's most ambitious experiments. So much of humanity's hope for a reasonable, survivable future is invested in the U.N that it can seem as if humanity averts its eyes when U.N personnel on the ground step badly out of line.

In Lebanon the discipline of Irish peacekeepers was good. There was the occasional flare-up at a checkpoint, a male ego impacting head-on against another male ego. But generally, we were good peacekeepers. We lacked the arrogance and baggage of soldiers from the former colonial powers, the cock-a-hoop armies stuffed with regimental pride. We took with us the docile, disempowered role we'd inherited in Ireland to the hills of South Lebanon. We were used to holding our fire back home, so we could hold our fire in Lebanon too.

In Lebanon, Irish U.N soldiers were willing to fight, and did fight on occasion in limited infantry engagements. The village of At Tiri in 1980 was one such event that became part of Irish army legend. Two Irish soldiers were kidnapped and killed in retaliation for the death of one of Maj. Haadad's militiamen. What began at At Tiri all those years ago continues to this day in international legal battles to find some kind of justice or closure for Irish fatalities in Lebanon.

Whether Irish soldiers had any personal or national reason to stand firm at At Tiri is as relevant as asking if Indian U.N soldiers had a reason to stand firm in Sierra Leone, or

Dutch U.N soldiers in Bosnia. Complex causal factors send national soldiers far from their homebases on humanitarian duties which can go bad very quickly. So much of humankind's instincts are warlike or hostile to others and so much popular and academic history is obsessed by war that peacekeeping becomes another prized addendum to war.

In the absence of the conditions and attitudes of the U.N's war in Korea the U.N Security Council and U.N leaders will struggle to incite a spirit of aggressiveness in its peacekeepers. Idealist sentiment for the U.N and what it does is not universal. In speaking with former peacekeepers from Ghana, Nigeria and Nepal I was struck by their pragmatism. It was a similar mindset to Fu Manchu's single-mindedness linking his U.N duty in Lebanon with double-glazed windows for his house back home in Kildare.

For African and Asian soldiers it's more about economics than shiny medals. If they travel to a U.N area of operations and don't risk their lives they get paid the same as if they do risk their lives. If they are killed on U.N peacekeeping duties their dependents back home will quickly be forgotten about.

There will not be anything like the provision for widows and orphans of servicemen from the richer nations. A soldier's death is economically as well as personally disastrous for African and Asian widows and orphans.

Idealism has its limits. The U.N soldier at a checkpoint stands emotionally outside the conflict they are policing. How can they be expected to have a fighting spirit to equal those caught up in a war when they have no stake in the fight? It's a curious offer, an invitation for soldiers from the less-developed nations who make up the bulk of the U.N's peacekeepers to get killed in a stranger's land. It can be perceived as yet another conjuring trick by richer nations to mesmerize poorer nations, to exploit further those who are already exploited.

A microcosm of the differing attitudes to soldiering from the rich nations as opposed to the poorer nations can be seen in the recruitment approach of the French Foreign Legion. Recruits from the poorer nations, often former French colonies, can be openly contemptuous of recruits from richer nations. After all they have an economic imperative for enlisting for five years in a tough military outfit. At the end of their service a French passport and the full citizen rights of a progressive nation awaits. Recruits from the richer nations have no such impetus. Already they have passports from societies of opportunity. The Legion for the recruit from the richer countries is but a self-ordained coming-of-age, another possible remedy to the stinging impositions of boredom, the pressures on the male ego and the urge to be heroic. Voluntary military service in the richer nations is not necessarily based on financial desperation or hunger.

Whatever the future of the U.N's peacekeeping operations on the ground the Irish army's roles in past missions and missions yet continuous are revered. Honour, the frailty of the human ego, the importance of remembrance ritual and military tradition make it thus. History's fickle hand dictated that as young Irish soldiers we were posted to South Lebanon rather than Gallipoli or the Somme, or to the modern counterparts of Gallipoli or the Somme. By 1969 and 1981 the wounds of both nationalist service personnel and personnel from Ireland who for one reason or other served the Crown had not healed. To what extent these wounds have healed today is open to interpretation.

With a focus on numbers our U.N role is better contextualised. Our U.N record is honourable and highly valued despite limited numbers. India has thus far committed one hundred and eighty thousand soldiers to over forty missions. In a recent mission we sent one hundred and fifty soldiers to the Golan Heights. It's unlikely the battles of At Tiri or Jadotville will be repeated with such smaller concentrations of soldiers, even when Irish soldiers under the U.N flag are convinced it's worth getting involved in gunfire with strangers in a land of strangers.

When war is glorified it's easier for the young and brave of heart to look for glory and meaning in war. To keep the whole shabby business of war and all its component parts going each new generation must be coached in the business and mystique of war. By opting out of political union with London we side-stepped much of the war-propaganda and indoctrination of young minds so fundamental to the enlistment of soldiers. In Irish schools the violent origins of our state were played down for fear of moulding young minds in the fanatic's cause. From 1969 onwards this softer reading of revolutionary history was more apparent.

We were taught little if anything of our grandfathers and great-grandfathers who fought in wars as British soldiers and very little about the IRA/IRB and Citizen's Army who were so instrumental in creating the state we were born and raised in. The more remote and abstract the history the better. In an echo of the history of Rome when Horatius and his men kept the bridge in the brave days of old the story of Sergeant Custume was told and re-told with reverence.

During the siege of Athlone in the Williamite Wars Custume rallied volunteers to tear down the planking on the main bridge over the Shannon which would give access to Ginckel's Williamite army. Sergeant Custume's call for volunteers resounded in Irish national school classrooms centuries after his bravery.

Are there ten men here who will die with me for Ireland?

Custume and his comrades died on the bridge and Athlone was saved. It was the fearless Sergeant Custume on the bridge at Athlone and the mythological figures from ancient Ireland like Cu Culainn that we knew as heroes in our classrooms.

References to the men of 1916 were more muted and a division was always drawn between the Old IRA from the 1919-1922 era and the Provisional IRA born from the turmoil of 1969. Rory Og O'More sent the Elizabethan soldiers to Hades and great reformers like Daniel O'Connell and Charles Stuart Parnell were Irish heroes who used oratory and unfaltering canniness to confound perfidious Albion. History was as one-sided and simplistic as the national history of any people. It was passed on viscerally, mined into the consciousness of the growing child.

The Irish policemen and soldiers killed and wounded during the Easter Rising of 1916 were not mentioned. Likewise, the thousands of Irish soldiers who enlisted in the illustrious Irish regiments and fought in WW1 and WWII and lesser wars were not mentioned. Only their immediate families remembered and grieved them. The rest of us remembered and grieved Padraig Pearse and the other martyrs of 1916. National history must always be written by the winners, as much as it must be reductive, visceral and one-sided.

Post October 7th attack on Israel. London.

In the confusion of this age there's a truth that seems too straightforward for minds fattened by the tumult of the internet to fully grasp. It's a truth that's referenced in one of Isaac Bashevis Singer's short stories. In 'I Place My Reliance on No Man' the story's main character Rabbi Jonathan Danziger has reached a critical moment in his life.

The rabbi stood alone, his hands clasped, his gaze wandering from wall to wall. He would make his departure from the synagogue where he prayed for so many years. It was all so familiar: the twelve signs of the zodiac, the seven stars, the figures of the lion, the stag, the leopard and the eagle, the unutterable Name of God, painted in red. The gilded lions on the top of the Ark stared at the rabbi with their amber eyes while their curved tongues supported the tables with the Ten Commandants. It seemed to the rabbi that these sacred beasts were asking: Why did you wait so long? Couldn't you see from the start that one cannot serve God and man at the same time?

Lebanon. 1981.

In the early nineteen eighties popular history as the Irish people knew it had not remembered or forgiven the Redmondites who fought in the British army in WW1 to honour the Home Rule Bill passed in the British parliament in September 1914. We didn't despise these men because we knew nothing about them. They were the invisible men from an era dominated by the martyrs of 1916 and the romanticised birth of the modern Irish state.

For those raised in the old garrison towns occupied by the British army in Ireland it was harder to fully shake off the influence of the defunct Irish regiments. Certain names, impressions and symbols resonated at a level deeper than conscious thought. The Inniskillings, Munsters, Connaught Rangers and South Irish Horse. The famous Dublins with their headquarters at Naas and the Cavalry barracks at Newbridge. The angel and harp insignia of the King's Irish soldiers. We knew at a subliminal level such references were very personal to us. But our education and socialisation had erased all mention of them. The English were our enemies and were always our enemies. The Irishmen from the Irish regiments were our enemies too, traitors who'd sided with England in her imperial adventures and endless wars. We had somehow become our own enemies, Catholic Irish people despising fellow Catholics because the winds of history had changed so quickly.

In the Irish army's 49th Battalion in UNIFIL we had veterans of the British army. In A Company we'd had a corporal who'd served with 2 Para. He wasn't a guy to boast about serving in such a tough outfit but his comrades in A Coy knew about it and respected him because of it. The nuances of Irish history followed us to Lebanon and occasionally unveiled a strand or two of our national historical narrative as inconsistent or flawed. For many of us the sight of a winged harp or the mention of an Irish regiment brought a pang of regret or pride which we quickly put out of our heads. We were Irish national soldiers after all and our military history independent of 1916 and the battles of At Tiri and Jadotville didn't exist.

It took quite a number of years and much more water under the bridge for the maturation of the Irish mind to arrive at a point where it was not threatened by its own history. The Provisional IRA's campaign achieved in almost three torturous decades of armed conflict what we could have achieved in a re-run of the Pettigo-Belleek battles in 1969, or at the introduction of internment in 1971 when we equally had a moral right to cross the border. After the Good Friday Agreement the civil, legal and political institutions in Northern Ireland were re-constituted so as Catholic citizens were upgraded from second-class citizenship to a parity of rights and dignity with their Protestant fellow citizens. The gestures of reconciliation were profound and deeply moving. The youngest ranger from the Royal Irish Regiment stood to attention in solidarity with a corporal from the Irish army's Cavalry Corps at the Messines Ridge commemoration tower in Flanders.

The Island of Ireland Peace Park, or Irish Peace Tower, is a war memorial in Messines, near Ypres in Flanders, dedicated to soldiers from Ireland who died or were wounded in WW1. It was unveiled in 1998 by Queen Elizabeth II, President Mary McAleese and King Albert II of the Belgians. It is an important milestone of reconciliation between the two distinct identities on the island of Ireland. It couldn't have existed in 1969 when Jack Lynch sent the Irish army to the border, or in 1981 when we were forming up for Lebanon. The growing co-operation and joint commemorations between the British military and the Irish Defence Forces is a very hopeful and healing factor in the overall reconciliation between nationalist Ireland and the British state.

An even more poignant act of remembrance was organised in Dublin's Glasnevin Cemetery in July 2014, attended by President Michael D. Higgins and the president of the Commonwealth War Graves Commission, the Duke of Kent. A Cross of Sacrifice was erected to commemorate Ireland's war dead and wreaths were laid by the president and by the Duke of Kent. Irish soldiers from the British army's Royal Irish Regiment paraded with soldiers from the Irish army. The speeches were eloquent and honourable, the military music and drill of a high standard. President Higgins touched the hearts of those present with his poetic eulogy to the Irish war dead-

We cannot give back their lives to the Irish dead, nor whole bodies to those that were wounded, or undo the disrespect that was shown to those that fought, or their families … but we honour them now even at a distance, nor would it be appropriate to interrogate their reasons for enlistment. If they could come back, no doubt they would have questions to ask why it was and how it came to be that their lives were taken ...

The only deficit was on the part of An Garda Siochana, who allowed protestors to stand close enough to the commemoration for their jeering and shouted insults to spoil the decorum of the ceremony. On a very important state occasion and ritual of remembrance the Gardai lacked the self-awareness and professionalism to move the jeering protestors far enough away for their insults and jeers to go unheard.

This was a cemetery after all, a place of consecration and sanctity. And the President of Ireland along with the Duke of Kent were present and speaking as the voice of the Irish people and as the voice of the body with responsibility for preserving the graves of fallen Irish soldiers across the globe. It was yet more solemn and ritualistic because of the curious nuances of Irish history which relegated so many Irish citizens who'd served in the British military to unmarked graves and to disrespect.

And while this important state ceremony of remembrance was taking place two Garda officers were seen having a good old gossip nearby. And the howls and jeers of protestors were heard throughout the entire ceremony. Any police force in the world would have had the sensitivity to move the protestors back far enough so as they were yet free to protest but without their shouts and jeers disrupting the solemnity of the ceremony. Was it complacency, laziness or unprofessionalism from the Gardai rather than a deliberate insult to our president and the others who were there?

It might have had something to do with the Irish national character in bloom, if we believe nations can have shared characteristics. Allowing a rabble of jeering protestors to disrupt the president during a sensitive commemoration service is a recognisable trait to anyone who experienced the chaos of our arrival in Lebanon. We've travelled a long distance as a people but certain parts of Irish institutional life and how we behave in public have yet some ways to travel.

In this age there is a lesser need to club each other senseless with our final vocabularies from history. There's no need for this generation or the generations to come to interrogate Collins' motivation for ordering the execution of the British army general Sir Henry Wilson. With representatives like Wilson the British administration at the time could hardly expect any great expressions of love or devotion from ordinary Irish people. Wilson's role in the Curragh Mutiny of 1914 was an act of sedition against the crown, but as a Protestant landowner and in Collins' words a violent Orange partisan he went unpunished. In fact, soon after his dishonourable role in the Curragh Mutiny he was promoted to even higher office.

Wilson's family bought their land in County Longford under the Encumbered Estates Act of 1849, yet another act of official state aggression against Irish peasants who had only just survived the Famine. The hateful exploitation of the Irish poor and working classes by opportunistic land-grabbers, both English and Irish, was resisted by Charles Stewart Parnell and Michael Davitt's Land League. Later the Congested Districts Board and the Department of Agriculture founded in 1899 redressed a degree of the impoverishment and humiliation following on from the Encumbered Estates Act.

The rational mind unfettered from the indoctrination of propaganda can only marvel at the exploitation of the Irish and their resources by England and by England's agents in Ireland. Why would the Irish of the time not be angry enough to organise in resistance? What saintly patience or Christ-like compassion were the Irish peasants driven off their land by agents of their English king presumed to have? Any one policy of England in Ireland or any one single parliamentary act against the interests of the people of Ireland was enough to morally legitimise a thousand risings and rebellions.

As a point of interest Sir Henry Wilson advised London on the developments at Pettigo-Belleek in 1922. His prejudiced reports to Lloyd-George influenced the decision to send two British infantry regiments backed up by an artillery battery to Pettigo-Belleek after the actual exchanges had ended. These front-line formations crossed the border to attack a Free State army post at Pettigo and kill seven unsuspecting national soldiers who had assumed the border exchanges were over.

Such musings are tempered now by happenings at home in Ireland and elsewhere. There are expressions of humanity and conciliation from many sides of an ancient argument. With so much history subsumed in our deeper consciousness we were naturally predisposed to standing shoulder to shoulder with the exploited people of the world. We were the perfect peacekeeping soldiers for UNIFIL, in a hurry to comfort the successors of the evictions at Clongorey in the hilly villages of Southern Lebanon.

Like any soldiers serving under the tricolour if we were obliged to fight in a re-run of Pettigo-Belleek for the defence and honour of nationalist Ireland we would have done so. Because of politics, human vulnerabilities and the delicate relationship between the Irish state and the United Kingdom this could not happen in 1969, even though it would have been morally correct and in hindsight the wisest action to take. Instead, we were sent to places like Cyprus to serve under the blue flag of the U.N. Later, as Irish nationalist martyrs died on hunger strike, we went to Lebanon.

The Spiritual Death of an Irish Soldier

On the day before we travelled to Beirut for to fly back to Ireland something happened. I was waiting for the quartermaster to show up so as I could hand back in my rifle. Several vehicles from the French UNIFIL contingent drove into our camp. Their uniforms fitted their athletic forms like latex gloves on a surgeon's strong hands. Blue berets were cocked to one side of their shaved heads and silver paratrooper's wings were pinned to their breasts. They were probably Foreign Legion as one of their jeeps had the insignia of the Africa Korps from WWII on its sides. Maybe that was some kind of in-joke from the Germans serving among them.

A few of the Dubliners of A Coy had uncles and fathers who'd deserted the national army in the nineteen forties for to cross the Irish Sea and enlist in the British Army. There was a possibility that one of them served in the Eight Army in North Africa and faced the same Afrika Korps the French paras were referencing in chalk on their jeeps. Such curious things went unremarked upon as the French silently entered our camp and parked in front of the company building.

They didn't stay long but the aura they brought with them stayed longer. They were configured for war or at least armed action of some kind, with index fingers never far from the triggers of their assault rifles. Eyes scanned their surroundings with a readiness that announced to anyone looking on that they were ready for the worse that might happen. They were not peacekeepers but professional soldiers ready at a moment's notice to fight and die if need be for the honour of France. They'd been taken off peacekeeping duties after complaints about their aggressiveness and given the job of driving trucks for UNIFIL.

As they were parked up one of our officers appeared with a camera in one hand. He didn't have anything on his head, no beret or forage cap, and was wearing Jesus sandals. He seemed like an inoffensive fellow who probably lived a fulfilling life in the middle-class Dublin suburbs. You could imagine him in a waxed jacket and woollen scarf knitted by a doting mother or wife, walking the family labrador on Seapoint or Sandycove before placidly heading on back to the kind of homelife most people dream about having.

Using the simple French he'd learnt in one of the better schools in Ireland back then he asked the young paratroopers if they minded if he took some photographs. They barely responded but didn't seem to mind. The gentle and refined captain then orbited the parked jeeps, taking photos, going down on one knee for a few shots. His features intensified as he took shot after shot. Clearly, he took photography seriously. In a pre-internet world it was a poplar thing to do.

In minutes it was over. The paratroopers readjusted the machineguns fitted to their jeeps and tightened their berets to the sides of their shaven skulls. Then they were gone. The harmless-looking captain, who didn't appear to have an ounce of aggression or military elan in him, ambled back to his quarters seemingly quite pleased with what he'd captured through the lens of his camera. He carried the confidence of a correct and connected life in his easy steps. He surely knew people back home or was married into a family that the other battalion officers recognised as a part of the social credentials that put them at a distance from the rank and file.

Ancestors had softened the path for this inoffensive man, created wealth and status that could be handed down to the generations that came after them. It'd be easy to picture him in the officer's mess, holding the soupspoon in the right way and without trying very hard impressing his fellow officers with his connections and social life back home. Lebanon was something he could tell his social circle about, something different to add to after-dinner chit-chat.

Much like in Ireland, in Lebanon we were observers, looking on as the armed forces of other nations carried through their plans and campaigns with killing instincts honed through the generations and ready to erupt at a moment's notice. We were morally stunted on the sidelines, a role we'd grown used to back home after the battles of Pettigo-Belleek had faded into the recesses of our national consciousness.

I felt the weight of the F.N rifle in my hands, a weapon I'd never fire in anger. History had set a trap for us, cradled us in a free state of sorts from where we looked out at the world like children watching adults going about serious business. Our captain with his Jesus sandals and single-lens reflex camera looked at the French paratroopers in awe, as if they were a different species. In a sense they were. We hadn't crossed the border in '69 when we had every moral right to do so. Instead, the crisis was taken on by a different body of Irishmen. There was no way of taking a photograph of that.

As we had separated ourselves from the British and whatever their regiments were doing we only had one possible role that might justify our arms. That involved us taking another run at Pettigo-Belleek, an act of madness that was more than morally justified by the brutalities of '69. We didn't do that. We avoided the only fight we were morally and constitutionally obliged to take on. In sitting around in South Lebanon watching the agonies of a conflict we had no stake in we'd traded whatever right we had to call ourselves Irish soldiers for an easy life in the Irish hinterlands, for U.N jaunts that paid for second-hand cars and double-glazed windows and for a tin medal with the crest of the U.N stamped on the front of it.

Now and then an Irish soldier died in an accident or on account of a health crisis or was killed by one of the militias and was offered as a kind of oblation, proof that we were willing to die for something. But everyone knew we'd abandoned our kith and kin in the North for the sake of a good drink-up at the weekends and a simple, turf-smoked life in an improving but stagnant and morbidly conservative twenty six county state. We guarded men in Portlaoise prison who were well up for a re-run of Pettigo-Belleek and we took the jeers of Free state bastard with a laugh.

Critics gave Irish soldiers in '69 no hope if they'd have stepped over the border, much as they gave the national soldiers along with their irregular IRA comrades no hope at Pettigo-Belleek in 1922. But they'd have opened eyes around the world to what was happening to Irish Catholics in what was then an Orange statelet out of step with the principles of the modern democratic world. They'd have been driven back across the border by superior numbers and force but they'd have left a mark big enough for the world to notice and to intervene in a meaningful way. Graves of Irish soldiers would have been offered to the Irish people as a sacrifice and as proof that serious change was needed. Maybe the decades of guerilla war that followed could have been avoided. Who can say?

Morally we were obliged to act. We didn't act. And that hangs around the neck of Irish national soldiers years and decades later.

Looking at it in more detail it's obvious that every agency of note at the time was infiltrated by British intelligence. Because of that it would have been almost impossible for anything useful to be done. The abysmal morale, weak leadership, poor organisational structure, low numbers, combat unreadiness and toleration for so many alcohol-dependent, sick and low-grade soldiers in the army at the time was enabled by a complacent political hierarchy determined to deny the army a role in the life of the nation. They were no doubt encouraged in their goals by British agents in Ireland.

All that failure swims in front of my eyes as I cradle my useless rifle for the last time. We came here as failures. Soon we'll return as failures but with a UNIFIL ribbon to pin to our uniforms. Just then a great sadness breaks from my soul and I'm happy to be alone with my thoughts for a little while. The futility of spending time out here in these hilly villages straddling the Lebanon-Israel border is choking me up. This is not our fight. It has nothing to do with us. Back home Irishmen have starved themselves to death in their struggle against British political power in Ireland. Others have taken to the boreens and dewy fields of the northern counties to continue the old battles in any way possible.

I sling the rifle over one shoulder and straighten my blue beret and walk to the barbwire marking the boundaries of our camp. A few locals are passing and I'm glad we're cut off from each other's thought life. I wouldn't like anyone to read my thoughts just now. I quietly sing the lines of an old song they used to play on RTE radio.

You fought for the wrong country, you died for the wrong cause, and your Da always said that it was Ireland's great loss. All those fine young men who marched to foreign shores to fight the wars, when the greatest war of all was at home.

I look out on the hills of South Lebanon for the last time and then my eyes begin to blur. Cries in Arabic can be heard from a nearby wadi. Probably some young fellows are larking about. I close my eyes tight-shut and when I open them again I sense something passing. Something important. I wasn't quite sure then but I'm sure now. What passed in front of me was whatever soldier's spirit I had inside me. We were not really Irish soldiers after all, or if we were we'd waited in the shadows when history called us forth to take our place on its stage.

We didn't step forward in '69 or '71 and now when Irish volunteers are starving to death in protest at British political power in Ireland and are taking to the wet fields of Tyrone and Armagh we're not stepping forward either. They've sent us out here to watch others play out the moves of a bitter conflict and in doing so hope we forget we're Irish soldiers without any serious part to play in the destiny of our divided and troubled island. At this moment, on the day before we're due to fly back home, all this is shaping up in my mind and I see how useless the whole thing is. Spiritually at least, the Irish soldier I am is dying in front of my eyes.

I know there's nothing more that can be done, except to get out of this place. To move. Shake off all the traces of the army I swore my life to at seventeen. To move on as so many others have moved on, passing the poisoned chalice to those who follow on behind us. There might even be some other kind of life at the end of all this. Maybe there's even a life beyond the doomed nights of unfulfillment in smalltown Ireland, a life worth living.

Postscript. Ireland. Sometime in the nineteen nineties.

The Irish U.N contingent in Lebanon seems a lifetime ago, my part in it insignificant and vague in a world of tears and war. At times it seems like something that happened in a dream. That long ago stint in the Irish military was one of those trials we go through in life that we mark off as probably necessary on some level or other, although we're not quite sure what it means. Even years later we may not be any closer to understanding what was going on. Maybe the kindest way of making sense of such things is to put it down to what we must go through in life to get us to where we are now, the routes of adolescence and early adulthood that lead to somewhere we're at least comfortable in our skin.

It's also a coming of age of sorts, a ritual that helps in a time when there's not much ritual. Learning how to handle and fire an assault rifle and running through rain and mud with guys the same age and from much the same social background is probably helpful to the growing mind. After all, how easy it is for the growing mind to take a wrong turning and go down a road where there's no way back. Such routines probably help at a time when most things don't help.

I'm back in Ireland for a funeral. It's a fine, bright Autumn day and after so many years in London the air of the Irish countryside is almost intoxicating. There's an ever-present musty smell from numerous turf-fires, an unmistakable beacon that lets the deepest part of us know where we are. Soon enough the turf-fires will disappear and that Ireland will be lost and gone forever. I'm at a distance from the other mourners, standing on a hillock overlooking the graveside. The sense of being an outcast is strong inside me as I bow my head and mumble in response to the priest's valediction.

The sense of out-sidedness I've worn all my life is strong just then, like the sense of out-sidedness carried by the Osu from my wife's Igbo tradition. On my birth certificate a name appears that's not unknown in the under-currents of shame cultivated in a more robustly Catholic age. Sister Hildegard. Sean Ross Abbey. As a Magdalene Laundry baby I'd a walkway of shame laid out for me before I even learnt to walk. A legacy of serious dysfunction and darkness of spirit shaped my outlook on the world and all in it. It was there as a merciless hex, a shame that deepened as my consciousness grew. It was felt with every knowing pause when shopkeepers and random adults I'd come into contact with asked my name. The shame of bastard children from poor families, who were only considered acceptable because they avoided having bastard children, was a deep and carefully cultivated shame.

As an outcast from a Magdalene Laundry the route of shame through the lower echelons of the Irish military and then onto the anonymity of an English city seemed a natural role, a route mapped out while I was still straddled in the charity of the Sisters of Mercy at Sean Ross Abbey. It felt like such an inherited and insidious mark on my existence in the world that it seemed pointless to even try to shake it off. I was a lower-caste citizen, a carrier of shame, someone unacceptable and inherently flawed. The sin of the father was very much visited upon the son.

The sense of being an outcast stuck with me like something nasty on the sole of one's shoe. The trope of Sister Hildegard collecting money from the traumatised families of her baby factory is never fully exorcised from the psyche. Although conceived in sin I was grateful to Catholicism for my life as if it wasn't the governing moral authority back then I'd almost have certainly ended up as a dead foetus in the disposal chute of some abortion clinic or other.

So I stood apart from the mourners, accepting the stigma of an outcast. What was I anyhow? Just some dysfunctional guy prone to dark moods who'd done a stint in our Free State peacetime military before disappearing into the impersonality of an English city. Just another outcast from the state's baby factories who ran away from the shame of generations of alcoholism and its pathetic outcomes and the taboo of a birth ordained by a loveless fuck. There were moments in the billets of the Irish army when that sense of out-sidedness was eased by the company of lads from Letterfrack and Daingean, and others who yet carried the marks of brutal assaults by the state's raging bullies, masquerading as teachers for want of anything better to do.

I stood alone with my thoughts, lost in the rituals of death and burial. It wasn't the loneliest I ever felt but it was up there among the loneliest moments. Just then someone touched my shoulder and called out my name. I looked around to see Fu Manchu smiling and holding out a hand of friendliness. We shook hands and then stood shoulder to shoulder as the coffin was lowered into the ground and the priest gave his final blessing. At those moments he was an earthbound angel, the universal big brother sticking around just in case something wrong happened.

There was a sense by how he stood there for those moments that he was sharing in my role as an outcast, standing loyally beside me as he had done years before in the hills of South Lebanon. As the mourners crossed themselves and begun to move towards the cemetery gates we followed on. For those moments I wasn't an outcast, wasn't on the outside looking in. Our brotherhood of imperfect souls raised a glass to us from wherever they were, from the old forts and barracks of a fallen empire or the hills of South Lebanon or some very distant place. We shook hands in farewell in the carpark, and I promised Fu Manchu I'd stay in touch. In the words of the old song London was calling and although it was wonderful to see him again Lebanon was a long time ago. I knew that chances are our paths will never cross again.

Printed in Dunstable, United Kingdom